MIGHTY
JUDGMENT

ALSO BY PHILIP SLAYTON

Lawyers Gone Bad:
Money, Sex and Madness in Canada's Legal Profession

PHILIP SLAYTON

MIGHTY
JUDGMENT

HOW THE
SUPREME COURT OF CANADA
RUNS YOUR LIFE

ALLEN LANE
CANADA

ALLEN LANE CANADA

Published by the Penguin Group

Penguin Group (Canada), 90 Eglinton Avenue East, Suite 700, Toronto, Ontario, Canada M4P 2Y3
(a division of Pearson Canada Inc.)

Penguin Group (USA) Inc., 375 Hudson Street, New York, New York 10014, U.S.A.
Penguin Books Ltd, 80 Strand, London WC2R 0RL, England
Penguin Ireland, 25 St Stephen's Green, Dublin 2, Ireland (a division of Penguin Books Ltd)
Penguin Group (Australia), 250 Camberwell Road, Camberwell, Victoria 3124, Australia
(a division of Pearson Australia Group Pty Ltd)
Penguin Books India Pvt Ltd, 11 Community Centre, Panchsheel Park, New Delhi – 110 017, India
Penguin Group (NZ), 67 Apollo Drive, Rosedale, North Shore 0632, New Zealand
(a division of Pearson New Zealand Ltd)
Penguin Books (South Africa) (Pty) Ltd, 24 Sturdee Avenue, Rosebank, Johannesburg 2196,
South Africa

Penguin Books Ltd, Registered Offices: 80 Strand, London WC2R 0RL, England

First published 2011

1 2 3 4 5 6 7 8 9 10   (RRD)

LIBRARY AND ARCHIVES CANADA CATALOGUING IN PUBLICATION

Slayton, Philip
Mighty judgment : how the Supreme Court of Canada runs your life / Philip Slayton.

Includes bibliographical references and index.
ISBN 978-0-670-06927-9

1. Canada. Supreme Court. 2. Political questions and judicial
power—Canada. 3. Judicial review—Canada. 4. Canada. Supreme
Court—Biography. 5. Judges—Selection and appointment—Canada.
I. Title. II. Title: How the Supreme Court of Canada runs your life.

KE8244.S52 2011   347.71'035   C2011-900466-6
KF8764.ZA2S52 2011

FOR RAYMOND AND VALERIE

THERE'S A MIGHTY JUDGEMENT COMING,
BUT I MAY BE WRONG
YOU SEE, YOU HEAR THESE FUNNY VOICES
IN THE TOWER OF SONG

—Leonard Cohen, *Tower of Song*

CONTENTS

PART II

MIGHTY
JUDGMENT

The Voice Passed Down from the Mountain

Terri-Jean Bedford is a professional dominatrix. She has said the best years of her life were spent tying up and spanking male clients in her north Toronto bondage bungalow.[1]

In the fall of 2009, a lawyer for Bedford and two other sex workers argued in a Toronto courtroom that laws limiting sex-trade workers' ability to protect themselves were contrary to section 7 of the Canadian Charter of Rights and Freedoms.[2] Section 7 guarantees a person's right to liberty and security. Bedford's lawyer asked the judge to invalidate Criminal Code provisions that made it illegal to run a bawdy house, communicate for the purposes of prostitution, and live off the avails of prostitution. These provisions, he said, increased the risk of violence to prostitutes. These laws, he continued, drove prostitutes onto the streets and denied them the protection of a manager, bodyguard, or chauffeur. The result was to make their trade much more dangerous, exposing them to people like Robert Pickton, the convicted serial killer of Vancouver streetwalkers.[3] About a year later, all these arguments were accepted by Madam

Justice Susan Himel of the Ontario Superior Court of Justice, who struck down the impugned Criminal Code provisions in a September 2010 judgment.[4] The federal government appealed her decision to the Court of Appeal for Ontario. Whatever happens there, it is widely accepted that the case will eventually move on to the Supreme Court of Canada.

Should all that goes with prostitution be legal in Canada? What is the role of the law in regulating morality? These questions will finally be settled, far away from Terri-Jean Bedford's suburban bondage bungalow, by the Supreme Court sitting in a magisterial and remote courtroom in the severe city of Ottawa. Nine largely unknown and unelected elite lawyers, of unquestioned sobriety and impeccable careers, will decide what to do about sex workers. The chances are good that the Right Honourable Beverley McLachlin will still be chief justice when that happens. And the indomitable Terri-Jean Bedford may be in the courtroom too. In a strange turn of events, the Charter of Rights will have brought together two women from very different worlds, dominatrix and chief justice.

That fall, while sex laws were being discussed in a Toronto courtroom, a question of an entirely different kind landed in the Supreme Court's lap. On October 16, 2009, Justice Minister Ron Nicholson announced that the federal government would ask the court whether the government had the constitutional power to create a national securities regulator. This superficially dry and technical question is intensely political, with some provinces— notably Quebec and Alberta—determined to hang on to their provincial securities commissions. One newspaper report predicted, "Quebec will react with fury. Premier Jean Charest … will howl. That howl will be echoed in Alberta …"[5]

Bondage and bonds, passion and politics: just about every question we care about ends up at the Supreme Court of Canada, the most important but least known branch of our government.

The Supreme Court is Canada's court of last resort. There is nowhere to go afterwards. It hears appeals from provincial courts of appeal and from the Federal Court of Appeal. It was created and is governed by the Supreme Court Act. Most scholars (but not all) agree that the Act is not an entrenched part of Canada's constitution. It's a federal law like any other, and like any other can be amended by Parliament. No amendment of the Constitution, with its onerous requirements, is necessary to change the way the Supreme Court operates.[6] This means that reform of the court is easy, at least in principle. And there *should* be reform, as I propose in this book's Conclusion.

The Supreme Court Act provides for a chief justice and eight other judges, appointed to serve until age seventy-five by the Governor in Council (which is legal-speak for the cabinet, and which, in reality, means the prime minister acting alone). Three of the judges must be from Quebec; there are no other geographic requirements in the Act, although a convention has developed of having three judges from Ontario, one from the Atlantic provinces, one from the Prairies, and one from British Columbia. The court must agree to hear an appeal (there are limited exceptions to this requirement in certain criminal law matters when the court must hear an appeal whether it wants to or not). Section 40 of the Act says that leave should be granted when the court "is of the opinion that any question involved ... is, by reason of its public importance or the importance of any issue of law or any issue of mixed law and fact involved in that question, one that ought to be decided by the Supreme Court ..." Section 53 permits the federal government to ask the court for what is, in effect, a legal opinion on certain "important questions of law or fact" (this is the provision under which the government asked for an opinion on a national securities regulator).

The court has a staff of slightly over two hundred and an annual budget of about $30 million.[7] The 2008 Public Service Employee Survey rated it the best place to work in the public service (tied with the Atlantic Canada Opportunities Agency).[8] In 2009, it released seventy judgments.[9] The 2010 trend suggests there will be fewer; an analysis at the beginning of October showed that "the top court has decided just 35 cases from Jan.1 to Sept. 23, 2010 ... its lowest output during that period in decades."[10] In fact, the number of judgments released annually has been decreasing steadily for some time. In 1990, there were 144; in 2007, only 58. The U.S. Supreme Court has experienced a similar trend.[11] There has been considerable speculation about why this is happening.[12] Some have argued that neither court is as important as some people think, and that both are growing less important day by day; the big decisions, so the argument goes, are made elsewhere. Others have said that Canadian Supreme Court judges have become lazy. I don't agree with either suggestion. Our Supreme Court justices are the most important decision-makers in Canada, and, as befits Canadians with such grave responsibilities, they are working away like beavers.

———

Who are the judges of the Supreme Court? One of the best answers comes from Dahlia Lithwick, a former Canadian who writes on U.S. legal matters. Lithwick wrote of the Canadian Supreme Court, "The justices include all sorts of quirky outliers, including women, people with French accents, and men with fantastic hair."[13] Few Canadians could be so precise and accurate about their court.

A while ago, before I began this book, I had dinner in Vancouver with a friend who is a senior and distinguished member of the British Columbia bar. After a drink or two, for the fun of it, we tried to list all nine Supreme Court of Canada judges, scribbling their names down on a paper napkin as they popped into mind. We managed to get them all, but it took a while. "What about U.S. Supreme Court justices?" said my friend, getting into the spirit of the thing and knocking back another gin martini. "Let's make a list of those guys!" That proved easier. Roberts, Scalia, Breyer, Ginsburg, Alito: they tripped off the tongue. "Don't forget Clarence Thomas!" said my friend. "He's a good one!" People in the trendy Yaletown restaurant, quietly finishing business deals or starting romances, or both, looked up as we shouted out the names of distinguished jurists. Perhaps they recognized the names of some of the American judges. It was a pretty safe bet that no one could have named even one judge of the highest Canadian court.[14] For Canadians, my friend and I did pretty well naming U.S. Supreme Court judges. A C-SPAN poll in 2009 revealed that more than half of Americans could not name even one.[15] A 2010 survey said that 65 percent couldn't name one judge and that only 1 percent could name all nine.[16]

"And what about that naked judge?" my friend, who had been silent for a moment or two, suddenly asked. "What about him?" I knew what he was talking about. In the spring of 2006, an article in the travel section of the *San Francisco Chronicle* reported that the owner of a cruise line specializing in nude cruises had said its clientele included "at least one Canadian Supreme Court justice." Kirk Makin wrote in *The Globe and Mail*: "Some Supreme Court judges seek relief from work stress in the comfort of their families. Others love nothing more than to curl up with a good book. And could it be, for at least one of them, a nude romp on the high seas was just the ticket?"[17] The identity of the naked judge, if he or she ever existed, remains unknown.

Even if we Canadians can name one or two of our Supreme Court judges, most of us don't know the constitutional role of the court, what kind of issues it decides, or how it does so. That may be largely because the work of the Supreme Court is severely under-reported by the popular media. A retired judge of the court told me: "Media coverage is very weak. And the few reporters there are always rely on one or two 'usual sources' who seem to be expert on everything. Generally, they're law professors. One day they're an expert on constitutional law. The next day they're an expert on labour law. Or you name it. It's always the same few guys that get rung up." There are only two or three print reporters who pay careful attention to what the court does, and there is no serious reporting by television, radio, or emerging electronic news media.

The situation is different in the United States, where there are many knowledgeable and sophisticated analysts of the U.S. Supreme Court reporting to the general public. Some of them directly affect the court's work. Jan Crawford Greenburg has described the influence of Linda Greenhouse, who reported for many years on the U.S. Supreme Court for *The New York Times*. The "Greenhouse Effect," writes Greenburg, is a phrase used "to describe the temptation a justice faces to drift left to appeal to the press, and to … Linda Greenhouse in particular."[18] But the extent and quality of Supreme Court media coverage in the United States can be exaggerated. Dahlia Lithwick commented in 2005 that on becoming a Supreme Court reporter, she had been "stunned that oral argument is covered so reverently by the media." The conse-quence was that the court ended up "being the voice passed down from the mountain."[19]

Canadian law professors, of course, have a great interest in the Supreme Court, teach courses about it, hold conferences to discuss its work, and write about the court in books, law review essays, and occasional newspaper articles.[20] But, with few exceptions, what they write is intended for each other. Some of it is not even remotely accessible to non-lawyers, and there is an increasing trend toward theoretical quantitative analysis that even most lawyers cannot comprehend. And a lot that is written by law professors is, let's face it, very dull. In the United States, by contrast, there is a constant supply of excellent popular accounts of the highest American court—Jeffrey Toobin's *The Nine*,[21] for example, and Jan Crawford Greenburg's *Supreme Conflict*.[22] These books enable citizens who are not lawyers to understand the U.S. Supreme Court much better, and they fuel great and appropriate public interest in what the Supreme Court does (although I haven't forgotten those polls which showed that more than half of Americans could not name one Supreme Court judge). In March 2010, Adam Liptak, *The New York Times*' Supreme Court correspondent, described the interest in a case before the U.S. Supreme Court: "Mike Sachs likes to be the first person in line for big Supreme Court arguments, and he was feeling pretty confident when he arrived at the court Monday morning around 8, 26 hours before the court would hear a big gun control case. But he found a couple from California already set up in lawn chairs."[23] Liptak reported that, for any case, court police hand out numbered placeholder cards to people in line, and that there is a separate line for those who will settle for a three-minute glimpse of proceedings.

Beverley McLachlin is the current chief justice of Canada. One of her constant public themes has been the need for Supreme Court transparency. She returns to this topic repeatedly. In a 2004 article, for example, published in Australia's *Deakin Law Review*, McLachlin vigorously endorsed what is sometimes called the "open court principle." She wrote, "Openness signifies that the public and the press have free access to the courts of justice and are entitled to attend and observe any hearing. It signifies that court records and documents are available for public examination. The rule of openness entails that reasons for judgment are public and, therefore, subject to the scrutiny of the parties, the media, the bar, legal scholars and, ultimately, the populace. And, under the open courts principle, the public and the press may freely discuss and publish accounts of court proceedings, hearings, examinations and decisions."[24]

In some limited ways, the Chief Justice has delivered the goods on transparency. A new policy for access to formal court records came into effect in 2009. The Supreme Court, the policy says, "will provide public access to its court records in a manner that balances the constitutional requirement of open courts against other rights and interests of the public and participants to judicial proceedings, namely privacy and security of individuals and the proper administration of justice." Appeal documents are now available through the Supreme Court's website. Court hearings are broadcast live on the web, and recent broadcasts are archived online. Judgments, of course, have been easily available for some time, free of charge, on the internet. At the personal level, Chief Justice McLachlin has given many speeches over the years, although typically to traditional and safe audiences—universities, bar associations, the Empire Club, etc. (One of the RCMP officers who protects her has said, "If there's a person in the room that isn't laughing or clapping when everyone else is as a member of the audience, you have to wonder."[25]) It is estimated that she delivers between thirty-five and fifty speeches annually.[26] Some of her fellow judges have criticized her for talking and travelling too much. When I interviewed McLachlin in her elegant Supreme Court office, she was careful to say, "My job is here. I try to avoid overbooking. Sometimes I have to cancel engagements."[27]

But broad and troubling transparency issues remain. Despite routine genuflections to transparency, and the formal initiatives mentioned above, the justices are secretive about what they do. They are sensitive to criticism. They care very much what people say about them. A retired justice told me: "Judges who have been academics are the most sensitive to outside criticism. Those who have been litigators don't mind it quite as much. They're used to having their arguments picked apart." The attitude of Bora Laskin, who was an academic for most of his life and who became chief justice in 1973, illustrates this retired judge's point. In his biography of Laskin, legal historian Philip Girard writes: "In spite of being a lifelong champion of free expression and a vigorous critic of all societal institutions including the courts, he became extraordinarily sensitive to any perceived slights on himself or his office."[28] A retired judge told me, "The judges really care what people say, even the chief justice, although she hides it better than the others." When I quoted what Girard said about Laskin to Chief Justice McLachlin, she quickly replied, "That isn't true about me."

It doesn't help matters that Canadians are highly deferential to authority and public institutions. This enables those who run these institutions to get away with disclosing only what they want, handing out tidbits of information that are gratefully accepted by citizens who have been taught to expect little. Bob Woodward, the famous American journalist best known for his role in uncovering the Watergate scandal, is co-author of *The Brethren*,[29] the first modern mass-market book about the U.S. Supreme Court, published in 1979 and still in print. Woodward gave a speech in Calgary in April 2009. He talked about his journalistic methods, which, judging by newspaper accounts of what he said, consist mostly of good old-fashioned nosiness combined with shoe leather. Woodward described to the gathering how easy it is in the United States for a journalist to get access to the highest governmental sources. For a book on the Iraq war, he remarked, he interviewed George W. Bush for more than seven hours. Tom Flanagan, former chief of staff to Stephen Harper, was also part of the Calgary program that evening. The *Financial Post* reported his comment to Woodward that "no prime minister in Canada would give you seven minutes ... There's like light years of difference between Canada and the United States." Woodward's response?

"What I worry about is secret government ... Democracies die in darkness."[30]

It's easy to accept Woodward's point when it comes to Canadian politicians. Does it also apply to Canadian courts? Should judges, including the chief justice of Canada, be more freewheeling in communicating with the public and the media? Does the Canadian judiciary have something to learn from, say, Justice Antonin Scalia of the U.S. Supreme Court? Scalia, known popularly as "Nino," is sometimes described as the Arnold Schwarzenegger of American jurisprudence and is both admired and heavily criticized for candidly expressing his strong views, in and out of the courtroom. In 2008, for example, he was interviewed for an hour by Lesley Stahl on the CBS program *60 Minutes*.[31] Nino told Stahl: "I can be charming and combative at the same time. What's contradictory between the two? I love to argue. I've always loved to argue. And I love to point out the weaknesses of the opposing arguments. It may well be that I'm something of a shin kicker." Scalia's not the only U.S. Supreme Court justice happy to have a big public presence. In July 2010, for example, the publisher Alfred A. Knopf announced that it had acquired the rights to Sonia Sotomayor's memoir. Sotomayor had been on the court less than a year. In September 2010, Justice Stephen Breyer published a book discussing how Supreme Court judges have decided difficult cases (and severely criticizing his colleague Scalia's approach to constitutional law).[32]

I talked to an eminent litigator about all this, someone who has appeared before the Supreme Court of Canada many times. As we ate lunch in a rather louche downtown Toronto restaurant, with horse races being shown on an enormous flat-screen television and tellers taking off-track bets, I asked him: Should Canadian judges belly up to the public bar with less compunction? Should our judges be more muscular in public? More like Nino? He was appalled at the idea, although I wasn't quite sure why. Was it just because of that good old Canadian reserve and deference to authority? No, he assured me, it was about preserving respect for judges and safeguarding judicial independence. A retired Supreme Court judge made another and more practical point to me, supporting reticence. "If you say anything to the media, someone will get upset and complain to the Canadian Judicial Council. They have to look into it, and you have to hire a lawyer, and write letters. It's better to just keep quiet. I've been burnt."

When I began writing this book, I thought I knew what its main arguments would be. The Supreme Court of Canada was an undemocratic institution, and needed reform. It was intolerable that nine upper-middle-class well-fed lawyers with narrow backgrounds and similar points of view, not elected by anybody and appointed by the prime minister with no meaningful legislative oversight or review of the process and choice, sitting on the bench until the age of seventy-five and unassailable during their tenure, almost completely unknown to the Canadian public, should make decisions fundamental to Canadian social and political life. The court's undemocratic nature was accentuated by its liking for secrecy, and by the failure of the media to report fully and properly on its work. Something had to be done, and a good start was to bring this bad situation to everyone's attention.

Fired up, I got to work. I began in the summer of 2008 by reading a lot of Supreme Court judgments. That gave me pause. I didn't always agree with the reasoning or the results of those judgments, but you had to be impressed by the justices' honest and intelligent struggle to understand and resolve complex issues. Also, there's something to be said for a decision-making process that delivers to the public a very detailed written explanation of why a decision was made. The summer of 2008, you may remember, was followed by an autumn and winter in which the Canadian parliamentary system seized up, and elected politicians, seemingly occupied with grandstanding and scheming, appeared uncertain about how to deal with a grave economic crisis. By contrast, the careful deliberation of nine smart people, elected or not, didn't seem like a bad way of solving a problem. In 1981, before a parliamentary committee considering the Charter of Rights and Freedoms, Jean Chrétien, then justice minister, said: "I think we are rendering a great service to Canadians by taking some of these problems away from the political debate and allowing the matter to be debated, argued, coolly before the courts with precedents and so on. It will serve the population, in my judgment very well.'"[33] Was Chrétien right?

Although, although … As I read more and more Supreme Court judgments, there was something familiar about them that bothered the erstwhile law professor in me. One evening I realized what it was. Most of the judgments seemed like essays written by diligent B students, the well-meant work of worthy souls working late into the night. They went on and on, as B-student essays tend to do. It seemed as if the intended audience was law professors (who, in due course, would reply in learned articles); it was professorial approval that the judges wanted most of all. The judgments were crammed full of references to cases, books, law review articles, sometimes sociological and economic data, often from foreign jurisdictions as well as Canada, references demonstrating lots of hard work and a desire to be thorough. (The former Lord Chief Justice of England and Wales, the late Tom Bingham, has noted, "The length, elaboration and prolixity of some common law judgments … can in themselves have the effect of making the law to some extent inaccessible."[34]) On the whole, the judgments were not well written, tending to the pedantic and plodding. And, as a retired Supreme

Court judge pointed out to me later, there was little theoretical rigour and precious little understanding that law is a social science. Where was the flash of insight or originality that marks the essay of an A student? Where was the ability to get quickly to the heart of the problem, and to deal with it imaginatively and succinctly? Where were the ideas that led into the future? But then, as Justice Louis LeBel said to me when I interviewed him,[35] "Whatever style we adopt, there is someone who won't be happy. Professor Weiler used to complain that our judgments were too short. Now some say they're too long."[36]

The first part of this book describes, in theory and practice, how judges of the Supreme Court of Canada make fundamental law for the country and decide essential social and political questions. I give a number of detailed examples of this—decisions dealing with abortion, for instance, or assisted suicide, or group sex in a public place, or the duties of public-company directors faced with a takeover bid. Then, because it matters so much who becomes a judge of the Supreme Court, I discuss the appointment process, and offer profiles of justices now sitting on the bench. The penultimate part of the book discusses the internal dynamics of the court. What is the process of decision-making? How do judges deal with each other? What is the role of the judges' law clerks? Most of this discussion is based on interviews with Supreme Court judges (retired and currently sitting), lawyers, law clerks, and close observers of the Supreme Court.

Five words sum up today's Supreme Court of Canada. *Powerful:* There can be no doubt that the court is supremely powerful, in a way not realized by most Canadians. It decides just about everything we care about. It runs our life. *Paternalistic:* Perhaps unavoidably, the process of judgment-giving has the flavour of law-making for the masses who need it, the handing down of laws by nine Solons. *Competent:* Justices of the Supreme Court do a good job (few argue with this). *Undemocratic:* The judges are appointed by the prime minister, with no meaningful review by Parliament or anyone else, and have the job to age seventy-five. *Secretive:* Supreme Court justices do not like attention, or any discussion, except the most formal and polite, about what they do.

Should the Supreme Court be reformed? Having now written the book, I think I was right at the outset about the main arguments, although the extent of desirable reform may be mitigated by the diligent and valuable job that the Supreme Court does today. In the Conclusion, I propose changes of both law and attitude that would make the Supreme Court of Canada a better fit with Canadian democracy. These changes are long overdue.

PART I

———❖———

ONE

Law Out of Their Guts

In the summer of 1998, Dugald Christie, a fifty-seven-year-old Vancouver lawyer, bicycled to Ottawa.[1] He made this journey, long and arduous for an unfit man in late middle age, to burn his lawyer's robes on the steps of the Supreme Court of Canada. Christie was appalled by the failure of the justice system "to provide justice to the ordinary guy and especially the poor and disabled." He wanted to protest this failure, and he wanted to do it at the highest court in Canada. He went not to Parliament just down the street but to the place that he recognized as mattering more than any other when it came to law and the legal system.

The day before he burnt his robes, Christie visited the Supreme Court building on a reconnaissance mission. "The awesome majesty of that grand old building always takes my breath away," he wrote. "The statues outside have a symbolism and mystery that blend in perfectly with the stately granite construction and the Ottawa River lazily flowing behind it. Still in my shorts and bicycle clothes, I told the commissioner that I proposed to ignite my robes outside his building the next day."[2] And so he did, on September 10, 1998.[3]

The art deco building where Dugald Christie burnt his robes was designed by Montreal architect Ernest Cormier. It sits just west of the Parliament Buildings, on a bluff overlooking the Ottawa River. The statues on the front steps that were so evocative for Christie are by Toronto sculptor Walter S. Allward. One is called *Truth*; the other, *Justice*. At the back of the building there is a fountain, and a terrace overlooking the river. Inside, beginning with a cavernous and ornate entrance hall, there is a lot of marble.

Christie's breath may have been taken away, but not everyone reacts in this fashion. Some do not care for the Supreme Court of Canada building. They think it grandiose and cold, or out of place next to the Parliament Buildings, constructed as it is in a different style, or just too art deco, an intrusive type of design that is largely a historical curiosity. The building has been described as "powerful, dominating, even intimidating."[4] One retired Supreme Court judge commented to me that the court is too far from everything else, encouraging the isolation of judges. "You have to walk half a mile to buy a newspaper," he said. Others, including Christopher Hume, architecture critic for the *Toronto Star*, think differently. Hume considers the Supreme Court of Canada building one of the most impressive pieces of architecture in Ottawa: "I think it is a structure that expresses the dignity and *gravitas* of the Supreme Court but without resorting to the sort of gargantuanism you find in Washington."[5]

This peculiar building is where the nine judges of the Supreme Court of Canada hear cases, consult with each other, think about the law, conduct research, and write judgments. This is where they make law. This is where they govern Canada. This is where they run your life.

There are nine Supreme Court of Canada judges. A majority of them can do whatever it wants. Professor Dennis Baker of the University of Guelph has written plaintively, "Why, exactly, do five justices determine the law over the objection of four of their colleagues?"[6]

William J. Brennan Jr., a judge of the (also nine-member) United States Supreme Court from 1956 to 1990, was once asked by an eager law clerk what he thought was the most important law. He replied: "The law of five! With five votes, you can do anything around here." Later, Brennan got in the habit of making this point by simply holding up an open hand.[7] Linda Greenhouse, who for thirty years reported on the Supreme Court for *The New York Times*, puts it this way: "If there are five people who are just trying to get something done ... they're not too interested in other people's arguments once they have five votes."[8]

In Canada, a Supreme Court panel deciding a case may be only seven judges, or even just five.[9] (The panel's size—and its composition, if there are fewer than nine judges—is decided by the chief justice.) With a smaller panel, "the most important law" at the Canadian Supreme Court shrinks to the law of four, or even three. So it happens that sometimes *three* people, unelected and largely unknown, unaccountable to Canadians, make essential law for all. And they may disagree among themselves on the reasons for what they are doing.[10]

And sometimes, in a sense, it may be just one judge who makes the law. As we shall see, there are important Supreme Court judgments that have been decided by a five-to-four vote, or four-to-three. If one judge had voted the other way, the result—and the law—would have been different. "One vote away from victory," an unsuccessful appellant once said in a press release after such a decision.

Did Marshall Rothstein believe what he said? In February 2006, after it had been announced that Rothstein was the prime minister's choice to fill a vacant Supreme Court of Canada seat, he appeared before an ad hoc parliamentary committee.[11] The committee's job was to make a non-binding recommendation about Rothstein's suitability for the job. Rothstein told the members, "The court's job is really to take what you say about social issues and try to interpret it as best we can and apply it to the facts."[12] Did he really believe that the court simply applied the thinking of Parliament to particular facts in front of it? Did the parliamentarians, who sat there and listened, believe it? Whether they did or not, they liked what they heard. Rothstein got the committee's enthusiastic approval. (When I asked Justice Rothstein about this quotation, he said the context was important. He told me he was talking about the interpretation of specific statutes, not about the general principles of the Charter of Rights and Freedoms.[13])

Judges make law. Some people deny it. The most vociferous gainsayers, particularly in public, are judges themselves. They make their most enthusiastic denials in the process leading up to their appointment, particularly if they're being interviewed for the job by elected legislators resentful of the authority and security of non-elected officials. In private, of course, many judges tell a different story. One former Canadian Supreme Court judge said to me: "The Supreme Court is a court of policy. It is not there to fix errors of law. The court of appeal is the last place you can go to get an error fixed. We decide policy." Chief Justice McLachlin has recently written that the court is not a court of error, and that its principal role is to supervise "the growth and development of Canadian jurisprudence."[14]

John Roberts Jr., now chief justice of the United States, gave a famous example of candidate double-talk at his September 2005 Senate confirmation hearings. Roberts said: "I come before the committee with no agenda. I have no platform. Judges are not politicians. I will remember that it's my job to call balls and strikes and not to pitch or bat."[15] Many scoffed at this statement then, and many have since. "His umpiring turned out to have a decidedly conservative slant," Christopher Eisgruber, provost of Princeton University, has written.[16] The legal philosopher Ronald Dworkin commented that Chief Justice Roberts joined "an unbreakable phalanx bent on remaking constitutional law."[17] Richard Posner, a judge of the United States Court of Appeals for the Seventh Circuit, wrote of Roberts, "The tension between what he said at his confirmation hearing and what he is doing as Justice is a blow to Roberts's reputation for candor and a further debasement of the already debased currency of the testimony of nominees at judicial confirmation hearings."[18] Less than five years after the Roberts confirmation, an analysis in *The New York Times* said, "President Obama and Chief Justice John G. Roberts Jr. have emerged as the intellectual gladiators in a great struggle over the role of government in American society."[19] A few months later that paper editorialized, "In the most recent term ... the Roberts court demonstrated its determination to act aggressively to undo aspects of law it found wanting, no matter the cost."[20]

In her July 2009 Senate Judiciary Committee hearings, Sonia Sotomayor, nominated to the U.S. Supreme Court by President Obama, easily matched the disingenuousness of Chief Justice Roberts. Sotomayor said: "In the past month, many senators have asked me about my judicial philosophy. Simple: fidelity to the law. The task of a judge is not to make law—it is to apply the law."[21] Legal commentator Jeffrey Toobin commented in *The New Yorker*, "Coming from a jurist of such distinction, this was a disappointing answer." Toobin wrote: "Justices have a great deal of discretion—in which cases they take, in the results they reach, in the opinions they write. When it comes to interpreting the Constitution … there is, frankly, no such thing as 'law.' In such instances, Justices make choices, based largely, though not exclusively, on their political view of the issues involved."[22] Ronald Dworkin described Sotomayor's statement more harshly: "That empty statement perpetuated the silly and democratically harmful fiction that a judge can interpret the key abstract clauses of the United States Constitution without making controversial judgments of political morality in light of his or her own political principles."[23]

Are judges politicians in robes? Richard Posner asks this question in his book *How Judges Think*. Posner is a distinguished thinker about the law as well as an American appellate court judge. He writes, "Empirical scholars have found that many judicial decisions, by no means limited to the Supreme Court, are strongly influenced by a judge's political preferences or by other extralegal factors, such as the judge's personal characteristics and personal and professional experiences, which may shape his political preferences or operate directly on his response to a case."[24] Posner argues that judges are legislators when it comes to the "open area" where orthodox methods of analysis yield unsatisfactory or no conclusions. In the open area, "emotion, personality, policy intuitions, ideology, politics, background, and experience will determine a judge's decision."[25]

In a recent book,[26] American law professor Brian Tamanaha has taken Posner (and those who think like him) vigorously to task. Tamanaha believes that a false and distorting divide has arisen between formalism and realism in analyzing what judges do.

Formalists think judges apply the law; realists think they are politicians who make the law. But, in reality, few people, least of all judges, are really one thing or the other, or strictly believe in one or the other of the two models. Posner, writes Tamanaha, is fighting a straw man. Posner, says Tamanaha, writes "as if the classical legal formalist phantom—never real to begin with—is still thriving and must be slain for us to finally see the light."[27] The truth, according to Tamanaha, is to be found in "balanced realism," which unites skepticism and an emphasis on rules. It recognizes that judges sometimes make choices, while accepting that legal rules work.

Before she appeared in front of the Senate Judiciary Committee, Sonia Sotomayor, it seems, largely agreed with Posner's point of view. In a lecture in 2001, she said, "Personal experiences affect the facts that judges choose to see ..."[28] She said, "I would hope that a wise Latina woman with the richness of her experiences would more often than not reach a better conclusion than a white male who hasn't lived that life." And at a 2005 panel discussion at Duke University law school, Sotomayor commented that a "court of appeal is where policy is made."[29] These statements proved highly controversial during the Senate hearings that eventually approved her nomination.

Posner considers justices of the U.S. Supreme Court as supremely powerful, more powerful than members of Congress: "When deciding constitutional cases Supreme Court Justices are like legislators in a system in which there is no judicial power to invalidate statutes and legislators once elected cannot be removed."[30] The U.S. Supreme Court, writes Posner, is "truly a political court, so that the analysis of the behavior of the Justices, especially in constitutional cases, should parallel that of the behavior of conventional political actors."[31] This is not to say that judges are completely free from constraints; they are constrained principally "by concerns for their reputation among people whom they respect but even more by their having internalized the norms and usages of the judicial 'game.'"[32]

Judges in Canada, who regrettably have not come under anything like the sophisticated scrutiny given their American counterparts, are no different.[33] We should regard the Supreme Court of Canada as a political court, and the judges as politicians. The court is a branch of government (although two of the former Supreme Court judges I spoke to insisted that it was part of "governance," not government; to me, this is an elusive distinction). The decisions of Canadian Supreme Court justices will often be determined or influenced, as Posner wrote, by their "emotion, personality, policy intuitions, ideology, politics, background, and experience." In a recent empirical study of the court, Professor Donald Songer writes, "The evidence is strong that in a substantial number of politically significant cases, the justices' private political attitudes and preferences influence their decisions."[34]

It's not just politics at work. Gender also influences a judge's point of view. The Chief Justice of Canada, Beverley McLachlin, admitted as much in a 2010 television interview.[35] Songer's study determined that "gender has emerged as a significant new basis for cleavages on the Supreme Court of Canada in the Charter era. In the pre-Charter era, conflict on the Court was structured by political party, region, and religion. In the post-Charter era, conflict is more frequently structured by gender ..."[36] (The reference to cleavages must be unintentional humour, since the Songer book is unrelenting in its dullness.) When I quoted these lines to Chief Justice McLachlin, she commented that gender seemed important until there were three or four women judges, and then no one seemed to think about it or care about it any more.[37] Songer's data suggests, for example, that female judges are more likely than male judges to support the prosecution in criminal cases.

The legal scholar Ian Bushnell, in *The Captive Court*, his 1992 history of the Supreme Court of Canada, wrote that he had thought of calling the book *The Anonymous Law-makers*. "Nothing could be more important ... than a look at the judges themselves," wrote Bushnell. "Public knowledge of them over the years has been virtually non-existent, and ... there is a notion within our society that there is something disrespectful and wrong about viewing them as individuals.... They have been law-makers, and they have made "political" decisions, and they should not be shielded from public view."[38]

In the late 1960s I was law clerk to Supreme Court Justice Wilfred Judson. An intemperate recent law graduate, I urged him one day to give an aggressive judgment based on some policy argument or other that appealed to me. Judson gestured to Parliament's Centre Block, visible through the windows of his chambers, and said, in a tired but patient way, "That's for them to decide." Most Canadian judges of that and earlier generations felt exactly this way. Parliament, not the courts, was the place where laws were made.

Now it is a different world. The 1982 Charter of Rights and Freedoms gave the courts power to strike down federal and provincial legislation for a wide variety of reasons. The Charter is part of Canada's constitution, and cannot be changed without great difficulty. An amendment of the Constitution must be approved by both Houses of Parliament and by two-thirds of the provincial legislative assemblies representing at least 50 percent of the national population.

All laws, federal and provincial, must comply with the Charter's provisions. "It placed the Supreme Court at the nexus of societal power and change," one group of commentators has written.[39] In 1982 "my job description changed overnight," Justice Antonio

Lamer, later the chief justice, said. "Suddenly we're told every law can be measured to the Charter."[40] Beverley McLachlin, Lamer's successor as chief justice, has put it bluntly: "If existing laws did not comply with the rights in the *Charter*, then those laws had to change. If government action did not comply with the *Charter*, then government had to change the way it acted."[41]

Since the Charter was enacted almost thirty years ago, the social fabric of Canada has been changed by the Supreme Court, and continues to be changed, often in astonishing ways. The process has been accelerated by Canadians who, since the Charter, have come to love recharacterizing political problems as legal questions. It is encouraged by politicians who enjoy ducking behind the Charter to avoid becoming entangled in controversial issues like abortion. Those who want to change the law move away from the political arena, where moral and social policy arguments can be considered head-on, and where due weight can be given to public opinion. They go to court, and make complex and technical constitutional arguments that obscure the real issues. This shift is a basic change in Canada's constitutional arrangements. "The Charter is the only tool a citizen has to fight government," a former Supreme Court judge told me. Many citizens have used this tool with vigour and determination. Judges have become the official opposition to government.

Post-1982 constitutional law has had a vast effect on our country. In 1988 the *Morgentaler* decision invalidated Canada's abortion laws. *Delgamuukw,* in 1997, determined the extent of Aboriginal title. The 2004 *Amselem* case decided that the state cannot in any way regulate personal religious belief, however eccentric. The *Same-Sex Marriage Reference*, also 2004, determined that the federal government can change the definition of marriage and give gays and lesbians the legal right to marry. *Chaoulli,* in 2005, struck down a Quebec law banning private medical insurance and changed the shape of Canada's health care system. In 2005, *Labaye* decided that group sex at a commercial club was not indecent. I discuss these and other cases in the next few chapters. They are only a few examples of what the judiciary has done.[42] This book is not a comprehensive survey of recent constitutional and other law. It is intended to demonstrate the vast scope of what the Supreme Court does, and its implications.[43] I make no mention, for example, of important labour law decisions,[44] or the court's tentative forays into environmental law,[45] or administrative law cases.

Supreme Court judgments do not just change the law in abstract ways. They have enormous practical implications. A good example is the 1999 case of *R. v. Marshall*,[46] which found that Aboriginal peoples in the Maritime provinces have a constitutionally protected treaty right to hunt, fish, and gather for the purpose of making a moderate livelihood. The financial consequences of this decision have been detailed by Nova Scotia constitutional litigator Alex Cameron in his book *Power Without Law*.[47] He observes that hundreds of millions of dollars of taxpayers' money have been spent to implement the treaty right affirmed by the Supreme Court. "An entire policy of the federal Department of Fisheries and Oceans … has been calculated to meet this constitutional requirement."[48] Professor Dennis Baker has gone so far as to argue that the Supreme Court has accumulated legislative and executive power over the public purse.[49] Baker points out that it is difficult for an interest group to catch the attention of the government. But if the group can frame its demand as a constitutional right, "then the burdens and pay-offs dramatically shift. Despite the high costs of litigation, a judicial remedy is worth obtaining because it offers an indisputable, permanent, and almost immediately effective claim on public funds."[50]

It's not all about great issues of public policy with multi-million-dollar stakes. Suppose you are wrongly suspected of planning to throw a pie in the prime minister's face. The police detain you, in breach of your Charter rights. You sue and demand damages. You can get them. Section 24(1) of the Constitution Act authorizes the court to grant such remedies to individuals for infringement of Charter rights as it "considers appropriate and just in the circumstances." If an individual's Charter rights are denied, he can be given money in compensation.

On August 1, 2002, Prime Minister Jean Chrétien was in Vancouver. The Vancouver Police Department received information that someone was going to throw a pie at him. They mistakenly thought that Alan Ward, a known activist, was the prospective pie-thrower. They arrested Ward and took him to a police lock-up where he was strip-searched. A few hours later, the police— realizing they had made a mistake—released Ward. He sued. In 2010 the Supreme Court unanimously upheld an award of $5,000 in "constitutional damages" for unreasonable search and seizure in breach of Ward's section 8 Charter rights.[51] The court laid out the three interrelated functions of a damages award: "The function of *compensation*, usually the most prominent function, recognizes that breach of an individual's *Charter* rights may cause personal loss which should be remedied. The function of *vindication* recognizes that *Charter* rights must be maintained, and cannot be allowed to be whittled away by attrition. Finally, the function of *deterrence* recognizes that damages may serve to deter future breaches by state actors."[52] The strip search, inherently degrading and humiliating, was unnecessary; compensation for Ward was appropriate. We can now expect a flood of damages claims from individuals who argue that their Charter rights have been breached. One example arises from police treatment of protesters at the June 2010 G-20 Toronto Summit. In September 2010 two of the protesters filed a class action suit against the Attorney General of Canada, the Toronto Police Services Board, and the Peel Police Services Board. One allegation is violation of Charter rights. The protesters are seeking $115 million in damages.[53]

Some say, nonetheless, that the importance of the Supreme Court is exaggerated. It would be easy to make a list of vital contemporary issues that the court has never considered and is not likely to—for example, Canadian involvement in Afghanistan and other foreign policy and defence matters (although the court recently strayed into foreign policy in the *Khadr* case, when it came close to ordering the government to seek extradition of a Canadian held in the Guantánamo Bay U.S. military prison—see below). A leading Canadian journalist, who follows the court closely, put a stark point to me in private conversation. "The great Charter cases are over. Nobody gives a damn any more about the Supreme Court. It's just not that important." Chief Justice McLachlin sometimes seems to agree. She said at the beginning of 2010 that many contentious Charter rights were resolved before her time as chief justice and that much of the last decade has been devoted to fine tuning.[54] Law professor Frederick Schauer argued in a 2006 *Harvard Law Review* article[55] that the U.S. Supreme Court is not as important as people think. He wrote: "Overestimating the salience (and perhaps even the intrinsic importance) of Supreme Court adjudication ... is one of the recurring pathologies of American legal scholarship."[56] Could it be the same in Canada?

Canadian legal scholars, pursuing a vested interest, succumbing perhaps to Schauer's "recurring pathology," may be inclined to exaggerate the importance of the Supreme Court of Canada. Practising lawyers do not suffer from this ailment. A prominent Saskatchewan lawyer, with much experience in the legal trenches, wrote to me, "I find the court to be indifferent to 90% of practitioners in Canada ... The Charter's relevance to 90% of lawyers is trivial. The judgments are just too long to be efficiently usable by ordinary practitioners." This lawyer considered that Supreme

Court justices mostly write for an audience of law professors (who repay the compliment by writing books about the Supreme Court), and resented the dominance of Charter cases: "The SCC seems to have lost interest in achieving uniformity of principles for the common law. How many cases on common law issues (tort, conflicts, contract) does it render in a year?"

It is easy to forget that the Supreme Court of Canada is not just a Charter-based constitutional court but also a court of general jurisdiction. As my Saskatchewan correspondent implicitly suggested, it has vast powers, perhaps underused, to make and remake private law. An example is the controversial 2008 *BCE* case.[57] In *BCE*, a Supreme Court panel of seven judges unanimously overruled the Quebec Court of Appeal that, in a five–nothing decision, held that a special committee of BCE's board of directors failed to give proper consideration to the interests of bondholders when it approved a leveraged buyout. This Supreme Court decision was hailed (mostly by those who benefited from it), in a circus-like atmosphere, as one of the most important judicial decisions of the last few decades. Chief Justice McLachlin has said that case was one of her proudest accomplishments.

Some Canadians, particularly those on the political right, think the Supreme Court has usurped the power of other branches of government. In 2003, more than twenty years after the Charter became part of the Constitution, a retired law professor, Robert Martin, wrote an incendiary book called *The Most Dangerous Branch: How the Supreme Court of Canada Has Undermined Our Law and Our Democracy*.[58] Martin argues that the Supreme Court, in hot pursuit of a left-wing agenda, has derailed the legislative process in an egregious way. Nigel Hannaford of the *Calgary*

Herald referred in 2009 to "the subtle replacement of the will of Parliament ... by the will of the Supreme Court of Canada ..."[59] Others, mostly on the left, believe that the will of the majority can easily become the tyranny of the majority, and that only the courts, defining and enforcing minority rights, stand in the way. Recent polling suggests that the Canadian public likes the Charter and how judges have used it. "It's what I'd call a big patriotic symbol for the country," one pollster reported in 2007.[60]

Professor Kent Roach, of the University of Toronto, has advanced a middle-of-the-road view. In his book *The Supreme Court on Trial*, Roach writes, "Canadians are losing sight of the genius of the *Charter*, which gives *both* judges and legislatures robust roles in determining the way rights are treated in our free and democratic society."[61] He argues that critics of judicial activism overestimate the extent to which judges have been able to read their own preferences into law.[62] Justice Louis LeBel, when I interviewed him,[63] referred to a dialogue between the judiciary and the government. "We judges hope the executive branch will take what we say into consideration," he said modestly.

Concern about the judiciary infringing upon the legitimate powers of other branches of government is not unique to Canada. Anthony King, a Canadian who lives in England, has written a book called *The British Constitution*.[64] King argues that a new constitution has emerged in the United Kingdom since the 1970s. Britain's governing arrangements, he thinks, have been "substantially transformed." One important reason is the incorporation of the European Convention on Human Rights into British law, limiting parliamentary sovereignty and giving judges new powers. Oxford professor Stein Ringen, reviewing King's book in *The Times Literary Supplement*, commented, "With its new powers, the judiciary woke up from 'a long sleep', started to assert itself, and the senior judges metamorphosed into a political class of activists."[65] Another Oxford professor, Vernon Bogdanor, has argued similarly in his recent book *The New British Constitution*.[66] Bogdanor believes that the replacement in 2009 of the judicial committee of the House of Lords by the new Supreme Court for the United Kingdom as the final U.K. court of appeal will accelerate this trend, encouraging a wholly separate judiciary to take on the executive branch. In the United Kingdom, the final court of appeal is now explicitly and gloriously independent from Parliament. To drive home the point, it has moved out of the Parliament Buildings into the renovated Middlesex Guildhall across the way.

Many in Canada would say, echoing Stein Ringen, that Canadian senior judges have woken up from a long sleep and have become a new political class of activists. In a recent New Zealand law review article, three legal scholars described Canada's judges as "by most accounts, the most judicially activist in the common law world—the most willing to second-guess the decisions of the elected legislatures ..."[67] An important new development is an apparent judicial willingness to second-guess the government in an overtly political way. In 2010, in the case of *Canada (Prime Minister) v. Khadr*,[68] the Supreme Court of Canada poked a finger in the eye of the executive branch, albeit with a degree of delicacy and restraint. Omar Ahmed Khadr is a Canadian citizen who has been detained for many years at Guantánamo Bay. It is alleged by the Americans that he was a member of al-Qaeda and killed a U.S. soldier in Afghanistan. In 2003 agents from Canadian intelligence services questioned Khadr and shared the results with U.S. authorities. In 2004 a Canadian official interviewed Khadr again, knowing that he'd been subjected to sleep deprivation techniques to make him less resistant to interrogation. A unanimous Supreme Court found that Khadr's Charter rights had been violated in several ways. It came within a hair's breadth of ordering the government to request Khadr's extradition from the United States, but backed off at the last minute. "Consistent with the separation of powers and the well-grounded reluctance of courts to intervene in matters of foreign relations, the proper remedy is to grant Mr. Khadr a declaration that his *Charter* rights have been infringed, while leaving the government a measure of discretion in deciding how best to respond...."[69] Subsequently, the Federal Court insisted that the government find ways to remedy the violations of Khadr's constitutional rights. The Khadr case seems a harbinger of increasing Supreme Court opposition to government, rejigging our constitutional arrangements yet further.[70] Meanwhile, in August 2010 a Guantánamo military judge ruled that all Khadr's confessions were admissible as evidence, no matter how they were obtained. Then Khadr pleaded guilty to a variety of charges in exchange for eight years' imprisonment, most of them to be served in Canada; thus was the federal government's dilemma resolved.

In the United States the struggle between the executive and judicial branches goes back to the beginning of the federation, and has been robust in the extreme. If anything, the judiciary has had the better of it. In the 2010 case of *Citizens United v. Federal Election Commission*,[71] the U.S. Supreme Court ruled five to four that corporations have a constitutional right to spend money to support or oppose political candidates. In doing so, it struck down part of the well-established McCain-Feingold campaign financing law. President Obama went so far as to criticize the *Citizens United* judgment in his State of the Union Address on January 27, 2010. Justice Samuel Alito, who was present, mouthed "not true" as Obama was speaking, and was caught on camera doing so. Pulitzer Prize winner and historian James MacGregor Burns, in his book *Packing the Court*, writes, "The Supreme Court's long supremacy over the Constitution has often led Americans to look to the justices for leadership ... It has led them to identify the court with the strength of the constitutional order and of the nation itself."[72] But

Burns is appalled by the ascendancy of a court he regards as elitist and undemocratic. He proposes that a president refuse to accept Supreme Court verdicts striking down progressive legislation and seek a constitutional amendment rejecting judicial supremacy.

In Canada the Supreme Court has asserted its post-Charter constitutional power in a variety of impressive ways, but, as *Khadr* shows, is not yet quite ready to stare down the executive branch and provoke a constitutional crisis. I believe the crisis will come.

"Why do we have any confidence that the courts have any idea what they are doing, when it comes to significant issues?" asks Osgoode Hall law professor Allan Hutchinson.[73] In Charter cases, the courts are criticized for usurping the prerogative of the executive and legislature and settling social and economic policy without any particular skill, experience, or insight in such matters. In private law litigation, they are accused of not understanding properly the life of the ordinary citizen, or of an inability to grasp business constraints and complexities. Judges, after all, are lawyers, trained in a narrow art, and normally live a restricted and cosseted existence. They know the law (some of it, at least). What else do they know? Few have much experience with what many people like to call "real life."

Supreme Court judges struggle with complex issues that have no clear or easy solutions. They will always reach a result—they are required to do so—but may be seriously divided. Even members of a majority may disagree about the reasons for the decision they have reached. Often judgments show Sisyphean efforts to grasp an issue, citing cases from around the common law world, papers by non-legal academics, the reports of government task forces, anything that seems to bear even remotely on the point. The

sense, sometimes, is of a person in a state of anxiety, reaching for
something just out of his grasp. The result can be judgments that
are too long and apparently erudite, and in which the main point
is obscured.

Supreme Court watchers agree that being a judge of that court
is a hard task. One senior lawyer described it to me as a "terrible
job," boring to boot. Another said it was hard to see how someone
seventy years old, or older, could possibly put in the long hours that
the job required: "It's a tremendous amount of work." A Supreme
Court judge has to cover a vast range—the complete range—of
legal fields, attempting expertise in everything, something no
lawyer or law professor would ever try. Chief Justice Beverley
McLachlin told me, "It takes a special kind of person, someone
with a keen curiosity and a lot of energy."[74] Dahlia Lithwick
praised retired U.S. Supreme Court Justice David Souter's 2010
Harvard commencement address for making plain that judging is
really, really difficult.[75] Canadian Supreme Court Justice Marshall
Rothstein told me: "One hundred percent of the cases here are
hard. It's intellectually very demanding. It's hard to get traction."
He added, "I roll into the office about 8 A.M. Three or four judges
are here ahead of me."[76]

If judges make law, we should know where they came from,
who they are, and what they think. After all, we know a lot about
members of Parliament, or we can find it out if we have a mind
to do so, and that is not seen as irrelevant or improper. Some of
this book attempts to describe sitting judges of the Supreme Court
of Canada. This is not an easy task, because judges and those
around them guard their privacy to an unreasonable extent, given
their status as high public officials. Richard Posner has written of
justices of the U.S. Supreme Court: "Cocooned in their marble
palace, attended by sycophantic staff, and treated with extreme
deference wherever they go, Supreme Court Justices are at risk of

acquiring an exaggerated opinion of their ability and character. In a democratic society of great size and complexity, it is difficult to justify giving a committee of lawyer aristocrats the power ... to create out of whole cloth, or out of their guts, large swatches of law that as a practical matter they alone can alter."[77] Can this also be said about judges of the Canadian Supreme Court? Are our judges lawyer-aristocrats creating law out of their guts?

TWO

A Brief History

The Supreme Court wasn't always supreme. Before the 1982 Charter of Rights and Freedoms, it was a sleepy institution, working on the fringes of Canadian life. It was not even Canada's final court of appeal until 1949. Until then, that responsibility belonged to a court sitting far away, in imperial London, the Judicial Committee of the English Privy Council. For much of its history, Canada's Supreme Court was undistinguished in its work, often criticized, sometimes reviled. For the first seventy-five years of its life, it did very little. From 1949 until 1982, it occasionally stirred, but not a great deal. Then, in 1982, with the Charter, everything changed.

The Supreme Court of Canada was created on September 17, 1875, by a Canadian statute, the Supreme Court and Exchequer Act.[1] Creation of the court tidied up a piece of business left over from Confederation eight years earlier. After considerable debate and confusion about the legal possibilities, the right of appeal directly from provincial courts to the English Privy Council was left untouched. There was also to be an appeal to the Privy Council from the new court. The right of appeal to the Privy Council left the new Supreme Court of Canada, despite its grand name, as an intermediate court at best. Final decisions about the law were still to be made in the mother country, many days away by ocean liner.

The 1875 statute provided for six Supreme Court judges, appointed for life, two of whom had to be from Quebec. That meant in practice, for political reasons, that at least two had to be from Ontario, although this was not required by the Act. The remaining two judges had to "represent" everywhere else. The quorum to hear a case was set at five. The first members appointed to the new bench, by Liberal Prime Minister Alexander Mackenzie, were William Buell Richards, William Ritchie, Henry Strong, Jean-Thomas Taschereau, Télesphore Fournier, and William Henry.

Richards, who had been chief justice of Ontario's Court of Queen's Bench, was made the first chief justice of Canada. By all accounts, he was a popular man and a well-liked judge, known for an excellent wit usefully employed to embarrass pompous lawyers.[2] Strangely, Richards earned his law degree in the United States, at St. Lawrence Academy in Potsdam, New York. (The successor institution to St. Lawrence Academy, The State University of New York at Potsdam, today trumpets Ritchie as its most distinguished alumnus.[3]) Ritchie, formerly the chief justice of New Brunswick, had "robust good health" and a "splendid physique"[4] but was considered rude. Strong, from Toronto, became known for his "opinionated criticisms of his colleagues, outbursts of temper, and discourteous treatment of counsel"[5] and was described by some as lazy and irresponsible; lazy or not, he served on the court for almost thirty years. Taschereau, a Quebec judge whose brother was that province's archbishop, served for only three years, during which time he continued to live in Quebec City, violating the

Supreme Court Act's Ottawa residency requirement. Taschereau was eulogized at his death in 1893 as "a tireless worker, yet a most likeable and urbane man ... cheerful, affable, hospitable, a most articulate conversationalist."[6] Fournier, a federal politician from Quebec who had been minister of justice and who'd introduced the legislation creating the Supreme Court, was a distinguished judge of the court for twenty years. Henry, a former Attorney General from Nova Scotia, a one-time mayor of Halifax, and a Father of Confederation, served on the Supreme Court until his death in 1888. Henry was thought to be not too bright, and in 1880, two of his fellow judges, including Strong, complained that his judgments were "long, windy, incoherent masses of verbiage, interspersed with ungrammatical expressions, slang and the veriest legal platitudes inappropriately applied."[7] No judges were appointed initially from either Manitoba or British Columbia (Alberta and Saskatchewan had yet to join Confederation), and no one in those provinces seemed to mind; perhaps that was a measure of how unimportant most thought the new court.

The newly appointed judges got down to work after a fashion, no doubt with the irascible and lazy Henry Strong bullying his colleagues while doing little himself (at the beginning, there was not much for anyone to do: at the Supreme Court's first sitting it had not a single case, and the justices adjourned immediately). In the first years of its life, the court sat in the Railway Committee Room of the Parliament Buildings. The physical facilities were extremely poor: "Here was a beggarly institution. No offices were planned for the justices; all the staff were to share just one room; and there was to be no separate permanent library."[8]

Not much happened until the 1877 term, when there were two interesting cases. In the first, the court decided that a Quebec by-election was void because of undue influence exerted on electors by Roman Catholic priests opposed to the Liberal party;[9] in the second, it struck down on constitutional grounds an Ontario law purporting to require a licence to sell beer wholesale for consumption in the province.[10] Of the following year, the 1878 term, Ian Bushnell has written "that it should have been quickly forgotten."[11] Few cases were heard, judges were often away, thus preventing a quorum being formed, and Ritchie and Strong fell to serious feuding. Strong picked his adversary poorly, for Ritchie, known to be at least as rude as Strong, was to become chief justice the following year. Meanwhile, the court was met with increasing criticism from the legal profession, the public, and politicians. Parliament debated its abolition more than once.

In 1882, the court moved from the Railway Committee Room to a two-storey Gothic revival building nearby on Bank Street that until then had served as stables. The court was to stay in the one-time horse barn until 1946. The building was not highly thought of by its new inhabitants: the court registrar complained in 1897, "The present condition of the building is filthy and quite unfit for the purpose for which it is used. Even the walls of the Court room are water stained, dirty and cracked, and some of the Judges' rooms look as if they were positively going to pieces so large and numerous are the cracks."[12]

Severe criticism of the court's work continued, not always confined to criticism of weighty legal matters. One complaint was "that judges would engage in conversations upon the bench while the case was going on, in a loud enough tone to be easily heard throughout the courtroom. These conversations were even worse for not being about the case."[13] The bad-tempered Henry Strong served as chief justice from 1892 until 1902.[14] With his departure, it is said, personality conflicts on the court declined significantly.

In his history of the Supreme Court, Ian Bushnell character-izes 1903 to 1929 as "the sterile years." The court marched along "the road of mechanical jurisprudence and sterility of the judicial

function."[15] He continues: "In the main, the judges were deciding who won and who lost in the litigation, and there was no contribution made to the law."[16] There was considerable turnover of judges; difficulty in finding suitable candidates to fill vacancies; and disunity on the bench, demonstrated by a multitude of individual judgments. There was also some highly questionable conduct that suggests the flavour of the times. In the 1921 case of *Gold Seal Ltd. v. Alberta (Attorney General),*[17] deciding whether the Canada Temperance Act was properly proclaimed into force in Alberta, Justices Anglin and Mignault consulted privately with the federal Minister of Justice Charles Doherty before the decision was handed down. Justice Duff, later to be chief justice, described what happened in a 1925 letter to Viscount Haldane, the British Lord Chancellor. Doherty, wrote Duff, obtained from Anglin and Mignault "information as to their own opinions and the opinions of their colleagues and the probable result of the appeal, and as a consequence legislation curing the defect was introduced before our judgment was delivered."[18] For judges to consult with the government in this way on a case not yet finally decided (or at any time) was an egregious breach of the principles of judicial independence and impartiality.

In 1927, the number of judges was increased from six to seven. The quorum was five, and experience had shown that in a court with aged justices, some of whom did not take their jobs all that seriously, and many of whom spent much of their time away from Ottawa, a complement of one above the quorum number was not enough. At the same time, a mandatory retirement age of seventy-five was legislated, applying even to sitting judges.[19] One, John Idington, aged eighty-six, was thereby forced to resign.

The 1928 *Persons* case[20] was a low point in the history of the Supreme Court. The question in the case was, could a woman be appointed to the Senate? The British North America Act empowered the governor general to appoint "qualified Persons" to the

Senate but it was a question in some minds whether women were "Persons." Five prominent Canadian women from Alberta, known to history as "The Famous Five," asked the government to seek the Supreme Court's opinion. This it did, by way of a reference. In answering the provocative question, Chief Justice Anglin, for a panel of five judges, said women didn't qualify for appointment, relying heavily on his own peculiar version of history. He noted, "By the common law of England ... women were under a legal incapacity to hold public office, referable to the fact ... that in this country in modern times, chiefly out of respect to women, and a sense of decorum, and not from their want of intellect, or their being for any other such reason unfit to take part in the government of the country, they have been excused from taking any share in this department of public affairs." Snell and Vaughan comment, in their history of the Supreme Court, that "the restricted views by the five justices, the narrowness of the definitions involved, and the unexpressed but apparent insistence of the justices that change be instituted through legislatures rather than courts stand out in the reasoning of the justices."[21] The Privy Council in England reversed this incoherent and shameful decision.[22] Lord Sankey, delivering the judgment, made clear that times had changed and that the reasoning of an earlier age no longer applied to new circumstances. Appeals from the Supreme Court of Canada to the Privy Council suddenly seemed like a very good idea. (Curiously, Chief Justice Beverley McLachlin defended the Supreme Court's *Persons* decision in a 2010 speech, saying that the court had to follow precedent and had no choice in the matter.[23]) There are statues of The Famous Five in downtown Calgary and on Parliament Hill. There are no statues of Chief Justice Anglin or the other four Supreme Court judges who rejected their arguments.

Things were no better in the 1930s. The judges were aged and often ill and the court slipped even lower in public regard.

From 1933 to 1944, Lyman Duff presided as chief justice. Falsely esteemed then, and even today, Duff has been described by Justice Ivan Rand's biographer, William Kaplan, as "tormented, alcoholic, indebted, sycophantic, and impotent …"[24] Late in the decade, morale was given a fillip by long overdue plans to build an imposing new building for the court. Prime Minister Mackenzie King was personally interested in this project. It suggested a new and positive, although perhaps unjustified, appreciation of the judges' work and significance. The well-known Montreal architect Ernest Cormier was hired, and work began in 1937. The Queen laid the building's foundation stone on May 20, 1939. The court didn't move in until January 1946, delayed by use of the building for government offices during the war. The court's old home, which it had occupied since 1882, was duly condemned as a fire hazard, demolished, and replaced by a parking lot. A picture of the old court building hangs in the new building's basement.

Meanwhile, despite the obvious usefulness (sometimes, at least) of appeals to the Privy Council, driven home by the *Persons* reference, talk of their abolition remained constant, as it had since creation of the Supreme Court in 1875. Criminal appeals to the Privy Council had been eliminated in 1933, but civil appeals remained. In 1947, the Privy Council itself, in an appeal from an earlier reference to the Supreme Court, decided that the government of Canada was competent to end Privy Council appeals if it chose to do so. Self-government, thought the Privy Council, demanded nothing less.[25] Finally, it was time. There was momentous post-war change in Canada and the world. Newfoundland joined Confederation on March 31, 1949. India had become independent in 1947. Israel was created in 1948. The statute abolishing appeals to the Privy Council, establishing full Canadian judicial independence, was given royal assent on December 10, 1949.[26] At the same time, the number of judges was increased to nine, with three now to be appointed from Quebec. And, no small matter, the salaries of the justices were raised.

———

The do-nothing years were over, more or less. Now the Supreme Court was Canada's final court of appeal. Actually, not quite: cases which had begun before abolition of appeals to the Privy Council could still go to London. In the 1950s, there were still a few Canadian litigation lawyers who enjoyed what had once been one of the pre-eminent perks of their profession, Atlantic crossings on a great Emperor steamship of the Canadian Pacific line, a suite at one of London's best hotels, weeks enjoying the pleasures of the Imperial capital, all paid for by a hopeful client. As late as the 1980s, there were still Canadian barristers who, over brandy in their club, fondly reminisced about their leisurely trips to London. The last Canadian case was heard by the Privy Council in 1959.[27] Counsel for the appellants in the "last case" was William Stevenson, later to be a Supreme Court of Canada judge for a brief period (he resigned because of poor health).

For the Supreme Court itself, in the austere and northern city of Ottawa, the 1950s seemed quiet, although some might disagree with this characterization. William Kaplan, in his biography of Ivan Rand, who sat on the court from 1943 to 1959, writes, "If the Supreme Court of Canada has had a heroic age, it was the 1950s ..."[28] Kaplan is impressed by the court's development during these years of "the implied Bill of Rights," particularly in the three cases of *Boucher v. The King,*[29] *Saumur v. The City of Quebec,*[30] and *Roncarelli v. Duplessis.*[31] These were the "Jehovah's Witnesses cases" that found the law of sedition inapplicable to the handing out of religious pamphlets (*Boucher*), denied a province or municipality the right to prevent the handing out of such pamphlets (*Saumur*), and vindicated a restaurateur whose liquor licence was cancelled because he provided bail to a large number of Jehovah's Witnesses charged with various offences (*Roncarelli*). Kaplan's praise of the court seems somewhat overdone, particularly given his own conclusion that "the concept of an implied Bill of Rights was always dubious" and "could not be constitutionally maintained."[32] Chief Justice Beverley McLachlin has said, "The protection of the implied bill of rights was limited, and uncertain. It was limited in the rights it protected. It was applied in only a few cases."[33]

By the end of the 1950s, the Supreme Court bench was dominated by ultra-conservative judges.[34] Ronald Martland of Alberta, a practising lawyer and former Rhodes Scholar who had studied at Oxford University in England with brilliant results, and Wilfred Judson of Ontario, a trial judge, were appointed in early 1958. Roland Ritchie of Nova Scotia, another practising lawyer who had studied at Oxford and was known to be conservatively minded, was appointed the following year to replace Ivan Rand (Roland was the brother of Charles Ritchie, the eminent Canadian diplomat and diarist). All three were picked by John Diefenbaker. "With the arrival of the 1960s," says Bushnell, "it did not take long for the non-creative, conservative nature of the bench to display its continuing domination of the institution."[35]

In 1962, Diefenbaker appointed his friend and former classmate Emmett Hall, a so-called Red Tory, to the court. Hall was chief justice of Saskatchewan, and chaired a commission on health services that in 1964 recommended a universal health care system for Canada.[36] Another Ontario trial judge, Wishart Spence, liberally inclined, was appointed by Prime Minister Lester Pearson in 1963. In 1967, Louis-Philippe Pigeon, a Quebec practising lawyer known as a strong defender of the integrity of Quebec's Civil Code, became a member of the court.

When I arrived in 1969 to be Wilfred Judson's law clerk, the other judges, in addition to the six just mentioned, were John Cartwright of Ontario, the chief justice, and Gérard Fauteux of Quebec, both appointed at the end of 1949 when the number of judges was increased from seven to nine, and Doug Abbott, also from Quebec. Abbott had been appointed in 1954 by Prime Minister Louis St. Laurent, whose finance minister he had been for many years; he went directly, and controversially, from the cabinet to the court. To a young law graduate like myself, the judges seemed an odd bunch. The Chief, John Cartwright, was a remote man of impeccable manners and grooming, conservative and old-fashioned. Doug Abbott was affable and, as a good ex-pol, roamed the Supreme Court hallways looking for a hand to shake. Martland had good humour and openness. Judson was an austere immigrant from the north of England and a former Latin teacher with a narrow conception of a judge's role. Ritchie, whom I helped when Judson was away ill for a few weeks, was good company. When I subsequently taught at the McGill law school, Ritchie visited and lectured on judicial law making. The pipe-smoking Spence was, ironically, a breath of fresh air. Pigeon was aggressive and shrill about his views, constantly badgering the other judges, sometimes shouting at them from their office doorways, generally making the point that they didn't understand Quebec's civil law. The judges didn't speak to each other very much.

In the year I was a Supreme Court law clerk, from September 1969 to August 1970, two significant things happened. In November 1969, the court delivered the *Drybones* decision.[37] In 1960, John Diefenbaker had introduced the Canadian Bill of Rights.[38] This was an ordinary federal statute, not a constitutional amendment, but it did purport to limit federal legislative power. Drybones, an Indian, had been convicted under the Indian Act with being drunk off the reserve. On an appeal, Drybones argued that, since he had been convicted under a provision that applied only to Indians, and one that provided more severe penalties than those that applied to non-Indians under other rules, he had been denied equality of law as promised in the Bill of Rights. The court of appeal found unanimously against him, and the case went to the Supreme Court. It reversed the lower court, six to three. Indians could not be treated differently from anyone else, said the majority, in a judgment delivered by Ritchie. Cartwright, Abbott, and Pigeon dissented. *Drybones* is the only case in which the Supreme Court struck down a law for breach of the Diefenbaker Bill of Rights.

The other significant event was a surprise appointment. In March 1970, John Cartwright resigned. Predictably, he was succeeded as chief justice by Gérard Fauteux. Much less predictably, the vacant Ontario seat was filled by Bora Laskin. This appointment was unexpected for several reasons: most of Laskin's career had been spent as a law professor, he was a Jew (the first to be appointed to the Supreme Court), and he had no experience at all in private practice (when appointed, he was a member of the Ontario Court of Appeal). Prime Minister Pierre Trudeau, also a former law professor, sent a message with this novel choice, and although it was not clear exactly what the message was, something was clearly stirring. Philip Girard, in his biography of Laskin, writes of his appointment, "With existing institutions and modes of thought under attack, Canadians were ready to give philosopher-jurists, like philosopher prime ministers, a try."[39] Girard comments, "The excitement surrounding the new judge was implicitly a criticism of the Court's sitting members, and they would have been less than human if they did not feel somewhat slighted."[40] It came as an even bigger surprise when Laskin was appointed chief justice less than four years later. Five judges more senior than Laskin were passed over for the job, including Ronald Martland, who as the most senior was the presumed successor to Fauteux.

One of the big problems at the court in those days was the inconsequential cases it was forced to hear because of an absurdly wide jurisdiction. Any civil matter involving more than $10,000 carried with it an automatic right of appeal, and the result was that the docket was cluttered with cases of no legal importance. The judges, forced to hear poorly argued cases of no legal interest, could be very bad-tempered on the bench. The workload was too great, and much of it, to no purpose. Once I was sitting in on a divorce appeal, with the estranged husband pleading his own case. He began describing a crucial day in his failed marriage. "In the morning, I got up and had oatmeal for breakfast." Wilfred Judson snapped, "I don't give a damn what you had for breakfast."

This problem of jurisdiction was fixed in 1975, opening the door a crack to the court as it has become. The Supreme Court Act was amended, requiring leave to appeal in civil cases; now, the court had to agree to hear a case before the matter proceeded. The Act said that the court should only agree to hear an appeal if it was "of the opinion that any question involved ... is, by reason of its public importance or the importance of any issue of law or any issue of mixed law and fact involved in such question, one that ought to be decided by the Supreme Court or is, for any other reason, of such a significance as to warrant decision by it."[41] This change of jurisdiction, almost unnoticed at the time, laid the foundation for what was to come.

What came was the Charter. Canada's new constitution, which included the Charter of Rights and Freedoms, was proclaimed by the Queen on April 17, 1982, on Parliament Hill in Ottawa. After more than a hundred dull and undistinguished years, the Supreme Court of Canada was transformed from, at best, a peripheral presence in government to a supremely powerful institution at the heart of Canada's affairs. Now things got exciting. Now judges had the power to strike down legislation that they considered incompatible with the constitutionally guaranteed rights and freedoms of each individual. Now the Supreme Court could decide social, economic, and political issues that affected every Canadian. Now the Supreme Court began to run our lives.

THREE

Life and Death

Questions of life and death engage profound emotions and are of intense political interest. In a democracy, we might expect such questions to be settled by political means, by elected representatives sitting in Parliament, and only after vigorous public debate. Yet in Canada they have often been answered by Supreme Court judges: nine men and women appointed by the prime minister who are little known to the average citizen, serve in the shadows for decades, and carefully guard their remoteness. The Supreme Court has decided what abortion laws Canada should have (none); that private health care insurance should be available (no matter that it may damage the public health care system); that, in some circumstances, a minor cannot be forced to have a medical procedure repugnant to her religious beliefs (even though the procedure would save her life); and that it remains a crime to help someone commit suicide (though the person who wants help is perfectly rational). Supreme Court judges, sometimes, decide who lives and who dies. They draw, and redraw, the social, economic, and political map of Canada.

The 1988 *Morgentaler* decision was the first big Charter case. It dealt with abortion, arguably the hottest issue of them all. Many Canadians believe abortion is equivalent to murder. Others consider it a legitimate expression of a woman's right to control her body. No social and political question has been more passionately addressed from church pulpits, or more vigorously debated at the nation's dinner tables.

In 1988, a five-judge majority of the Supreme Court, four men and one woman, decided that provisions of the Criminal Code regulating abortion, passed by Parliament almost twenty years earlier, were unconstitutional and of no effect.[1] They expected that Parliament would fill the void they had created with new legislation, but Parliament failed to oblige. Kent Roach, of the University of Toronto faculty of law, has called the *Morgentaler* decision "a spectacular example of the Court having the last word ..."[2] The result is that Canada has been left as the only Western country with no abortion laws of any sort. Both therapeutic and elective abortions are widely available, in the big cities at least. Many are paid for by provincial health plans.

Henry Morgentaler is famous as the doctor at the centre of the Canadian abortion debate for more than forty years. In 1969, Morgentaler began openly performing illegal abortions in Montreal. According to section 251 of the Criminal Code, added to the Code that same year of 1969, an abortion was legal only if it was provided in a hospital and if a hospital committee composed of at least three doctors had certified that the pregnancy endangered the life or health of the pregnant woman. Morgentaler's abortions did not comply. In 1970, he was arrested. He was acquitted in a jury trial, but the Quebec Court of Appeal sensationally overturned the jury verdict and Morgentaler went to jail for ten months. Later, he and two colleagues set up a clinic in Toronto to perform abortions upon women who had not obtained a hospital committee certificate. In 1983, Morgentaler and his colleagues were charged with conspiracy to violate the Criminal Code. They were acquitted by a jury, but the Court of Appeal for Ontario reversed the jury verdict, echoing what had happened in Quebec. Morgentaler and his colleagues appealed to the Supreme Court of Canada.

The Supreme Court heard the case in October 1986. There was a sense of drama in the air. Many Canadians were watching, something the justices were not used to. The case was an early test of what the court was going to do with the recently passed Charter. One judge called *Morgentaler* the "big one." Seven judges sat on the panel—Chief Justice Brian Dickson, and Justices Jean Beetz, Willard ("Bud") Estey, William McIntyre, Antonio Lamer, Bertha Wilson, and Gérard La Forest. Justices Julien Chouinard and Gerald Le Dain did not participate. Chouinard was ill (he died the following February), and Le Dain, who notoriously had difficulties with his workload, taking forever to produce judgments, was left off the panel to create the required uneven number. Chouinard and Le Dain were the only Catholic members of the court, and Chief Justice Dickson may well have been happy not to have them sitting.

At the beginning of the case, the likely outcome was far from clear. Morgentaler's key argument was that the abortion provisions of the Criminal Code were contrary to a variety of rights guaranteed by the Charter, in particular by section 7, which says, "Everyone has the right to life, liberty and security of the person and the right not to be deprived thereof except in accordance with the principles of fundamental justice." Some judges, new to the Charter like everyone else, uncertain how to interpret it or hesitant about flexing their fresh muscle, wanted to decide the case as narrowly as possible.

After hearing the arguments, the judges, as they normally do, adjourned to their book-lined conference room, directly behind the courtroom, to sit around an oval-shaped table and discuss the case, just as many ordinary Canadians had done at home around their dining-room tables.[3] Each gave a preliminary view of how it should be resolved, speaking, as was the custom then, in reverse order of seniority (this formal procedure has been modified in recent years, allowing for more give-and-take). The most junior justice, Gérard La Forest, spoke first. He said the question of abortion should be dealt with by Parliament. Bertha Wilson spoke next. The first woman to be appointed to the court, and at the time the only one serving, Wilson was passionate on the issue and favoured striking down the abortion law as an infringement of a woman's liberty. Bud Estey and Tony Lamer, speaking in turn, thought the law should be struck down but wanted to find narrower grounds than those urged by Wilson. Bill McIntyre did not believe that freedom of choice was enshrined in the Charter. Beetz appeared to agree with La Forest and McIntyre and did not want to strike down the Criminal Code abortion provision. The judges were split, three and three. Then Dickson, speaking last as chief justice, said the law should be struck down, to the surprise of some of the other judges. The conference concluded. It had been a close run thing, and opinions could still change.

Dickson circulated his draft reasons in June 1987. Meanwhile, Beetz had changed his mind: it now looked like it would be a five-to-two vote striking down the abortion provisions, although among the justices there were substantial differences of opinion about why this should be. Bud Estey had begun working on his own reasons, but suffered a stroke and couldn't finish them. McIntyre still hoped to change some minds. He sent Dickson a memorandum saying that the question was not whether abortion was a good thing or a bad thing but whether or not it was within the constitutional power of the government or Parliament to enact the section of the Code.[4] McIntyre thought the answer to this second question was yes. Although many judges were troubled by McIntyre's point, in the end no one budged. The law clerks— young hotshot graduates hired for a year to help judges with research, enamoured with the court's Charter powers which they'd just studied in law school, and thinking they knew more about the Charter than the judges they served—weren't troubled at all by McIntyre's point of view. But the opinions of law clerks, then as now, didn't much matter.

The court handed down its decision on January 28, 1988. It was five to two for Morgentaler. Chief Justice Dickson gave reasons for himself and Tony Lamer. He found the abortion provisions in the Criminal Code contrary to section 7 of the Charter: "Section 251 clearly interferes with a woman's bodily integrity in both a physical and emotional sense. Forcing a woman, by threat of criminal sanction, to carry a foetus to term unless she meets certain criteria unrelated to her own priorities and aspirations, is a profound interference with a woman's body and thus a violation of security of the person."[5]

But there was another issue. The words of section 7 would allow interference with security of the person if the interference was in accord with the principles of fundamental justice. Did that exception apply to the Criminal Code abortion provisions? Were they in accord with the principles of fundamental justice? In Dickson's mind, they were not; he thought the procedures for obtaining a therapeutic abortion set forth in the Code were arbitrary and unfair.[6] Nor were the Code provisions saved by section 1 of the Charter, which makes rights and freedoms subject to "such reasonable limits prescribed by law as can be demonstrably justified in a free and democratic society." Justices Jean Beetz and Bud Estey agreed with Dickson and Lamer, although, in a separate judgment delivered by Beetz, they used somewhat different reasoning to reach the same conclusion.

Bertha Wilson also agreed with the majority result but gave separate reasons. Her analysis was sweeping, her conclusions stark. The issue, Wilson said, was "whether a pregnant woman can, as a constitutional matter, be compelled by law to carry the foetus to term."[7] The answer was that she cannot: "The right to liberty contained in s. 7 guarantees to every individual a degree of personal autonomy over important decisions intimately affecting their private lives. The question then becomes whether the decision of a woman to terminate her pregnancy falls within this class of protected decisions. I have no doubt that it does."[8] Wilson also considered that the Criminal Code provisions violated not just the pregnant woman's right to liberty but also her right to security of her person. The provisions clearly were not in accord with the principles of fundamental justice, so the section 7 exception did not apply.

The tone of her judgment and her emphasis on liberty made Bertha Wilson a heroine to many. Others felt differently. As for Wilson herself, as her draft circulated, she believed at first that enough judges would sign on to make it the majority judgment. Wilson was bitterly upset when she realized this would not happen. She had misread the "old boys' club." The other judges excluded her from their closed-door discussions. She was particularly upset that Lamer did not concur with her reasons and is said to have commented, with uncharacteristic bitterness, "He can't be seen as a baby killer if he wants to be chief justice."

William McIntyre and Gérard La Forest, distressed by what they saw as an unwise attempt by the court to take power that rightly belonged to Parliament, dissented. McIntyre gave their reasons: "The proposition that women enjoy a constitutional right to have an abortion is devoid of support in the language of s. 7 of the

Charter or any other section …"[9] Later he made the key point that had been unaddressed but implicitly rejected by the majority judges: "The solution to this question in this country must be left to Parliament. It is for Parliament to pronounce on and to direct social policy. This is not because Parliament can claim all wisdom and knowledge but simply because Parliament is elected for that purpose in a free democracy and, in addition, has the facilities—the exposure to public opinion and information—as well as the political power to make effective its decisions."[10]

As the years went by, Bill McIntyre's pessimism about the effect of the Charter on Canada's constitution increased. The court, he thought, used its new power "to substitute its own social policy for that of the legislative branches throughout the country."[11] McIntyre came to be regarded as an arch-conservative. It was said that he left the court—in 1989, the year after the *Morgentaler* decision—because of his dislike of how the Charter was being used.[12]

In 2008, twenty years after the *Morgentaler* case, Morris Manning, Morgentaler's lawyer, described it as "not only a legal judgment, but as a great event of historical, social and political importance."[13] Other commentators observed on this anniversary that the *Morgentaler* case had merely created a legal void that had lasted two decades and which Parliament seemed unable to fill. "When it comes to abortion," wrote Andrew Coyne, "we are literally a lawless society: the only country in the developed world that does not regulate the practice in any way." Coyne argued that the Supreme Court judges in *Morgentaler* had not intended theirs to be the last word. They had expected legislation but several attempts to pass new laws had failed.[14] The political problem created by the *Morgentaler* decision had been discussed in seventeen cabinet meetings held in 1988.[15] The first was held the same day the decision was released. Minutes of that meeting recorded:

"Ministers noted the implications for the Charter of Rights and the movement of Canadian jurisprudence toward the U.S. style of legislating through the judiciary ..."[16]

There were respectable legal arguments on both sides in the *Morgentaler* case. McIntyre and La Forest were no mean jurists, and they disagreed with the majority decision. There were three separate judgments from the justices in the majority, each significantly different from the other two. The conclusion may have been clear, but there was no clear reason for the conclusion. The decision was five to two. Richard Posner has written of the U.S. Supreme Court, "Many of the landmark ... decisions were decided by close votes and would have been decided the other way had the Court been differently but no less ably manned."[17] The same is true of *Morgentaler*.

In July 2008, an ailing Henry Morgentaler was awarded the Order of Canada. "I deserve it," said Morgentaler. "Canada's highest honour has been debased," said the Roman Catholic archbishop of Toronto. "The Conservative government is not involved in either deliberations or decisions with respect to which individuals are appointed to the Order of Canada," said a spokesman for the prime minister.[18]

Because of the *Morgentaler* case, there are no legal restrictions on abortion in Canada. Neither are there significant financial barriers to a woman's access to abortion: in most circumstances, it will be paid for by public health insurance, the provincial health plans so beloved by Canadians. The national system of publicly funded health care, guaranteed by the Canada Health Act, is often said to define the Canadian nation—or, at least, to clearly distinguish it from the United States. A 2009 poll found that 86 percent of

Canadians surveyed supported "public solutions to make our public health care stronger."[19] Anything that might erode the public system is suspect and unlikely to attract much support.

Roy Romanow, former premier of Saskatchewan and head of the 2002 Commission on the Future of Health Care in Canada, wrote in the Commission's interim report that the Canada Health Act was "virtually untouchable by any politician."[20] But Romanow didn't mention the Supreme Court. The Canadian experience is that its medical system can be touched by judges. The court changed the system in 2005, when it ruled that Quebec legislation making it illegal for people to take out insurance to pay for health care services privately, rather than use the services available through the provincial plan, was unconstitutional.[21]

It began with George Zeliotis. A retired Montreal businessman, Zeliotis was in his seventies, and not well. He suffered from arthritis and needed a hip replacement. He waited and waited for surgery. Zeliotis was not the kind of man to stand in line and suffer in silence. His vociferous complaints about surgery waiting times made their way into the Montreal newspapers.

The complaints were seen by the right person. Dr. Jacques Chaoulli was born in France and had practised medicine in Quebec since 1986. He was eager to operate a private hospital. Like Henry Morgentaler, he was a doctor who liked to fight against the established rules of medical practice. Christopher Manfredi, a McGill political science professor, has commented, "Both Morgentaler and Chaoulli are ... lone crusaders, they're both kind of oddball in certain respects ..."[22] Chaoulli read the newspaper stories about George Zeliotis, recognized a fellow oddball, saw an opportunity, and contacted him. They were made for each other.

In Quebec, laws making it illegal to take out private insurance for publicly available health services effectively blocked creation of a private health care system.[23] Chaoulli and Zeliotis decided their best strategy was to challenge these laws as contrary to both the Quebec Charter of Human Rights and Freedoms[24] and the Canadian Charter. Chaoulli, who some years before had flunked out of law school after one semester, pleaded the case himself. The Quebec Superior Court ruled against them in 2000, and the Court of Appeal did the same in 2002.

The case was heard by seven judges of the Supreme Court in June 2004. In a judgment handed down a year later, four judges agreed with Chaoulli and Zeliotis, and three did not. Four judges changed Quebec's health care system, and, by implication, that of Canada.

Justice Marie Deschamps gave the first judgment. She said the prohibition on paying for private health insurance infringed "the right to personal inviolability and ... is not justified by a proper regard for democratic values, public order and the general well-being of the citizens of Quebec."[25] Inordinate waiting times, she said, violated the right to life and security. The laws under attack, she concluded, were contrary to the Quebec Charter. This, Deschamps cleverly said, made it unnecessary for her to go further and consider the Canadian Charter. She gave robust views on limits to the deference that courts owed the executive and legislative branches of government: "Deference cannot lead the judicial branch to abdicate its role in favour of the legislative branch or the executive branch.... The courts have a duty to rise above political debate. They leave it to the legislatures to develop social policy. But when such social policies infringe rights that are protected by the charters, the courts cannot shy away from considering them."[26]

Chief Justice Beverley McLachlin and Justices John Major and Michel Bastarache agreed with Deschamps's conclusion but arrived at it differently. In reasons written by McLachlin and Major, the three judges said that the laws under attack violated the Canadian Charter as well as the Quebec Charter: "The fact that the matter is complex, contentious or laden with social values does not mean that the courts can abdicate the responsibility vested in them by our Constitution to review legislation for *Charter* compliance when citizens challenge it."[27] They concluded, "Prohibiting health insurance that would permit ordinary Canadians to access health care, in circumstances where the government is failing to deliver health care in a reasonable manner, thereby increasing the risk of complications and death, interferes with life and security of the person as protected by s. 7 of the *Charter*."[28] The three judges also found that the laws prohibiting private health insurance did not fall within the section 7 exception, since they were arbitrary and therefore not in accord with the principles of fundamental justice.

The remaining judges—Ian Binnie, Louis LeBel, and Morris Fish—gave a powerful dissenting judgment, displaying obvious exasperation with their colleagues in the majority. (A lawyer who was a Supreme Court law clerk at the time told me that there was much personal acrimony among judges over the *Chaoulli* case.) The reasons, written by Binnie and LeBel, were blunt. The issue of private health care and insurance, they said, "has been the subject of protracted debate across Canada through several provincial and federal elections. We are unable to agree with our four colleagues ... that such a debate can or should be resolved as a matter of law by judges."[29] The case, they said, was about social policy, not constitutional law, and the questions it raised should be decided by the Quebec National Assembly, not the courts.

The *Chaoulli* case generated a storm of comment. Mark Kennedy wrote in the *Ottawa Citizen*, "Canada's top court has looked into the eyes of the country's political leaders and called their bluff.... judges are now driving the agenda on the future of medicare."[30] In the *Toronto Star*, law professor Errol Mendes commented, "The Supreme Court justices have strenuously denied that they are intruding into the political sphere ... Yet the impact of their decisions has been politically strategic in a most profound way. It demonstrates that as important as the Charter is to society, who gets appointed to the judiciary and the Supreme Court is even more important."[31] The initial reaction of the political establishment? "Horror on the scale normally reserved for a carnival freak," said one account.[32]

Since the decision in *Chaoulli* and in anticipation of similar challenges and changes in the other provinces, private health care insurance plans have been established across Canada,[33] although commentators have expressed surprise at the limited effect the decision seems to have had so far. Some say that the business case for major insurers to offer private health care insurance is weak.[34] Nonetheless, private health insurance and care are becoming increasingly respectable and more prominent. In Quebec, the province directly affected by *Chaoulli,* the role of private surgical clinics has expanded.[35] In Canada as a whole, premiums for private or group insurance now account for 12.8 percent of Canadians' overall health expenditures.[36] The general effect of these developments is yet to be seen, but they may be dangerous. One commentator on recent reforms to the U.S. health care system, which provide for mandatory expansion of private insurance plans, has argued that the investor-owned, for-profit health insurance industry "adds at least $150–$200 billion to the annual cost of providing health coverage to the American population." The extra cost is due to private health insurance companies' spending as much as 15 percent to 30 percent of their premiums to cover overheads, which include "extravagant salaries and bonuses for top management, dividends for shareholders, and retained corporate profit." As well, insurers dislike and resist any government regulation of their business.[37] These issues—the cost of private insurance and difficulty in regulating the industry—were not considered by the Supreme Court in its *Chaoulli* decision.

Three Supreme Court judges thought that the Quebec laws violated the federal Charter, and one said they were contrary to the province's own Charter. That was enough to presage change in the nature of Canadian health care. Three other judges were strenuously opposed to getting involved in what they saw as a policy matter, but their disagreement was of no consequence. The court had made a profound political decision, with little or no regard for its long-term consequences.

Sometimes medical care is not wanted. In 2009, the Supreme Court had to decide whether a fifteen-year-old girl could refuse vital medical intervention and in this way choose to die when her life could be saved. Faced with such an excruciating question, the judges tied themselves into knots, producing one of the worst decisions of recent years.

A.C. was almost fifteen, an excellent student, bilingual, a reader of Jane Austen.[38] On April 12, 2006, she was admitted to a Winnipeg hospital with severe gastrointestinal bleeding, a result of Crohn's disease. A.C. was a Jehovah's Witness. Her religion prohibited blood transfusions. A few months earlier, she had given written instructions that she was not to receive blood transfusions under any circumstances. Yet, when admitted to hospital that April, A.C. needed a blood transfusion badly.

Stanley Lipnowski was A.C.'s doctor. The day after she was admitted to hospital, he asked the hospital's Department of Psychiatry to assess her. The report, completed by three psychiatrists, said that A.C. was "alert and cooperative ... very well spoken. Mood 'fairly good' ... [B]right, [slightly] teary at times ..." It said, "States that even if she will die, she will refuse blood based on scripture 'to maintain a clean standing with God.'" Her parents told the psychiatrists that A.C. "treasures her relationship with God and does not want to jeopardize it, that she understands her disease and what is happening."

In the early morning of April 16, Easter Sunday, A.C.'s condition suddenly deteriorated. Her doctors thought she would die without a transfusion. In keeping with her religious faith, A.C. refused to have one. The Manitoba Director of Child and Family Services was alerted and decided that A.C. was a child under sixteen in need of protection under Manitoba's Child and Family Services Act.[39] He sought a court order authorizing doctors to administer blood transfusions. He said this was in A.C.'s "best interests," the phrase used in the Act.

Early that Easter Sunday morning, Winnipeg lawyer Allan Ludkiewicz was woken out of a deep sleep in his suburban home by a telephone call from A.C.'s father. A judge was about to hear an application for the order sought by the Director. A.C. needed legal help if her wishes, and those of her parents, were to be respected. Ludkiewicz threw some clothes on, jumped in his car, and began to drive downtown. His cellphone rang while he was driving. The hearing had already started. Ludkiewicz argued A.C.'s case on his mobile, driving down the Trans-Canada Highway. "Fortunately," he says, "there was not much traffic, it being Easter Sunday, and early in the morning." Ludkiewicz lost the argument. A.C. was given a blood transfusion and recovered. "That day, my tears flowed non-stop," A.C. later wrote. "Nothing can properly describe how I was feeling ... I could liken it to being raped and violated, but even those words do not express my feelings strong [sic] enough."[40]

Even though A.C.'s life had been saved, she and her parents were deeply upset. They believed that their religious beliefs had been trampled on. They decided to appeal the court order on principle. They argued that the Child and Family Services Act provisions were unconstitutional because they infringed A.C.'s rights, under Canada's Charter of Rights and Freedoms, to freedom of conscience and religion, to life, liberty, and security of the person, and to equal protection and equal benefit of the law. The Manitoba Court of Appeal unanimously dismissed the appeal. Indefatigable, A.C. and her parents moved on, to the Supreme Court of Canada. Their counsel told them that it would be a very tough case to win. After all, they were arguing that a child should be allowed to die when her life could be saved.

The Supreme Court heard argument in the case on May 28, 2008, and delivered its judgments more than a year later.[41] The Manitoba Child and Family Services Act was found to be constitutional by six judges (Ian Binnie was the lone dissenter) and the appeal was dismissed. In confusing judgments, which did little to guide those who might be confronted with this issue in the future, the majority hung their decision on an interpretation of "best interests," the phrase found in the Act. Paradoxically, the interpretation of "best interests" by four judges (Abella, LeBel, Deschamps, and Charron) might, in some cases, allow a child to decide to die.

Rosalie Abella gave the reasons for herself and Justices LeBel, Deschamps, and Charron. Abella said, "The interpretation of 'best interests' … requires that sufficient account be taken of a particular adolescent's maturity in any given medical treatment context."[42] There is a "tenacious" principle, she said, that competent individuals should be free to make decisions about their bodily integrity. The common law "has … abandoned the assumption that all minors lack decisional capacity and replaced it with a general recognition that children are entitled to a degree of decision-making autonomy that is reflective of their evolving intelligence and understanding."[43]

Abella continued: "If, after a careful and sophisticated analysis of the young person's ability to exercise mature, independent judgment, the court is persuaded that the necessary level of maturity exists, it seems to me necessarily to follow that the adolescent's views ought to be respected."[44] As to arguments on constitutionality, "When the 'best interests' standard is applied in a way that takes into increasingly serious account the young person's views in accordance with his or her maturity in a given treatment case, the legislative scheme ... is neither arbitrary, discriminatory, nor violative of religious freedom."[45] In other words, the statute used to force A.C. to have a transfusion was constitutional, but had it been interpreted correctly, giving due weight to A.C.'s best interests, and acknowledging her maturity, it would not have been used in that way. The law was all right, but, in the case of A.C., had been misapplied.

Chief Justice McLachlin, more cautious and traditional by nature, gave separate and different reasons for holding the Act constitutional. She said that the Act provided an all-encompassing statutory scheme regulating medical decisions for children and adolescents deemed to be in need of state protection. This scheme displaced the common law regarding medical decision making by so-called "mature minors," common law relied on by Abella. Constitutional analysis must centre on the statute, said McLachlin, which did not violate the Charter. It did not infringe upon liberty and security of the person in a manner contrary to the principles of fundamental justice, because "the legislative decision to vest treatment authority regarding under-16 minors in the courts is a legitimate response ... to heightened concerns about younger adolescents' maturity and vulnerability to subtle and overt coercion and influence."[46] Justice Rothstein agreed. Both McLachlin and Rothstein expressed great concern about the practicality of assessing case by case whether a child's maturity was sufficient that her medical wishes should be respected; the lack of practicality of such an approach was a good enough reason to reject Abella's analysis. For McLachlin and

Rothstein, the statute was not only constitutional but had been applied correctly in A.C.'s case.

Justice Ian Binnie was the lone dissenter, and a courageous one. He believed the relevant sections of the Manitoba Act were unconstitutional. A.C.'s wishes should be respected, even if that meant her death. Binnie, with understatement unusual for him, wrote, "This is a disturbing case." Further: "The *Canadian Charter of Rights and Freedoms* enshrines in our highest law the liberty and independence of a mature individual to make life's most important choices free of government intervention, provided there is no countervailing social interest of overriding importance."[47]

A lawyer who represented the Director of Family and Child Services told me that the Supreme Court missed the boat in the *A.C.* case. "They wanted to write a decision about the rights of children to control their medical care. They wanted to hear a case we didn't argue. The case was about whether a child has the right to commit suicide, and about the state's duty to protect the child. The judgments were off the point. Sure, a kid should be able to decide if they're going to go to the dentist, but not if they're going to die."

Public reaction to the *A.C.* decision was, for the most part, hesitant, perhaps because of the confusing nature of the judgments. But *The Globe and Mail* did not hold back editorially. "This is rights run amok," it thundered. "No 15-year-old or younger person should be permitted to die for her religious beliefs—or those of her parents, which may be the same thing."[48]

Who won the *A.C.* case? The statute was not struck down as unconstitutional, but some judges interpreted it as allowing mature minors to refuse essential medical care. Allan Ludkiewicz, one of A.C.'s three counsel, has no doubt who won. "We won," he says. "The Supreme Court accepted one of our two arguments, and awarded us costs. That's a win." A lawyer on the other side said Ludkiewicz and the Jehovah's Witnesses lost. "They're masters of spin. They put it out that they had won. They didn't. The decision will have no practical effect. No judge—ever—will allow a child to commit suicide."

———

Suicide is not a crime in Canada, but assisting suicide is. Sometimes a person who wants to die cannot kill herself without help, but she will not be able to find help because of the state of the criminal law. This is the dilemma that confronted the Supreme Court in the *Rodriguez* case.

Who owns my life? Sue Rodriguez wanted to know. In 1992, she was dying from amyotrophic lateral sclerosis (ALS, sometimes called Lou Gehrig's disease), a degenerative disease of the nervous system. She didn't want to live once she could no longer enjoy life. Rodriguez knew that by the time that happened she would be physically unable to kill herself. She sought a doctor to invent a machine that would allow her, although severely physically disabled, to commit suicide when she chose. But subsection 241(b) of the Criminal Code says that assisting suicide, unlike suicide itself, is a crime. Any doctor who helped Rodriguez kill herself would risk jail.

In 1992, Rodriguez asked the Supreme Court of British Columbia to declare the subsection invalid. Rodriguez said that it violated her rights under the Charter. She lost at trial, and before the B.C. Court of Appeal. In 1993, she lost again before the Supreme Court of Canada, but only by one vote—the court divided five to four.[49] The justices admired Rodriguez and, although the majority found against her, were deeply troubled by her case. Some of them talk about it still, with sadness, almost twenty years later.

Gérard La Forest, John Sopinka, Charles Gonthier, Frank Iacobucci, and John Major were the judges in the majority. They said that the law that made it a crime to assist a suicide was not unconstitutional. Sopinka gave their judgment. The issue, he said, was whether the provision of the Criminal Code that made assisting suicide a crime, and that prevented Sue Rodriguez from controlling the manner and time of her death, was contrary to section 7 of the Charter, which gives everyone the right to life, liberty, and security of the person. Sopinka summarized the argument of Sue Rodriguez: "The appellant asserts that her application is based upon (a) the right to live her remaining life with the inherent dignity of a human person, (b) the right to control what happens to her body while she is living, and (c) the right to be free from governmental interference in making fundamental personal decisions concerning the terminal stages of her life."[50] Sopinka concluded that the prohibition of assisted suicide "deprives the appellant of autonomy over her person and causes her physical pain and psychological stress in a manner which impinges on the security of her person."[51]

But that wasn't the end of it. Had Rodriguez been deprived of security of her person contrary to the principles of fundamental justice, a further Charter requirement if the law were to be found unconstitutional? Sopinka candidly acknowledged that "the principles of fundamental justice leave a great deal of scope for personal judgment …"[52] His own judgment (and that of the other four judges in the majority) was this: "Given the concerns about abuse that have been expressed and the great difficulty in creating appropriate safeguards to prevent these, it can not be said that the blanket prohibition on assisted suicide is arbitrary or unfair, or that it is not reflective of fundamental values at play in our society. I am thus unable to find that any principle of fundamental justice is violated.…"[53] The decisive point was the importance to society of preventing persons from encouraging and assisting suicide in abusive situations.

Chief Justice Lamer did not agree with the majority, although his disagreement was based on a quite different point. He found that the Criminal Code infringed the provision of the Charter that says, "Every individual is equal before and under the law and has the right to the equal protection and equal benefit of the law without discrimination ..." (subsection 15(1)). Wrote Lamer: "In my view, persons with disabilities who are or will become unable to end their lives without assistance are discriminated against by that provision since, unlike persons capable of causing their own deaths, they are deprived of the option of choosing suicide."[54] Could this discrimination be allowed under the first section of the Charter, which permits infringement of Charter rights if the infringement "can be demonstrably justified in a free and democratic society"? The principal fear, observed Lamer, was that the decriminalization of assisted suicide would increase the risk of persons with physical disabilities being manipulated by others. His reply: "I do not think legislation that deprives a disadvantaged group of the right to equality can be justified solely on such speculative grounds, no matter how well intentioned.... The fear of a "slippery slope" cannot, in my view, justify the overinclusive reach of the *Criminal Code* to encompass not only people who may be vulnerable to the pressure of others but also persons with no evidence of vulnerability, and, in the case of the appellant, persons where there is positive evidence of freely determined consent."[55] The Charter's section 1, then, did not permit the infringement of section 15. The Criminal Code's blanket prohibition of assisted suicide could not be justified.

Claire L'Heureux-Dubé and Beverley McLachlin also dissented. McLachlin gave the reasons for both of them. The case, she said, with all due respect to Chief Justice Lamer, was not about discrimination. It was about the manner in which the state may limit the right of a person to make decisions about her body. McLachlin wrote: "Parliament has put into force a legislative scheme which does not bar suicide but criminalizes the act of assisting suicide. The effect of this is to deny to some people the choice of ending their lives solely because they are physically unable to do so. This deprives Sue Rodriguez of her security of the person (the right to make decisions concerning her own body, which affect only her own body) in a way that offends the principles of fundamental justice ..."[56] In a brief additional judgment, Peter Cory also dissented. Said Cory: "The right to choose death is open to patients who are not physically handicapped. There is no reason for denying that choice to those that are."[57]

The five-to-four judgment of the Supreme Court of Canada was handed down on September 30, 1993. Less than six months later, on February 12, 1994, Sue Rodriguez committed suicide. The coroner's report said that she died from drinking liquid laced with morphine and the sedative Seconal. It said that Rodriguez had decided in mid-January of 1994 that she wanted to die on February 12. It is not known why she picked that date. An unknown doctor assisted her suicide. Criminal charges were never laid. The police looked the other way.

Whether assisted suicide should be illegal remains a potent and divisive issue. There have been other dramatic cases since *Rodriguez*.[58] Several private members' bills seeking to legalize assisted suicide have been introduced into Parliament but have gone nowhere. Had the Supreme Court in *Rodriguez* decided the other way, there would, as with *Morgentaler*, have been substantial changes to Canadian life. Assisting a suicide would be legal. Perhaps Canada would have become like Switzerland, where it is legal, under most circumstances, to help someone take their own life, and where foreigners go to take advantage of suicide clinics (so-called "suicide tourism"). The Canadian medical profession might have changed its ways.

"Sue Rodriguez was a noble litigant," one of the judges who sat on the case told me. "I wish we could have helped her." Another said, "This was my most difficult case. I can't help thinking that this was an issue that should have been decided by Parliament." Chief Justice McLachlin has said that *Rodriguez* was one of the most troubling cases she has heard in her years on the court, according to journalist Kirk Makin: "It is the sort of decision that motivates her to bounce ideas off colleagues or take long pensive walks."[59]

Life and death. The Supreme Court has not handled the issues well. In *Morgentaler,* an early Charter case, a split court showed itself uncertain how to exercise its newfound power and sent the explosive abortion issue back to a Parliament unwilling or unable to act. In *Chaoulli,* a four–three decision that threatened Canada's national medicare system, no single thread ran through the justices' reasons, and fundamental differences on the relationship between the judicial and legislative branches were on display. *A.C.* was a low point; what can one say of a decision when both sides think they won? As for *Rodriguez,* the saddest case of them all, which to this day preys on the minds of the surviving members of that panel— well, the court did the best it could, faced with impossible facts.

FOUR

The Bedrooms of the Nation

Sexual preference, gay marriage, and group sex are issues that have excited Canadian sensibilities. The Supreme Court has had almost as much difficulty with these issues as with those of life and death, but it has resolved them nonetheless, legally at least. Once again, here as there, it determines how we live our lives. The court has decided that gays and lesbians are protected by human rights legislation, even when that legislation, quite deliberately, as a political decision, says nothing about sexual orientation. It has decided that homosexuals can marry each other. It has decided that group sex in a commercially run club does not offend community standards. The court has spoken for Canadians on social policy affecting some of the most intimate details of our lives.

The 1998 *Vriend* case[1] was extraordinary. The Supreme Court, in the name of the Charter, overrode the clearly expressed political wishes of the Alberta legislature (infuriating the then premier, Ralph Klein). It did so to extend human rights protection to a gay man.

Delwin Vriend was twenty-five years old and a laboratory coordinator at King's College in Edmonton. King's is a private, fundamentalist Christian institution. By all accounts, Vriend was good at his job, and a respectable citizen. His parents were evangelical Christians who ran an organic farm. He had attended private Christian elementary and secondary schools, and belonged to the Christian Reformed Church. He had been a student himself at King's College, and knew what kind of place it was.

Delwin Vriend was gay. One day, in 1990, he wore a pink triangle to work. This symbol was used by the Nazis to identify male prisoners in concentration camps sent there because of their homosexuality. The president of King's College, Henk Van Andel, asked Vriend if he was homosexual. He said he was. Not long after, in early January 1991, the college's board of governors made a formal statement condemning homosexuality. Van Andel then asked for Vriend's resignation. Vriend refused to resign. He was fired for non-compliance with the college's policy on homosexual practice.[2] For good measure, when he fired Vriend, Van Andel told him that homosexual practice went against the teachings of the Bible.

Vriend appealed his dismissal and applied for reinstatement but was turned down. He had a difficult time of it. He left his church. He told his parents he was gay; they stood by him. He was unemployed for several months before getting a job with the AIDS Network of Edmonton.

Vriend complained to the Alberta Human Rights Commission that his employer had discriminated against him because he was gay. A seven-year legal battle began. The Commission told Vriend that he could not make a complaint under the Alberta Individual's

Rights Protection Act (IRPA)[3] because the Act did not include sexual orientation as a protected ground. This omission was quite deliberate. The Alberta legislature had refused on at least five occasions to amend the statute to include sexual orientation. The legislature did not want to protect gays and lesbians in this way.

Vriend and several gay groups challenged the constitutionality of various sections of IRPA, arguing they contravened the "equal before and under the law" provision of the Charter (subsection 15(1)). The important issue was whether the Charter could be used not just to strike down a legislative provision but to "fix" a legislative omission—to put words in a statute that the legislature had intentionally left out. The trial judge found that the IRPA provisions violated the Charter. She ordered that the phrase "sexual orientation," as a prohibited ground of discrimination, be read into several sections of the statute. "Reading in" is the controversial Charter remedy that allows a judge to fill legislative gaps. It permits a judge, for reasons of constitutional law, to rule as if there were words in a statute that are not actually there. But a majority of the Alberta Court of Appeal reversed the trial judge. Vriend and the others appealed to the Supreme Court.

The Supreme Court heard the appeal in November 1997 and gave judgment four months later. The decision of Chief Justice Lamer and Justices Gonthier, Cory, McLachlin, Iacobucci, and Bastarache was delivered by Cory and Iacobucci, in two separate judgments, each dealing with a different issue. Justice L'Heureux-Dubé largely agreed but gave separate reasons. Justice Major dissented in part. (Sopinka took no part in the judgment. He died a few days after the oral argument.) The court ruled that the contentious provisions of Alberta's IRPA infringed the Charter and the infringement could not be justified. The words "sexual orientation" were read into the prohibited grounds of discrimination in the statute, even though the legislature had deliberately left them out.

Cory, giving the first part of the majority's reasons, rejected the argument that courts must defer to a decision of the legislature not to enact a particular provision. That argument, he said, draws a "very problematic distinction ... between legislative action and inaction ..."[4] He made a familiar point: "It is not the courts which limit the legislatures. Rather, it is the Constitution, which must be interpreted by the courts, that limits the legislatures under the *Charter*."[5] Later, Cory made a particularly powerful observation: "If the mere silence of the legislation was enough to remove it from s. 15(1) scrutiny then any legislature could easily avoid the objects of s. 15(1) simply by drafting laws which omitted reference to excluded groups."[6]

Iacobucci, in the second part of the majority's reasons, discussed whether the violation of equality rights found by Cory could be justified by the "reasonable limits" exception in section 1 of the Charter. He had no difficulty in finding that there was no justification, and easily agreed that sexual orientation should be read into the provisions of the IRPA. With the introduction of the Charter, Iacobucci said, the Canadian people chose to replace a system of parliamentary supremacy with a system of constitutional supremacy, giving every person rights and freedoms that no legislature could take away. The courts' job was to mediate the constitutional system, settling disputes about the meaning of rights and deciding whether qualification or infringement of these rights could be justified. Iacobucci noted that some said judicial review was illegitimate because it was undemocratic, with unelected judges overruling elected legislators. Iacobucci responded: "[I]t should be emphasized again that our *Charter*'s introduction and the consequential remedial role of the courts were choices of the Canadian people through their elected representatives as part of a redefinition of our democracy."[7]

Justice Major, from Alberta, dissented in part. He was nervous about using the reading-in technique aggressively, at least in this case, and nervous as well about the court actively taking on the legislature. Major considered that the Alberta legislature should decide how to fix the statute—that was where the job had to be done, in the legislature—and that the declaration of invalidity should be suspended for a year to allow Alberta's elected representatives to figure it out.

Vriend was a remarkable decision. Judicial interference in democratic law-making reached a new height. Predictably enough, reaction to the Supreme Court's judgment was heated and varied. Radio talk shows were swamped by supporters and opponents of the decision.[8] Buckets of news ink were spilt.[9] In Alberta, there was a public outcry. Premier Ralph Klein received 3700 calls within a week of the ruling, and cabinet ministers received another thousand each.[10] A comment in the *Ottawa Citizen* said, "Gays and lesbians are the shock troops for the various forms of state-subsidized promiscuity.... With the Vriend decision ... the Supreme Court has sealed its rejection of chastity."[11] John Redekop, a professor of political science and a one-time national moderator of the Mennonite Brethren Church, was quoted as saying, "It's improper, bordering on outrageous. How one can say it is democratic for appointed officials to override the stated wishes of elected legislators boggles the mind."[12]

Many others, of course, enthusiastically supported the *Vriend* decision, and saw it as a legitimate application of the Charter. Two American political science professors who conducted a detailed study of Supreme Court decision making later concluded, "Vriend exemplifies a larger trend by the Court to extend equal protection to homosexuals in the post-*Charter* era, and both gay and religious discrimination claims have attained a higher degree of protection than other forms of bias recognized in the *Charter*."[13] Vriend's own comment was, "Ha, ha, Ralph Klein. I won. You lost."[14]

Delwin Vriend, having changed part of Canada's social and legal landscape, left the country in 2000. Sick of publicity and attention, he went first to San Francisco. He now lives in Paris with his partner. He has a computer job in the Paris suburbs but lives in the heart of the city, across the street from the Musée Picasso. In an interview with *The Edmonton Journal* in 2008, Vriend said if it hadn't been for the firing and the seven-year battle that followed, "he might not have found a way out of the strict version of Christianity of his upbringing that condemned homosexuality as contrary to its religious doctrine."[15]

In the *Vriend* case, the Supreme Court made clear that gays could not be discriminated against in the workplace, no matter what the politicians thought. The next issue on the gay and lesbian agenda was same-sex marriage. The government of Canada had made it clear that it was prepared to pass legislation providing for gay marriage. But the government needed political and legal help to smooth the way. It turned to the Supreme Court by way of a reference under section 53 of the Supreme Court Act, which permits the federal government to ask the court for what is, in effect, a legal opinion on certain "important questions of law or fact."

In July 2003, the Chrétien government asked the court three questions. Was Parliament free to define marriage to include same-sex unions? Would such legislation be consistent with the Charter of Rights and Freedoms (that is, would it deprive anyone else of his or her Charter rights)? Would the freedom of religion guaranteed by the Charter protect religious officials from being compelled to perform same-sex marriages if doing so was contrary to their religious beliefs? In January 2004, a fourth question was added to the reference: Was a definition of marriage that restricted it to opposite-sex partners lawful according to the Charter?

Some objected strenuously to the Supreme Court being asked these questions. The questions, they said, were political and should be dealt with by Parliament. There was widespread suspicion that the government had punted the matter to the Supreme Court because of its political sensitivity. The court, many thought, had been dragged into the political process in an unseemly way by a cynical executive branch. A retired judge who sat on the case told me, "This was an improper use of the reference process. Quite apart from anything else, three courts below had already struck down the opposite-sex definition of marriage. Why should we get involved?"[16] The court responded opaquely, and weakly, to these concerns in its *Reference re Same-Sex Marriage:* "The political underpinnings of the instant reference are indisputable. However ... these political considerations provide the context for, rather than the substance of, the questions before the Court."[17]

In December 2004, the court unanimously answered "yes" to the first three questions. It refused to answer the fourth, the one that was added on later, saying it seemed the government intended to proceed with same-sex marriage legislation regardless of the court's opinion. The government had already made clear that it supported gay marriage, and intended to legislate accordingly. There was no point addressing the fourth question.

The first question was whether Parliament could define marriage to include same-sex unions. Interveners before the court (groups permitted to appear and give their views on the issues at hand) had argued that the Constitution Act, 1867, entrenched the common law definition of marriage as it stood then. In 1867, marriage meant only one thing—a union between a man and a woman. The court replied that historically marriage and religion were thought to be inseparable, but thinking had changed. The court invoked the "living tree" metaphor, contrasting it with something called "frozen concepts." (It was Lord Sankey of *Persons* fame who enunciated the living tree doctrine of constitutional interpretation: "The British North America Act planted in Canada a living tree capable of growth and expansion within its natural limits.") The court said, "Canada is a pluralistic society. Marriage, from the perspective of the state, is a civil institution. The 'frozen concepts' reasoning runs contrary to one of the most fundamental principles of Canadian constitutional interpretation: that our Constitution is a living tree which, by way of progressive interpretation, accommodates and addresses the realities of modern life."[18] The judges decided that, given the "realities of modern life," Parliament was free to define marriage as a union between any two persons, including those of the same sex.

Was same-sex marriage consistent with the Charter? Yes, said the court, it was. Same-sex marriage would not take away anyone's Charter rights: "The mere recognition of the equality rights of one group cannot, in itself, constitute a violation of the rights of another. The promotion of *Charter* rights and values enriches our society as a whole and the furtherance of those rights cannot undermine the very principles the *Charter* was meant to foster."[19] As for the third question, the court found that the guarantee of religious freedom in the Charter "is broad enough to protect religious officials from being compelled by the state to perform civil or religious same-sex marriages that are contrary to their religious beliefs."[20]

Many were desperately upset by what the Supreme Court had done. Gordon Gibson, affiliated with the right-wing Fraser Institute, was particularly unhappy that the court had not answered the fourth question: "The first three were softball pitches. The fourth was the important one: Is the traditional law of marriage lawful under the Constitution? The court, disgracefully, refused to answer."[21] Gibson described the judges of the Supreme Court as "nine well-paid lawyers with jobs for life till 75, accountable to no one.... the court has become a law unto itself, above Parliament, above even the Constitution ..." Other commentators suggested that refusal to answer the fourth question showed appropriate judicial deference to Parliament, which had made its intentions clear.

The same-sex marriage reference led to the Civil Marriage Act,[22] which became law on July 20, 2005. The Act defines civil marriage as "the lawful union of two persons to the exclusion of all others," thus extending civil marriage to couples of the same sex. At legislative committee hearings considering the bill that became the Act, there was "fundamentally divided testimony on the merits of the legislation from witnesses representing various religious institutions and affiliated organizations or groups, advocacy groups for lesbians and gay men, spokespersons for traditional marriage, academics and legal experts."[23] *The New York Times,* calling the issue one that "divides the Canadian public down the middle," reported, "The vote in Commons followed weeks of heated debate infused with biblical references and emotional warnings about moral decay on one side, and promises of an expansion of equal rights on the other."[24]

Justice Louis LeBel has called this reference one of his "two toughest cases" (the other was *BCE*—see Chapter 7): "It was the sheer amount of work, the breadth of the constitutional issues that we had to address ..." And, he added, "the political context."[25] When I interviewed him,[26] LeBel said he was "not enthusiastic about the reference function. I much prefer the traditional fact-based litigation model, with the arguments on each side clearly set out." On the same-sex marriage reference, he said, "The big problem for me was the very large number of interveners. It got very repetitious." (Interveners included human rights commissions, civil liberties groups, and church associations.)

The Supreme Court's assigned role on same-sex marriage was to clear away political underbrush so that Parliament could move more easily. Tom Flanagan, long-time close advisor of Stephen Harper, has said, "I don't think same-sex marriage would ever have been legislated if the courts hadn't first given their decisions, which basically created a new status quo."[27] That was the Supreme Court's job, to create a new political status quo, and that is what it did.

———

With these important gay rights issues out of the way, the Supreme Court now turned its attention to heterosexual sex. Is group sex in a commercial club indecent?

Jean-Paul Labaye operated a Montreal sex club called L'Orage. People met there for sex. They watched or participated in cunnilingus, masturbation, fellatio, and penetration. On several occasions, witnessed by police, a woman had sex with several men, while other men looked on and masturbated. No money changed hands. Only paid-up members of the club (about eight hundred people) and their guests were admitted. Pre-membership interviews were conducted to make sure those thinking of joining understood just what went on at L'Orage.

In what has become known as the "Swingers Case," Labaye was convicted of keeping a common bawdy house. The Criminal Code defines a bawdy house as a place kept, occupied, or resorted to "by one or more persons for the purpose of prostitution or the practice of acts of indecency." The trial judge, applying his view of community standards, found what happened at L'Orage to be indecent. It seemed obvious. A majority of the Quebec Court of Appeal upheld Labaye's conviction. But, the Supreme Court of Canada thought differently, and Labaye's appeal from the Court of Appeal was successful.[28]

Chief Justice Beverley McLachlin gave reasons for the seven-judge majority (McLachlin, Major, Binnie, Deschamps, Fish,

Abella, and Charron). The reasons were murky, to say the least. The test for indecency, she said, was the community standard of tolerance. That was to be determined by the risk of harm resulting from the conduct. Harm—and not just community standards, which might simply enshrine points of view or prejudices—was what mattered. The analysis of harm was in two parts: "The first step is concerned with the *nature* of the harm. It asks whether the Crown has established a harm or significant risk of harm to others that is grounded in norms which our society has formally recognized in its Constitution or similar fundamental laws. The second step is concerned with the *degree* of the harm. It asks whether the harm in its degree is incompatible with the proper functioning of society. Both elements must be proved beyond a reasonable doubt before acts can be considered indecent under the *Criminal Code*."[29] The evidence, said the Chief Justice, failed to establish that the activities at L'Orage caused harm analyzed in this way. Community standards of tolerance were not offended. What took place was not indecent.

Bastarache and LeBel, in what the press called a "biting dissent,"[30] took a very different view, one that was much more straightforward and quite clear. "There is a single question that must be asked to find that acts are indecent and to determine whether a place constitutes a common bawdy-house: 'Do the impugned acts offend the standard of tolerance of the contemporary Canadian community, having regard to the place and context in which they occurred?'"[31] Serious harm, they said, is not the sole criterion for determining what the Canadian community will tolerate. They found that "the sexual acts in issue were indecent, given their context. In our opinion, the community does not tolerate the performance of acts of this nature in a place of business to which the public has easy access."[32] Bastarache and LeBel were obviously right about what the Canadian community would not tolerate. There was something slightly risible about the majority in this case, seven upstanding judges sitting in an austere Ottawa courtroom, deciding that group sex in a commercial club did not offend the community standard of tolerance.

Reaction in Canada to the Swingers Case was, of course, mixed. Canada's "Talk Sex with Sue" Johanson said she expected the ruling would prompt an outcry from the sexually squeamish. "Supreme Court swings the right way," proclaimed an editorial in Montreal's *The Gazette*.[33] Barbara Kay wrote in the *National Post*, "Expect far worse indecency with seven of nine Supremes decreeing ... non-judgementalism toward sexual degradation as the preferred Canadian value."[34] Michelle Dow, president of United Mothers and Fathers, said, "When the court says commercial swingers clubs are legal, our youth take that as an endorsement of random sex. It corrupts their ability to form stable, permanent families."[35]

Jean-Paul Labaye announced he would celebrate his victory by adding a Jacuzzi to his club facilities.

Sex clubs sprouted after *Labaye*. "Is Toronto in the middle of a sex boom?" asked *Xtra!*, Canada's gay and lesbian newspaper, in November 2010.[36] "Is the sight of writhing, naked tangled bodies draped over red vinyl sofas your idea of fun on a Saturday night?" the newspaper asked, as it described the available sexual cornu-copia. "All this horny nightlife was made possible by a landmark ruling by Canada's highest court," said *Xtra!* Ryan Cook, owner of a gay sex club called Urge, said the decision "opened up the possibility for us. Canada is far ahead of the rest of the world." Todd Klinck, co-owner of Goodhandy's, which describes itself as a "pansexual playground," said, "We opened as a direct result of the 2005 Supreme Court ruling."

These three cases paint a confusing picture. *Vriend* is the apogee of judicial intervention and is loathed by some for that reason. The judicial branch placed words in a statute that the legislature had explicitly rejected. The Supreme Court seemed supreme indeed. *Reference re Same-Sex Marriage* was quite different; there, a reluctant court, dragged into the political process by the executive branch, did the job asked of it, and greatly helped the cause of gay marriage. As for *Labaye,* only two justices, Bastarache and LeBel, were clear-sighted in their reasoning. The others, chary of the delicate issues, sought refuge in obscurantism.

FIVE

True Believers

Life and death, sex and marriage. The Supreme Court no longer toils in obscurity settling abstruse legal points, as it once did. Now it decides big questions about big subjects that Canadians care about a great deal.

Everyone has beliefs: religious convictions, for example, or gut views about the claims of Aboriginal peoples, or an *idée fixe* growing out of nationalistic passion, or a particular political view of the trade-off between human rights and national security. The Supreme Court tackles beliefs and the conflicts they inevitably provoke, sometimes poorly, sometimes with brilliance. Unexpectedly, it has been particularly adept politically, brokering cunning compromises between political differences, notably in dealing with Aboriginal land claims and Quebec separatism.

In the 2004 *Amselem* case,[1] the court decided that Charter-protected religious belief encompassed religious convictions of any kind, provided those convictions were sincerely held. The Canadian religious mosaic, as a result, remarkably, extends infinitely.

Moïse Amselem, his wife Gladys Bouhadana, Gabriel Fonfeder, and Antal Klein were Orthodox Jews. They owned condominiums in Montreal's luxury Place Northcrest. In September 1996, Amselem set up a succah on his balcony. A succah is a small temporary hut, open to the sky, in which Jews are supposed to live for several days during the annual religious festival of Succot. Place Northcrest's governing body (known as a "syndicate") requested the succah's removal. The syndicate said the succah was in violation of the co-ownership declaration, signed by Amselem and the other condominium owners, which prohibited decorations, alterations, and constructions on balconies.

The following year, 1997, hoping to avoid more trouble, Amselem asked the syndicate for permission to set up a succah for Succot. The syndicate turned him down. Amselem and his friends Fonfeder and Klein each set up a succah anyway. The syndicate applied to court for a permanent injunction prohibiting them from setting up succahs and permitting demolition of any already erected. The application was granted by the Superior Court. This decision was upheld by the Quebec Court of Appeal. The story seemed over.

But Amselem and his friends were not the kind to give up. They went to the Supreme Court of Canada. They said that the co-ownership declaration—which they had freely signed—denied them the freedom of religion guaranteed by the Charter. The Supreme Court gave its decision in June 2004. In an ill-conceived judgment, the court agreed with Amselem. It was a narrow decision, five to four. A lawyer in the case told me he realized early on that the result turned on John Major, the judge from Alberta. The other eight judges seemed committed to a position from the beginning, split evenly. The case was Justice Major's to decide, although he said later that he didn't realize it at the time.

Frank Iacobucci gave the majority judgment. Beverley McLachlin, Louise Arbour, and Morris Fish went with him. So, as it turned out, did John Major, the swing judge. Did the appellants' religious faith, correctly interpreted, require them to erect a succah? There had been evidence at trial that suggested not. But, said Iacobucci, a court is not qualified to rule on the validity of any given religious practice or belief, or to choose among various interpretations of the belief. A court can only inquire into the sincerity of a claimant's belief: "[A] court's role in assessing sincerity is intended only to ensure that a presently asserted religious belief is in good faith, neither fictitious nor capricious, and that it is not an artifice."[2] The appellants had a sincere belief that building a succah was a religious requirement. That was enough. The declaration of co-ownership infringed upon that belief, even though they had freely signed it, and therefore it denied the appellants their freedom of religion.

What about the rights of other Place Northcrest condominium owners, rights to peaceful enjoyment of their property and to personal security (it was claimed that succahs might obstruct fire escape routes), rights protected by the Quebec Charter?[3] Iacobucci said that the effects of erecting a succah on these rights "are, at best, minimal and thus cannot be reasonably considered as imposing valid limits on the exercise of the appellants' religious freedom."[4] He said the argument of the Place Northcrest syndicate "that nominal, minimally intruded-upon aesthetic interests should outweigh the exercise of the appellants' religious freedom is unacceptable. Indeed, mutual tolerance is one of the cornerstones of all democratic societies. Living in a community that attempts to maximize human rights invariably requires openness to and recognition of the rights of others."[5]

Michel Bastarache, Louis LeBel, and Marie Deschamps did not agree with Frank Iacobucci. Bastarache and LeBel, and particularly Bastarache, were angry and frustrated. In their opinion, sincere belief in a principle or practice was not enough. An obviously irritated Bastarache gave reasons for the three dissenters. "The approach I have adopted here," said Bastarache, "requires not only a personal belief or the adoption of a religious practice that is supported by a personal belief, but also a genuine connection between the belief and the person's religion."[6] In other words, the personal belief or practice had to be reasonably grounded in the religion's doctrine as generally understood. Most important of all to Bastarache was that freedom of religion was not absolute; it was limited by the rights and freedoms of others. Erecting succahs would infringe the rights of co-owners, found in the co-ownership declaration, to preserve the building's style and aesthetic appearance and to permit the balconies to be used as an exit in the case of fire. It should not be allowed.

Ian Binnie dissented as well, in a separate judgment and for another reason. He emphasized: "Buried at the heart of this fact-specific case is the issue of the appellants' acceptance, embodied in the contract with their co-owners, that they would not insist on construction of a personal succah on the communally owned balconies of the building. There is a vast difference, it seems to me, between using freedom of religion as a shield against interference with religious freedoms by the State and as a sword against co-contractors in a private building."[7] After all, Amselem and the others had freely agreed not to do what they did. How could they be allowed to agree to something and then later say their agreement meant nothing because it went contrary to their religious beliefs?

And so the Supreme Court decided that the law should protect any religious belief, no matter what, no matter how eccentric, provided that it was sincerely held. It decided that such a belief, in some circumstances at least, prevailed over property and security rights. It decided that such a belief could override a previous contrary promise freely made.

Julius Grey, a well-known Montreal civil rights lawyer, was one of the lawyers for the appellants. He later described the *Amselem* case as "a crucial and liberating moment in Canadian law ..."[8] Grey wrote that "the Supreme Court specifically denied any legal pertinence to accepted dogmas of Judaism, deferring to the individual faith and conscience of those who sought accommodation." Others felt differently about the case. Right-wing columnist John Robson wrote in Montreal's *The Gazette* that *Amselem* "conveys a freedom at once dangerously unbounded and utterly unreliable."[9] Continued Robson, if "an open-ended 'religious freedom' lets one disregard otherwise legally binding obligations, what freedom or security can any of us count on having?" Writing a couple of years after the decision, Brigitte Pellerin, also in *The Gazette,* called it "an atrociously bad, and dangerous, decision."[10] Pellerin went on, "The court avoided taking upon itself the task of deciding what Orthodox Judaism really requires, which is probably a good thing. Unfortunately, it substituted intensity of personal feeling, which is less a slippery slope than a cliff. What doesn't that standard allow?"

Amselem allowed all Canadians to insist that their sincere religious views and practices, no matter how eccentric or even absurd, be protected as a matter of human rights. A strange notion of religious freedom was allowed to trump a private promise freely made. It was a bad decision.

Five years later, in a startling four-to-three decision, as bad as or worse than *Amselem,* the Supreme Court took quite a different position on religious freedom. What had happened to the judges in the meantime to change their minds?

An Alberta driver's licence must have a photograph of the holder. For a time, there was an exemption from this requirement for people who objected on religious grounds to having their photos taken. About 450 people, most of them Hutterites, took advantage of this exemption. Hutterites believe that the Second Commandment ("Thou shalt not make unto thee a graven image, nor any manner of likeness ...") prohibits them from agreeing to be photographed.

In 2003, the Alberta government removed the photograph exemption in order—it was said—to reduce the risk of driver's licences being used for identity theft. The province offered to issue the Hutterites special licences without photos but on the condition that photos be taken anyway for placement in a central data bank. The members of the Wilson Colony of the Hutterite Brethren, many of whom needed to drive if the colony were to function, rejected this proposal and began proceedings against the Alberta government, alleging a breach of the religious freedom guaranteed by the Charter. They argued that if a colony member could not drive a car, which would be the effect of the government insisting on a driver's licence photograph, then the religious commune could not function properly, and its social, cultural, and religious way of life would erode.

The legal issue was whether the limit on religious freedom resulting from the photograph requirement was a reasonable limit "demonstrably justified in a free and democratic society," the exception to Charter obligations provided by section 1. Both the chambers judge and a majority of the Alberta Court of Appeal held that the infringement of freedom of religion was not justified and the section 1 exception did not apply. Seven judges of the Supreme Court heard an appeal in October 2008, and, in a four-to-three decision given in July 2009, startling to many, reversed the Court of Appeal and decided that Hutterites were not exempt from the requirement of a driver's licence photograph.[11] This was another one-judge majority, just as with the *Amselem* case, but having the opposite effect.

Chief Justice McLachlin, who had been in the *Amselem* majority, apparently had rethought her views on religious freedom during the five years since that case had been decided. In *Wilson Colony* she gave the judgment for a majority that took a different and much narrower position. The new majority consisted of herself and Justices Binnie, Deschamps, and Rothstein (Binnie and Deschamps had dissented in *Amselem*).

McLachlin agreed that there was a breach of the Charter (this was conceded by Alberta), but considered that the regulation requiring a photograph on a driver's licence was validated by the section 1 exception. "The goal of setting up a system that minimizes the risk of identity theft associated with driver's licences is a pressing and important public goal. The universal photo requirement is connected to this goal and does not limit freedom of religion more than required to achieve it. Finally, the negative impact on the freedom of religion of Colony members who wish to obtain licences does not outweigh the benefits associated with the universal photo requirement."[12]

McLachlin showed deference to the legislative branch: "Much of the regulation of a modern state could be claimed by various individuals to have a more than trivial impact on a sincerely held religious belief. Giving effect to each of their religious claims could seriously undermine the universality of many regulatory programs ... The bar of constitutionality must not be set so high that responsible, creative solutions to difficult problems would be threatened. A degree of deference is therefore appropriate ..."[13] As to the practical side of things, the majority considered that

Hutterites could hire drivers if they needed to go somewhere by car. (This point was later ridiculed by some commentators on the case, who regarded it as unrealistic and patronizing.)

But the court was badly fractured. Justices Abella, LeBel, and Fish disagreed with McLachlin. Abella gave the dissenting judgment, a judgment described in the press as "passionately argued."[14] She considered the infringement of religious freedom to be unjustified. "Unlike the severity of its impact on the Hutterites, the benefits to the province of requiring them to be photographed are, at best, marginal. Over 700,000 Albertans do not have a driver's license and are therefore not in the province's facial recognition database. There is no evidence that in the context of several hundred thousand unphotographed Albertans, the photos of approximately 250 Hutterites will have any discernable impact on the province's ability to reduce identity theft."[15]

Wilson Colony was another bad decision, badly received. A near-consensus quickly developed that the majority had made a mistake, and that Abella was right. Nathalie Des Rosiers, lawyer for the Canadian Civil Liberties Association, said the judgment was "a setback for religious beliefs in Canada."[16] In an editorial, *The Globe and Mail* called the decision "a step backward on religious freedom," and said that "the risk in exempting 250 Hutterites seems to be marginal and speculative compared with the actual damage to the community's religious freedom and autonomy done by Alberta's mandatory policy."[17] A year after the decision, Ian Mulgrew was writing in *The Vancouver Sun,* "The majority's reasons ... understated the nature and importance of the Constitution's guarantee of freedom of religion." Alluding to *Amselem,* Mulgrew added, "Our fundamental law requires only a sincere belief that a practice fosters an individual religious commitment ..."[18]

There were those on the right who took a different position.

Columnist Colby Cosh, writing in the *National Post,* contrasted what he considered McLachlin's "realistic" view, as a daughter of Alberta, with Abella's näiveté. "Any Albertan who has seen flocks of bonneted Hutterites wallowing in consumerism at West Edmonton Mall cannot help snickering a little at Abella's tribute to the supposedly unworldly eremetic ways of the Brethren."[19] In an editorial, the *Ottawa Citizen* said the majority made the right call: "The consequences for the Hutterites are not severe. It probably means they'll have to hire outsiders to drive for them."[20]

The Wilson Colony asked the Supreme Court for a rehearing. The court refused. The *Amselem* and *Wilson Colony* decisions are at opposite ends of the spectrum of religious tolerance. Both are bad decisions. The first is too generous. The second is not generous enough.

———

The question of Aboriginal title to lands in Canada incorporates beliefs of a different kind, and is bound up with an entire way of life. Aboriginal peoples have made vast land claims based on history. Other Canadians have found these claims disquieting, even threatening. In 1997, with the *Delgamuukw* case, the Supreme Court examined their validity thoroughly and cannily set out a framework for their adjudication.

The Gitksan and Wet'suwet'en Aboriginal "Houses," seven thousand strong, claimed 58,000 square kilometres in British Columbia. The claim was based on historical use and "ownership" of the territories. The Gitksan part of the claim was supported by an *adaawk,* a collection of sacred oral traditions about the nation's ancestors, history, and territories. The Wet'suwet'en had a *kungax,* a spiritual song or dance or performance, which tied them to their land. There was a feast hall where the Gitksan and Wet'suwet'en people told stories that reminded them of a sacred connection to the territories.

In 1993, the hereditary chiefs of the Gitksan and Wet'suwet'en Houses (Delgamuukw was one of them) took their land claim to court. They were unsuccessful at trial (which lasted an extraordinary 374 days[21]). They lost at the B.C. Court of Appeal. They were partly successful at the Supreme Court of Canada, which gave its reasons in December 1997.[22] The Supreme Court found that the trial judge had improperly excluded oral histories as evidence. It directed that there be a new trial. That was the technical part of the decision. More importantly, to give guidance to the judge at a new trial, the court discussed the nature of Aboriginal title and how it became part of the law of Canada. The Chief Justice of Canada, Tony Lamer, wisely, so most people thought, encouraged the parties to settle the matter through negotiation. There never was a new trial, but the "guidance" remained. The case is an example of the Supreme Court attempting to influence future events rather than making a final decision.

Lamer gave reasons for himself, Peter Cory, and John Major. Gérard La Forest delivered reasons for himself and Claire L'Heureux-Dubé; both agreed with Lamer's broad conclusion but disagreed with some of his reasoning. Beverley McLachlin concurred with the Chief Justice, and said she was also in substantial agreement with La Forest and L'Heureux-Dubé. Justice Sopinka died before the judgment was rendered.

The central question, Lamer said, was the nature and scope of the constitutional protection given common law Aboriginal title by subsection 35(1) of the Constitution Act, 1982, which says, "The existing aboriginal and treaty rights of the aboriginal peoples of Canada are hereby recognized and affirmed." Aboriginal peoples have the right to use land, but not for any purpose; the use, said Lamer, "must not be irreconcilable with the nature of the attachment to the land which forms the basis of the particular group's aboriginal title."[23] For example, "If occupation is established with reference to the use of the land as a hunting ground, then the group that successfully claims aboriginal title to that land may not use it in such a fashion as to destroy its value for such a use (e.g., by strip mining it). Similarly, if a group claims a special bond with the land because of its ceremonial or cultural significance, it may not use the land in such a way as to destroy that relationship (e.g., by developing it in such a way that the bond is destroyed, perhaps by turning it into a parking lot)."[24]

Nor, wrote Lamer, is Aboriginal title absolute. It may be infringed by the federal and provincial governments. The Constitution Act, 1982, however, requires that any infringement must further a legislative objective that is compelling and substantial, such as conservation of fisheries. The infringement must also be consistent with the special relationship of trust between the Crown and Aboriginal peoples. Infringements that might be acceptable include the development of agriculture, forestry, mining, and hydroelectric power, the general economic development of the interior of British Columbia, and the protection of the environment or endangered species. Chief Justice Lamer concluded his majority judgment by saying, "Let us face it, we are all here to stay." The decision, in the strictest sense, was about the admissibility of evidence. But more broadly, it offered legal and political advice to the people of Canada on how to deal with an explosive issue.

The *Delgamuukw* decision was unpopular in British Columbia. It conjured up the spectre of a handful of Aboriginal people taking land away from the vast majority now occupying it, and being allowed to do so for obscure historical reasons. The fear developed that economic development and investment in the province would be stifled by uncertainty created by the decision. The Supreme Court of Canada came under vigorous fire from the

West. A few days after judgment was given, Terry Morley fever-
ishly wrote in *The Vancouver Sun,* "A court in faraway Ottawa,
with modes of reasoning foreign to B.C. sensibilities, has revived
our colonial state and made itself and its subordinate judges our
effective rulers."[25] The Supreme Court, wrote Morley, had shown
"a reckless disregard for public opinion and popular sovereignty."
Columnist John Gray gave a more measured and serious appraisal
in a series of articles that appeared in *The Globe and Mail* a few
months later. One suggested that *Delgamuukw* threatened the
robustness of the B.C. economy.[26] In another, Gray reported,
"The Gitxsan and the Wet'sewet'en are still revelling in the
December court judgment that was, at least for them, as delicious
as it was improbable." The question now, wrote Gray, was, "Do
they take what they can negotiate with the federal and provincial
governments, or do they go to court and try for more?"[27] At about
the same time, Andrew Coyne described the consequences of
Delgamuukw as "an unholy mess." He wrote, "If the whole of the
province is now to be encumbered by a previously unsuspected
regime of aboriginal title, it rather makes hash of conventional
property relations."[28]

Almost fifteen years after the decision, its effect still seems
unclear. More power is in the hands of some Aboriginal peoples,
certainly, but it is power they do not seem to have used coher-
ently or to great effect. In October 2010, a First Nations lawyer
plaintively wrote in a British Columbia newspaper that not much
had happened as a result of the *Delgamuukw* judgment.[29] But, the
First Nations have more clout, lots of it. One newspaper commentator wrote in 2009, commenting on the effect of a series of
Supreme Court decisions: "From the Enbridge project (known as
the Northern Gateway) and the proposed Mackenzie Gas Pipeline
in the Northwest Territories to the Lower Churchill River hydro
development in Labrador and the development of wind power and

transmission lines in Southwestern Ontario, energy companies are facing people who are newly empowered as well as assertive."[30] They had been empowered by the Supreme Court.

***

Relations between Aboriginal peoples and other Canadians are tricky. Just as delicate is the relationship between Quebec and the rest of Canada. The unexpected political savvy of the court shown in *Delgamuukw* was also demonstrated in the 1998 secession reference. The court offered the country a way of thinking about a difficult subject, and a framework for dealing with a contentious issue.

In September 1996, the Chrétien government asked the Supreme Court whether Quebec could unilaterally secede from Canada.[31] Chief Justice Lamer considered the court's answer the most important decision in Supreme Court history.[32] In 2004, Beverley McLachlin described the reference as probably the most difficult and troubling decision that she had faced.[33] Another Supreme Court judge told me, "This was the greatest decision the court has ever made. It was tremendously wise." Another said, of all the decisions he was involved in, he was proudest of this one. "The Case of the Century," said a headline in *La Presse* at the time.[34] The future of Canada seemed at stake.

The case was heard in the middle of February 1998. On the first day of the hearing, more than one thousand protesting Quebeckers marched from Parliament Hill to the Supreme Court, chanting, "*Au Québec de décider* [for Quebec to decide]." Politicians attacked the government for "hiding behind the robes of judges on an issue only Québeckers should decide." "Street theatre and political rhetoric forged a passionate sideshow," wrote one reporter.[35] Professors of law argued through newspaper op-ed pages about whether the Court should decide the case at all.[36]

On August 20, 1998, Lamer gave the government the answer of a unanimous court (Lamer, L'Heureux-Dubé, Gonthier, Cory, McLachlin, Iacobucci, Major, Bastarache, and Binnie).[37] Quebec could not unilaterally secede from Canada. But the answer was nuanced. There was something for everybody. The Supreme Court showed political astuteness. One retired judge told me, "It's not just what we said; it's how we said it."

Tony Lamer began, "This Reference requires us to consider momentous questions that go to the heart of our system of constitutional government." There were, he said, four relevant principles that were the lifeblood of the Constitution: federalism, democracy, constitutionalism and the rule of law, and respect for minorities.[38] Lamer discussed each principle at great length. Part of the discussion was about why the Constitution is entrenched beyond simple majority rule. "By requiring broad support in the form of an 'enhanced majority' to achieve constitutional change, the Constitution ensures that minority interests must be addressed before proposed changes which would affect them may be enacted."[39] ("Enhanced majority" refers to the requirement that a constitutional amendment be supported by two-thirds of the provinces having at least 50 percent of the population.)

Quebec secession would mean an amendment to the Constitution, continued the judgment, and that requires negotiation, but negotiation would have to be conducted in accordance with the four principles. "In the event secession negotiations are initiated, our Constitution, no less than our history, would call on the participants to work to reconcile the rights, obligations, and legitimate aspirations of all Canadians within a framework that emphasizes constitutional responsibilities as much as it does constitutional rights."[40]

"The judgment," wrote two learned commentators, "has been read as a statute that lays down the road map to referendum and secession. If one of the Court's goals was to secure a central place for the judgment in the ongoing debate over the future of the country, that goal has surely been met."[41] The court had assumed and discharged a political role of great importance. In 2004, Beverley McLachlin described how the court had approached the reference: "Everybody had to collaborate. It was a real collaborative effort in the true sense. Everybody talked, everybody listened while we worked out what we could say about these profoundly difficult questions that would be true to the Constitution."[42]

There may have been something more behind the collaboration described by McLachlin. Chief Justice Lamer was not well during this period. He was drinking heavily. The RCMP, responsible for the chief justice's security, unofficially expressed concern about his conduct to other Supreme Court justices. An unofficial committee of three judges, Charles Gonthier, Peter Cory, and John Major, went to see Lamer and told him that things must change. It was decided that during oral argument there would be no questions from the bench: the risk of embarrassing behaviour by the Chief Justice seemed too great.

Frank Iacobucci came up with the idea of all judges jointly writing the secession reference reasons, with each judge—except Lamer—responsible for a section. Gonthier wrote the core of the judgment, and formulated the four principles. If anyone was the father of the Secession Reference opinion, it was Gonthier. The judges frequently conferenced and exchanged notes as the judgment progressed, a rarity. The decision was written by committee. Lamer had little or nothing to do with it.

But Lamer's reasons for the importance of the reference, expressed in the judgment, seem sound, however and by whom they were put together. Laying down the four principles that must govern any negotiations about Quebec secession was a political masterstroke.

Secession is one kind of threat to Canada. There are other dangers. If the country is threatened by terrorists, extreme measures may seem necessary. Yet, the country is free and democratic, and it is hard to justify draconian steps. In the *Charkaoui* case,[43] the Supreme Court had to work out this delicate balance.

On the afternoon of Wednesday, May 21, 2003, in Montreal, Adil Charkaoui, a twenty-nine-year-old immigrant from Morocco and a permanent resident of Canada since 1995, dropped off his wife and nineteen-month-old daughter at a family member's home. Then he set off in his car for the Université de Montréal, where he was studying for a master's degree in education. Suddenly, he was pulled over by police. Charkaoui's first thought was that perhaps he'd been speeding, or it was some kind of routine traffic stop. Ten police officers converged on his car from all directions. He was arrested. There was nothing routine about this.

The government suspected Charkaoui was a member of an al-Qaeda terrorist cell. He had travelled to Asia in 1998, probably to Afghanistan and perhaps to Pakistan, for reasons that were not clear. He had dubious friends, some believed to be Islamic extremists. He was detained under provisions of the Immigration and Refugee Protection Act (IRPA).[44] They allowed the Minister of Citizenship and Immigration and the Minister of Public Safety and Emergency Preparedness to issue a certificate permitting detention of a permanent resident or foreign national deemed to be a threat to national security. The certificate and detention were subject to review by a judge. The person named in the certificate might be deprived of some of the information that led to the certificate being issued.[45]

In prison indefinitely, likely to be deported, Charkaoui began a series of extraordinary constitutional challenges. Their essence was that the security certificate regime deprived him of his section 7 implicit Charter right to know the case he had to face. One of Charkaoui's lawyers was Julius Grey, the aggressive and experienced civil rights lawyer who had represented the appellants in *Amselem*. The government's position was that information justifying the Charkaoui security certificate could not be released for reasons of national security.

Human rights and national security claims can easily compete. In *Charkaoui v. Canada* they had to be balanced. Chief Justice Beverley McLachlin laid out how that was to be done in the Court's unanimous judgment delivered on February 23, 2007: "One of the most fundamental responsibilities of a government is to ensure the security of its citizens. This may require it to act on information that it cannot disclose and to detain people who threaten national security. Yet in a constitutional democracy, governments must act accountably and in conformity with the Constitution and the rights and liberties it guarantees. These two propositions describe a tension that lies at the heart of modern democratic governance." This, perhaps, was an instance of what Justice David Souter of the U.S. Supreme Court had in mind when he said, "Judges have to choose between the good things that the Constitution approves."[46]

The judges had little sympathy for the government's position. When government lawyer Bernard Laprade suggested that national security trumped all other interests, because without it all rights are theoretical, Louis LeBel replied, "If we don't have the rest, we'd be living in North Korea."[47] Beverley McLachlin said in her reasons, "The overarching principle of fundamental justice that applies here is this: before the state can detain people for significant periods of time, it must accord them a fair judicial process ..."[48] The secrecy of the IRPA scheme, she said, denied the accused the opportunity to know the case against him, and thus the ability to defend himself. The judge's ability to come to a decision based on all the relevant facts and law was undermined. The current procedure, she concluded, "fails to assure the fair hearing that s. 7 of the *Charter* requires before the state deprives a person of life, liberty or security of the person."[49]

The Chief Justice thought that Canada's national security could be protected in ways that did not impair the rights of non-citizens to the same degree; a better balance could be struck between the protection of sensitive information and the procedural rights of individuals. She said: "Precisely what more should be done is a matter for Parliament to decide. But it is clear that more must be done to meet the requirements of a free and democratic society."[50]

The effect of this ruling, striking down the IRPA scheme as unconstitutional, was suspended for one year to give Parliament time to rewrite the legislation. Charkaoui, after two years in detention, remained under strict bail conditions, forced to wear a GPS ankle bracelet. In February 2008, new legislation came into force. It provided for security-cleared lawyers to protect the interests of non-citizens facing deportation or constraints on their freedom based on undisclosed evidence. These "special advocates" would be able to view confidential information but could not disclose it to the accused. The new regime, many say, has the same flaws as the old one. One lawyer who appeared in the *Charkaoui* case told me, "The court paid homage to liberal views, but didn't go far enough. It should have just done away with certificates. The new laws don't do it." In a second *Charkaoui* case, following the new legislation, the Supreme Court required the government to give full information to reviewing judges and special advocates, and instructed judges, if it were necessary, to summarize that information and give the summary to the named person.[51]

The indefatigable Adil Charkaoui fought on: "In a six-year battle of legal attrition, he outlasted dozens of spies, border guards, and government lawyers who aligned against him, scuttling their bid to keep him in thrall, and winning back his liberties one by one."[52] The fight seemed over in September 2009, more than six years after Charkaoui was first detained. A Federal Court judge, Danièle Tremblay-Lamer (widow of former Chief Justice Antonio Lamer), halted proceedings to have him deported and freed him from a variety of restrictions, including the wearing of a GPS bracelet.[53] This followed her ruling earlier in the year that secret evidence against Charkaoui could be disclosed publicly without harming national security, and the subsequent decision by government lawyers to withdraw much of the evidence rather than disclose it (the government said it was particularly concerned about endangering sources and disclosing investigative methods). *The Globe and Mail* commented, "It is galling that a suspected terrorist from Morocco is free to roam Canada because of a dispute between the country's spy service and a judge."[54] The *Toronto Star* felt differently. "Turning such people loose," it said, was "certainly not ideal, but it may be the least bad option available."[55]

After the case, the issue seemed to weigh on Chief Justice McLachlin still. In a speech to the Ottawa Women's Canadian Club on September 22, 2009, she said that the fear of terrorism "may lead governments to curtail civil liberties and seek recourse in tactics they might otherwise deplore ... that may not, in the clearer light of retrospect, be necessary or defensible."[56] In an editorial, the *National Post* approved of the Chief Justice's political comment. "She's right," the editorial said.[57] Others thought she was overstepping her role. The tension remained. Charkaoui was free. Was Canada safe?

Thus the Supreme Court draws the face of the country. It decided, by a one-judge majority, that religious freedom has enormous scope, can prevail over other rights, and can even nullify contractual commitments (*Amselem*). Later, also by a one-judge majority, it backed away substantially from this position (*Wilson Colony*). It gave heft to the concept of Aboriginal title to land, and handed the Aboriginal peoples a powerful negotiating strategy (*Delgamuukw*) and the people of Canada a way of thinking about the issue. It said Quebec could not secede unilaterally, taking a central part in Canada's most important political debate (*Reference re Secession of Québec*). And it decided that, in the contest between national security and human rights, human rights win (*Charkaoui*).

SIX

True Crime

The *Charkaoui* decision leads us to the criminal law decisions of the Supreme Court, where the judges struggle with a similar dilemma: they must decide how far bad people should be protected in the name of human rights.

In an interview she gave in 2010 to mark her tenth anniversary as chief justice, Beverley McLachlin picked two decisions she said had given her particular satisfaction as a jurist.[1] One was the *BCE* case (discussed in the next chapter). The other was the 2009 criminal law case of *R. v. Grant*,[2] which, with three similar cases decided at the same time (the "Grant companion cases"), has been described as the most important criminal law decision in years. The Osgoode Hall Law School blog "The Court" named the *Grant* case the 2009 "Criminal Judgment of the Year," "Charter Judgment of the Year," and "Judgment of the Year."[3]

The four *Grant* cases affirmed a new law-and-order approach by the Supreme Court. In three of them, the court ruled that evidence the police had obtained using questionable methods was admissible. In the fourth, police conduct was so egregious that the court sided with the accused. Previous law had given greater protection to the criminally accused. Kirk Makin commented in *The Globe and Mail,* "The Supreme Court of Canada has moved to silence critics of the Charter of Rights by reducing the thousands of cases where evidence is tossed out on the basis of police violating the rights of an accused person."[4] In this, the Canadian Supreme Court mirrored the U.S. Supreme Court: in its 2009–2010 term, the U.S. court "narrowed earlier decisions barring the use of evidence obtained through police misconduct."[5]

Criminal law cases loom larger at the Supreme Court than many realize. By the numbers, they dominate the docket. In 2009, 25 percent of cases heard were pure criminal cases, and a further 15 percent were officially classified as "Charter (criminal)." The next largest category of cases, at 11 percent, was constitutional law (excluding Charter cases), the category traditionally associated with the court's work.[6] Criminal cases also tend to dominate press coverage and the public imagination, often because they have simple (and sometimes lurid) facts that everyone can understand and have opinions about. They frequently concern the police, the most visible manifestation of state power for the average citizen and a source of unending interest to just about everyone. Justice Ian Binnie got the point right in his *R. v. Grant* reasons: "While the uniformed police embody society's collective desire for public order and livable and safe communities, they also present a serious and continuing risk to the individual's right to be left alone by the state …"[7]

Criminal cases also offer a tasty opportunity for any group, including an appellate court, to divide ideologically. Like any citizen, a judge may be for "law and order," sympathetic to the victim and generally favouring the state and the police in the battle against crime. Or he may be partial to the rights of the accused, seeking to rein in the police—for example, by excluding evidence obtained using dubious techniques. The Supreme Court has been a ground for this ideological battle in the last two decades or so, swinging back and forth from one position to the other. A law clerk from the mid-1990s told me that in those years, when Antonio Lamer was chief justice, there was considerable conflict within the court on criminal law, with many five-to-four decisions, but with the precarious outcome generally favouring the accused. "It was crazy then," a retired Supreme Court judge said. "There was permanent conflict. There was no common sense. It was driven by a desire to be politically correct, to please law professors at the Toronto law schools."

In recent times, things have moved to the right. The law clerk I talked to said: "The court has evolved. Its composition has changed. Lamer retired, Sopinka died. They had been the leading writers in this area. The court has become more conservative on criminal matters, on constitutional guarantees for criminal defendants." Queen's law professor Donald Stuart, a respected authority on criminal law,[8] said in a 2009 speech at a Canadian Bar Association conference that the Supreme Court had "decimated the right to remain silent ... In this respect, Canada is out of step with the law in other countries. There are also some worrying signs that a law-and-order bias is creeping into some recent Charter rulings which divided the court....The disturbing reality is that our Supreme Court has now clearly given the police huge authority to use tricks and inducements in interrogations."[9]

Three of the four *Grant* cases affirmed a law-and-order agenda. They favoured the police at the expense of the accused. It seems that, in Canada, after all, bad people (except, perhaps, terrorists) cannot count on much protection from the law of human rights.

Donnohue Grant, a young black man, was walking down the street in Toronto's Greenwood/Danforth district. It was lunchtime on Monday, November 17, 2003. Police constables Worrell and Forde were patrolling the district, dressed in plainclothes and in an unmarked car. Constable Gomes was also on patrol, in uniform, driving a marked police car. Constable Worrell noticed Donnohue Grant and thought that he was behaving suspiciously.

Worrell decided that "maybe we should have a chat with this guy and see what's up with him." At the radioed suggestion of Worrell and Forde, Gomes got out of his car and stepped into Grant's path. Gomes asked Grant "what was going on" and then for his name and address. Grant, behaving nervously, adjusted his jacket. Gomes didn't like that and told Grant to "keep his hands in front of him." Worrell and Forde pulled up in their car, joined Gomes, and blocked Grant's path. The three police officers were large men. Gomes and Grant had the following exchange:

Q: Have you ever been arrested before?

A: I got into some trouble about three years ago.

Q: Do you have anything on you that you shouldn't?

A: No. (Pause.) Well, I got a small bag of weed.

Q: Where is it?

A: It's in my pocket.

Q: Is that it?

A: (Male puts his head down.) Yeah. Well, no.

Q: Do you have other drugs on you?

A: No, I just have the weed, that's it.

Q: Well, what is it that you have?

A: I have a firearm.[10]

Grant was arrested.

At trial, Grant was convicted of five firearm offences. The Ontario

Court of Appeal dismissed an appeal. A seven-judge panel of the Supreme Court heard the case in April 2008 (Justices Bastarache and Rothstein were absent; Bastarache had recently announced his resignation, to take effect soon, and Rothstein's absence made the panel the required uneven number). Judgment was given in July 2009. Grant lost. The Chief Justice and Justice Charron gave joint reasons, concurred in by Justices LeBel, Fish, and Abella. Binnie and Deschamps gave "partially concurring" reasons. (Judges who "concur" with a judgment agree with the result, but want to have their own say.) The judgments were complicated.

The threshold question, said McLachlin and Charron, "is whether the appellant was detained before he produced the firearm and was arrested. If he was detained, the detention was arbitrary; all parties are agreed that the police lacked legal grounds to detain the appellant. Further, if detained, Mr. Grant was entitled to be advised of the right to counsel at that point...."[11] (Section 10(b) of the Charter says, "Everyone has the right on arrest or detention ... to retain and instruct counsel without delay and to be informed of that right ...")

Was Grant "detained" before the gun was found? That depended on the meaning of the word "detention." McLachlin and Charron said that "detention" refers to a restriction of the individual's liberty by a significant physical or psychological restraint. Psychological detention occurs if a person would reasonably conclude that he had no choice but to comply. What it is "reasonable" to conclude depends on a variety of factors—the nature of police conduct, for example, and the characteristics of the individual such as age, physical stature, minority status, and level of sophistication.[12]

Applying these principles, McLachlin and Charron considered that Grant had been detained from the moment Constable Gomes told him to keep his hands in front of him. They wrote, "A reasonable person in his position (18 years old, alone, faced by three physically larger policemen in adversarial positions) would conclude that his or her right to choose how to act had been removed by the police ..."[13] The detention was arbitrary and therefore contrary to section 9 of the Charter, since as the police themselves acknowledged there was no good reason to detain Grant before his self-incriminating statements. There was a further Charter breach because the requirement that a person be advised of his right to counsel immediately upon being detained was ignored. These were the legal consequences of three burly policemen confronting an eighteen-year-old.

But Grant was a man with a gun. Despite the Charter breaches, was the gun nonetheless admissible in evidence? If not, his convictions would not stand. The Charter says that where "a court concludes that evidence was obtained in a manner that infringed or denied any rights or freedoms guaranteed by this Charter, the evidence shall be excluded if it is established that, having regard to all the circumstances, the admission of it in the proceedings would bring the administration of justice into disrepute" (section 24(2)). Three lines of inquiry, said McLachlin and Charron, must be considered in assessing the effect of admitting evidence on the reputation of the administration of justice—the seriousness of the state conduct, the breach's impact on the accused's interests, and the importance to society of having the court rule on the incident.[14]

It was clear that Grant's gun was discovered as the result of an unlawfully obtained statement. Did this bring the administration of justice into disrepute? McLachlin and Charron applied the "three lines of inquiry" doctrine. Police conduct was not egregious. The impact of the Charter breach on the accused's interests was not at the most serious end of the scale. The value of the evidence uncovered was considerable.[15] Admission of the gun, they concluded, would not bring the administration of justice into disrepute.[16]

Ian Binnie did not agree with his colleagues on the detention issue. He thought their approach placed too much emphasis on the claimant's perception of psychological pressure. He described the court's approach as claimant-centred.[17] When, he asked, does a simple interaction between the police and a citizen crystallize into a detention? Given the cautious and respectful nature of Canadians, they are likely to feel obliged to obey the police in circumstances when they do not need the assistance of legal counsel. Such circumstances should not be regarded as "detention." Binnie wrote, "I believe more attention should be paid to the *objective* facts of the encounter between a police officer and members of the public ..."[18]

Marie Deschamps had a similar point of view. Like Binnie, she was against a "claimant-centred" approach and wasn't interested in "subjective" facts. It didn't matter to her what the detained person thought and felt. What mattered was "the societal interest in protecting constitutional rights and the societal interest in the adjudication of the case on the merits."[19] But, despite their problem with the majority's view of detention, both Binnie and Deschamps agreed with the majority on the disposition of the *Grant* case. The gun should be admitted into evidence.

There's nothing new about the gun-as-evidence problem. Forty years ago, long before the Charter, when I was law clerk to Justice Judson of the Supreme Court, I worked on a gun case.[20] A man suspected of shooting a gas station attendant in the course of a robbery told the police he had thrown the murder weapon into a swamp. The police looked in the swamp and found the gun. The trial judge found that the suspect's statement was induced by trickery, duress, and improper inducements and said that to admit the gun into evidence would bring the administration of justice into disrepute. The court of appeal agreed. In a six-to-three decision (Judson was in the majority), the Supreme Court overturned that decision and decided the gun should be admitted, saying the only test was the weapon's relevance as evidence. The majority were also impressed that parts of the murderer's confession were proven true when the gun was found in the swamp. That resolved doubts about the statement's reliability. The pre-Charter decision in this case might seem to belong to a long-ago age, but the result in the 2009 *Grant* case was similar.

The other three *Grant* cases, the so-called "companion cases," dealt with roughly the same issues as *Grant* itself, with reasons handed down on the same day by the same justices. In two of them, the court sided with the police and found no Charter breach. But in the third case, police conduct was considered so improper that the judges sided with the accused.

In *R. v. Suberu*[21] detention was, once again, the principal issue. Musibau Suberu had been arrested for fraud and told his rights, but before that point he had had some "preliminary interaction" with the police. Constable Roughley had responded to a call about a person attempting to use a stolen credit card at a Cobourg, Ontario, liquor store. He was told that there were two male suspects. Roughley entered the liquor store and saw another police officer talking to an employee and a male customer (who, as it turns out, was Suberu's accomplice). Suberu walked past Roughley and said, "He did this, not me, so I guess I can go." Roughley followed Suberu outside and, while Suberu was getting into the driver's seat of a minivan, said, "Wait a minute. I need to talk to you before you go anywhere." Roughley then asked Suberu a few questions.

Did the "preliminary interaction" fall within the definition of "detention"? Should Roughley have told Suberu of his Charter right to retain and instruct counsel when the "preliminary inter-action" took place? For the majority judges, the answer was no, because Suberu had not been detained at that time. He had not been denied right to counsel when he should have had it. His fraud conviction should stand. McLachlin and Charron delivered majority reasons to that effect, with LeBel, Deschamps, and Abella concurring.

An exasperated Binnie disagreed; he thought that if one applied the claimant-centred analysis that McLachlin and Charron had themselves formulated in *Grant*, it was clear that Suberu had been detained. Said Binnie, "Generally speaking, the police mean what they say when they direct a citizen to stay put. As Constable Roughley acknowledged in this case, if Mr. Suberu had not heeded the officer's direction not to leave the parking lot at the crime scene, Constable Roughley would "likely" have pursued him in the patrol car and stopped Mr. Suberu's van in the street ..."[22] In very brief reasons, Morris Fish agreed with Binnie.

In *R. v. Shepherd*[23] McLachlin and Charron once again gave joint reasons; this time, all the judges agreed. Shepherd had been charged with impaired driving. The arresting policeman saw him go through a stop sign, driving over the posted speed limit. The officer activated his siren and flashing lights and chased Shepherd for more than three kilometres. When Shepherd finally pulled over, the officer observed that he had red eyes, smelled of alcohol, and appeared lethargic and fatigued and that his movements and speech were slow and deliberate. The officer thought the accused was intoxicated and, after reading him his rights, made a breathalyzer demand. At trial, Shepherd sought to exclude his breath samples on the basis that they were obtained in violation of the Charter. He argued that the arresting officer lacked reasonable and probable grounds to demand the breath samples. The Supreme Court considered that there was ample evidence to support the officer's subjective belief that Shepherd's ability to drive was impaired by alcohol. Accordingly, the officer's breathalyzer demand was lawful.

The exception in the Grant quartet was *R. v. Harrison*.[24] The issue was whether cocaine, discovered because of an unconstitutional detention and search, should have been admitted into evidence. The police had pulled over Harrison's rented car without reasonable grounds. The officer had noticed that the car had no front licence plate but realized almost immediately that, because it was registered in Alberta, it did not require one; he proceeded to pull Harrison's car over anyway. The officer arrested Harrison when he discovered his driver's licence was suspended, then searched the car and found drugs. McLachlin gave reasons for all the judges except Deschamps, who dissented. The Chief Justice disagreed with both the trial judge and the Ontario Court of Appeal, who thought the cocaine should be admitted as evidence. She applied the *R. v. Grant* "three avenues of inquiry" and concluded the evidence was not admissible.

McLachlin was heavily influenced in *Harrison* by what she saw as appalling police conduct. There had been a "brazen and flagrant" disregard of the appellant's Charter rights against arbitrary detention and unreasonable search and seizure. "These are protections that law-abiding Canadians take for granted and courts must play a role in safeguarding them even where the beneficiaries are involved in unlawful activity. In the circumstances of this case, it is my view that the admission of the evidence would bring the administration of justice into disrepute."[25]

Justice Deschamps dissented, and vigorously, almost angrily, reiterated the views she had expressed in *Grant*. She said of the judges in the majority, "They attach excessive weight to the officer's conduct and disregard the fact that the impact of the violation on the interests protected by the *Canadian Charter of Rights and Freedoms* was limited."[26] If the simpler test she had laid out in *Grant* were used, she said, the result would be different. What should have been emphasized was not the predicament of the accused but the interests of society. Facts were objective, not subjective.

And so, it seemed, police powers were in the ascendant. Evidence obtained illegally by the police was admissible except in the most egregious circumstances. Fighting crime trumped constitutional nuance. But, as it turned out, for a little while at least, things were not quite that clear.

"A man found with cocaine walked free. Next time it could be someone with a gun."[27] So *The Globe and Mail* thundered editorially, all riled up over the December 2009 Supreme Court judgment in *R. v. Burke*.[28]

Abede Burke had been arrested by the Montreal police without a warrant. When the police stopped him (he was riding a bicycle), they thought he had been involved in a home invasion. They had mistaken Abede Burke for his brother; there was a warrant out for the brother. Abede Burke told the police it was his brother they were after, but they paid no attention and, warrantless, arrested him instead. The Criminal Code says that a peace officer may arrest someone without a warrant if he has reasonable grounds to believe that one is in force (section 495(1)(c)). Following his arrest, the police searched Abede Burke and found a bag of crack cocaine in his pocket. He was charged with possessing cocaine for trafficking. The trial judge acquitted Burke, finding that the officer did not have objective grounds for the arrest because he had not investigated the accused's claim of mistaken identity. The trial judge said that the arrest was illegal, the subsequent search was unreasonable, and the evidence was therefore inadmissible. The court of appeal agreed (with a dissent).

The Supreme Court, taking a rest from the law-and-order agenda, agreed with the trial judge. Morris Fish gave brief reasons for himself and four other justices (LeBel, Abella, Charron, and Rothstein). Fish said that the judge had found no reasonable grounds to believe that there was a warrant for Abede's arrest. Her reasons "explain in detail why she found the evidence of the arresting officer inconsistent, contradictory and wanting as to the circumstances surrounding the respondent's arrest."[29] Justice Thomas Cromwell and Justice Deschamps disagreed. They thought that Justice Chamberland, who dissented in the Quebec Court of Appeal, had got it right when he said of the trial judge's analysis, "It would require the officer to be certain, or at least persuaded, that the person about to be arrested is the one against whom a warrant of arrest is in force, rather than simply to have reasonable grounds to believe so."[30]

Did this decision, a few short months after *Grant,* show the court was having second thoughts about police powers? Was *The Globe* right? Next time, would it be a man with a gun who walked free?

——◆——

Be careful when you put out the garbage. Calgary police suspected that Russell Patrick was operating an Ecstasy laboratory in his house. They reached through the airspace, across his property line, and grabbed garbage bags on a stand just inside that line waiting to be collected by the garbagemen. In them, they found articles typically used to manufacture the illegal drug. They went and got a warrant and searched Patrick's home. He was charged with drug offences.

Patrick contended that without the garbage the police would not have been able to obtain the warrant. He said the evidence had been gathered in breach of his section 8 Charter rights ("Everyone has the right to be secure against unreasonable search or seizure"). Given the seriousness of the breach, the admission of such evidence, he said, would bring the administration of justice into disrepute. As there then remained insufficient evidence upon which a properly instructed jury could convict, he argued that he should be acquitted of all charges.

The trial judge held that there was not a reasonable expectation of privacy in the items seized from his garbage and that the search warrant was valid. The court of appeal, with a dissent, agreed. The Supreme Court handed down its reasons in April 2009, with Justice Binnie writing for six judges (himself, McLachlin, LeBel, Fish, Charron, and Rothstein). Abella gave separate concurring reasons.[31] Binnie's judgment is vintage Binnie, eloquent in places, and humorous; clearly he was enjoying himself.

Binnie observed that a homeowner might have no interest in the physical possession of garbage but nonetheless might have a very strong interest in keeping private the information embedded in its contents. "In that case, the question is whether he or she has so dealt with the items put out for collection in such a way as to forfeit any reasonable expectation (*objectively* speaking) of keeping the contents confidential."[32] Binnie observed that we should not speak lightly of garbage:

> Residential waste includes an enormous amount of personal information about what is going on in our homes, including a lot of DNA on household tissues, highly personal records (e.g., love letters, overdue bills and tax returns) and hidden vices (pill bottles, syringes, sexual paraphernalia, etc.).... a garbage bag may more accurately be described as a bag of "information" whose contents, viewed in their entirety, paint a fairly accurate and complete picture of the householder's activities and lifestyle. Many of us may not wish to disclose these things to the public generally or to the police in particular.[33]

The question, said Binnie, is whether people generally have a privacy interest in the concealed contents of an opaque and sealed "bag of information." He said, "I believe that they do."[34] But, in this case, when Patrick placed his garbage bags for collection in the open container at the back of his property adjacent to the lot line, he had "abandoned" his bag of information. "The bags were unprotected," said Binnie, "and within easy reach of anyone walking by in a public alleyway, including street people, bottle pickers, urban foragers, nosey neighbours and mischievous children, not to mention dogs and assorted wildlife, as well as the garbage collectors and the police."[35] Patrick had lost any objectively reasonable privacy interest. And so, "the taking by the police did not constitute a search and seizure within the scope of s. 8, and the evidence (as well as the fruits of the search warrant obtained in reliance on such evidence) was properly admissible."[36]

Justice Abella concurred in separate reasons. She emphasized that "the privacy of personal information emanating from the home, which has been transformed into household waste and put out for disposal, is entitled to protection from indiscriminate state intrusion. Such information should not be seen to automatically lose its 'private' character simply because it is put outside for garbage disposal. Before the state can rummage through the personal information from this ultimate zone of privacy, there should be, at the very least, a reasonable suspicion that a crime has been or is likely to be committed."[37]

It's a conservative court all right, at least when it comes to the criminal law as seen by a majority of the justices. The December 2009 *Burke* case seemed like an aberration just a few months later, with the arrival in July 2010 of the pro-police decision (but only by four justices to three) in *R. v. Cornell*.[38]

Justice Fish (in dissenting reasons for himself and Justices Binnie and LeBel) described what happened in Calgary at the Cornell residence at about 6:00 P.M. on November 30, 2005: "Loaded weapons in hand, nine masked members of a police tactical unit smashed their way into the appellant's home in a residential Calgary neighbourhood. They forced the appellant's brother, who has a mental disability, face-down to the floor and cuffed his hands behind his back. They dented the front door with their battering ram and broke the door frame ..."[39]

The police had been issued a search warrant (but did not have it with them) and were looking for cocaine, which they found. Cornell, the accused, later argued that the drugs were discovered by unreasonable search and seizure and, because of the Charter, should not be admitted into evidence. The trial judge and court of appeal disagreed that the search and seizure was unreasonable, and Cornell was convicted of possession of cocaine for the purpose of trafficking.

A bare majority of the Supreme Court didn't buy Cornell's Charter argument either. Justice Cromwell gave reasons for himself, Chief Justice McLachlin, and Justices Charron and Rothstein. The search, he said, was conducted reasonably in the circumstances. The police believed that the house was being used by a violent criminal gang and that evidence might be quickly destroyed if they announced their presence in the usual way.

But Fish, for the minority, did not think that these police beliefs were reasonably founded. In reasons, which took Cromwell to task, he wrote, "There is no evidence that the officers considered that their safety was at risk or that evidence was likely to be destroyed when they executed their search at the Cornell home."[40] Fish particularly found police use of balaclava masks to be offensive. "The tactical team wore balaclavas *because that is what they always did.* And their avowed reason for proceeding that way was to intimidate and psychologically overpower those inside, in part by creating an 'overwhelming sensory uniformed kind of appearance' ... Gratuitous intimidation of this sort—psychological violence entirely unrelated to the particular circumstances of the search—may in itself render a search unreasonable."[41] Finally, wrote Fish, the invading officers should have had the search warrant with them. "This is not a technical or insignificant breach of the law. It is a violation of a venerable principle of historic and constitutional importance."[42] The search and seizure was unreasonable, said Fish, and with some passion, and the evidence therefore should be excluded.

Any doubts that the Supreme Court is now a law-and-order court, although desperately split on the basic issue of civil liberties versus police powers, were put to rest in October 2010 by the *Sinclair, McCrimmon,* and *Willier* decisions,[43] the so-called "interrogation trilogy." *The Globe and Mail* commented editorially on the cases: "The right to counsel and the right to silence have been taken out to the parking lot and given a good working over ... Our highest court has unjustifiably and surprisingly weakened those rights."[44] The past president of the Defence Counsel Association of Ottawa, Mark Ertel, said, "It's crazy." Paul Burstein, head of the Criminal Lawyers' Association, called the state of the law following the rulings "absurd."[45]

The first case in the trilogy involved Trent Sinclair, who killed Gary Grice on November 21, 2002, in a hotel room where both men had been drinking liquor and using cocaine. Sinclair was arrested about three weeks later. He quickly and briefly consulted with a lawyer of his choice. Then he was questioned at length by the police. During questioning, on five separate occasions, Sinclair said he wanted to speak to his lawyer again but was told he couldn't. Later, Sinclair confessed to the crime and was convicted of manslaughter. Sinclair argued that the Charter imposed a duty on the police to discontinue questioning a detainee who has indicated a desire to speak with counsel again. Sinclair said that because he was denied this right the statements he made were not admissible into evidence.

Chief Justice McLachlin and Justice Charron gave judgment for a bare five-judge majority (Deschamps, Rothstein, and Cromwell agreed with McLachlin and Charron). The purpose of the section 10(b) Charter right to counsel, they said, was principally to ensure a detainee was advised of his right to remain silent and that he understood he need not cooperate with police. It did not carry with it the right to receive ongoing advice about how to deal with police questions. A detainee was not entitled to have a lawyer present during the interview. If there was a material change in his circumstances (for example, if the investigation took a new and more serious turn), he did have the right to "reconsult" his lawyer to seek advice on whether to continue to cooperate, but only then. Trent Sinclair, said the judges, had always understood that he had the right to remain silent, and the right to reconsult had not arisen in his case. What he had said was admissible.

In his dissent, Ian Binnie, using what Kirk Makin of *The Globe and Mail* called a "blunt, near-mocking tone,"[46] said a detainee was entitled to further advice from counsel during a police interview if, objectively speaking, he reasonably needed legal assistance, perhaps because of "unfolding information," and that the need was or should have been apparent to the police. "It cannot be correct to limit the role of defence counsel under s. 10(*b*) ... to urge silence regardless of what may emerge in the course of the interrogation ... this much could be accomplished by a recorded message: You have reached counsel. Keep your mouth shut. Press one to repeat this message."[47]

LeBel and Fish also dissented, giving separate reasons, with Abella concurring. They said, "A close reading of the interaction between detainee and police interrogator demonstrates the need for ongoing assistance of counsel, in the context of the relentless custodial interrogation that occurred in this case."[48] Their view of McLachlin and Charron's reasoning: "Their conclusion tends to erode the very basic principles of Canadian criminal law, particularly the protection against self-incrimination and the presumption of innocence."[49] Nor did they agree with Binnie's "intermediate position": "Detainees are constitutionally entitled to consult counsel without having to persuade their interrogators that their wish to do so is *valid* or *reasonable*."[50]

The facts were similar in the second case, *McCrimmon*, with the judgments following the *Sinclair* pattern, except that this time Binnie joined the majority, finding that McCrimmon's requests for legal counsel during police interrogation (which were denied) were not reasonably justified by objective circumstances. In *Willier*, the last of the interrogation trilogy cases, all nine judges agreed on the disposition. The issue was whether the Charter right to counsel had been denied when the detainee could not reach the lawyer of his choice and—at the suggestion of the police—consulted the legal aid lawyer on duty (and expressed satisfaction at the advice received). All the judges found no breach of the Charter right in these circumstances.

Part of an ideological back-and-forth, the *Grant* cases (with one exception) had seemed to strengthen police powers, resiling from

1990s Supreme Court jurisprudence that went in the other direction. But the reasons given in the four cases were inconsistent, some of them not well written, and all of them murky in places. As Justice Binnie noted, the claimant-centric position of the majority in *Grant* seemed to be rejected by the same judges in *Suberu.* In *Burke* a few months later the court apparently had second thoughts about the whole thing and let the man with the cocaine go free. But then *Cornell* backed off *Burke,* taking us back to the confused land of *Grant.* (Why, exactly, was Chief Justice McLachlin so satisfied with the *Grant* decision?) With the interrogation trilogy, a bare majority of the court made clear that it was the police they favoured, but a deep fissure appeared, with Binnie, LeBel, Fish, and Abella lining up with the accused and against increasing police powers. It is a troubled court, when it comes to crime.

SEVEN

Money Talks

The Supreme Court has more than the Charter of Rights and Freedoms on its plate. In a Charter-mad legal system, it's easy to forget that the court continues to do something it has done since its inception—decide private disputes[1] (as well as settle disagreements, mostly over money, between citizens and the state). It's easy to forget the importance of a generally held belief that private-sector promises will be enforced, a belief backstopped by the courts; without such a belief, the economy would collapse. In 2009, about 40 percent of the Supreme Court's cases involved private disputes of one kind or another.[2]

What a circus![3] On the morning of Tuesday, June 17, 2008, while the Supreme Court was hearing the *BCE* case,[4] the trading volume of BCE shares doubled, the stock price moving with every question asked from the bench. The courtroom was full of people hunched over their BlackBerry smartphones, thumbing out every question and answer to keep their distant corporate masters fully informed. The market responded in real time to every nuance of courtroom debate. Thirty people had stood in line most of the night as paid sitters, holding spots for lawyers or hedge fund executives. The Supreme Court had never seen anything like it.

In May 2008, the Quebec Court of Appeal, in a unanimous five-judge decision, held that a special committee of BCE's board of directors had failed to consider the interests of certain bondholders when it approved a leveraged buyout.[5] The bondholders had argued that the increased debt contemplated by the buyout agreement would reduce the value of their bonds. The proposed transaction would increase the value of BCE shares by 40 percent but decrease the value of the debentures by 20 percent, because of a downgrade of those debentures to below investment grade; this, said the bondholders, was not fair. Corporate executives and their lawyers inveighed against the Quebec court's decision from the moment it was released. Al Hudec of the law firm Farris in Vancouver, one of the smartest and most experienced commercial lawyers in the country, wrote on *The Globe and Mail* website, "I do not believe there is a mergers and acquisitions lawyer in Canada who, before the Court of Appeal decision, would have advised the BCE Special Committee that it had a duty to balance the interests of BCE's shareholders and bond holders ..."[6]

The Quebec Court of Appeal handed down its judgment on May 21, 2008. All commentators agreed that, were the decision to stand, the BCE buyout would be dead. Under various agreements, the transaction had to close by the end of June. The only hope for BCE was to obtain leave to appeal to the Supreme Court, argue the appeal, and have the court of appeal decision overruled, all in less than six weeks. How likely was that? Very unlikely.

First of all, it would be a strong judicial statement for the

Supreme Court even to grant leave to appeal from a unanimous court of appeal sitting five judges (a normal panel is three), let alone overrule its decision. Second, the facts and legal arguments were complex. At trial (which lasted twenty-eight days), there were thousands of exhibits, tens of thousands of pages of affidavits and other documents, over a thousand pages of written arguments, and twenty-five volumes of authorities. How could the Supreme Court possibly make sense of all that in the time available? Third, the Supreme Court is not considered a strong commercial court. Only two of the justices, Binnie and Rothstein, have serious claims to knowledge and experience in the area (and Rothstein's is largely in the specialist areas of tax and intellectual property). The temptation to duck must have been strong. And then, there was the human factor. It was June when the *BCE* case arrived. As summer begins, a judge wants to go to his cottage and fire up the barbecue just like anybody else.

Immediately following the Quebec Court of Appeal's decision, BCE sought leave to appeal to the Supreme Court. A few days later, the court gave the parties until May 30 to file the application for a hearing and responses, and said that it would hear the case on June 17 if leave were granted. On June 2, leave was given; the appellant was instructed to file its papers by June 6; the respondent, by June 10. The hearing was on June 17, with the Supreme Court sitting seven judges. Justices Fish and Rothstein were absent, reducing the number of commercially experienced judges to one, Justice Binnie (it is said that Rothstein had a conflict arising from his personal investment holdings). Three days later, the court gave its decision, with reasons to follow. The Quebec Court of Appeal was unanimously overruled. Predictably, the corporate and commercial world (or most of it) applauded.

Beverley McLachlin was very pleased with the court's performance in the *BCE* case, or so she said at the August 2008 annual meeting of the Canadian Bar Association. Kirk Makin wrote, "There was no mistaking Chief Justice Beverley McLachlin's pride as she boasted about the high point of the Supreme Court of Canada's work year—a quick resolution to the spring appeal in the proposed $35-billion takeover of BCE Inc."[7] McLachlin told the assembled CBA delegates that the *BCE* case was an "extreme example" of how relevant and timely the Supreme Court could be. Makin commented, "Timely and relevant are words the business community has rarely associated with the Supreme Court."

McLachlin's attachment to the *BCE* case is curious. Perhaps it is akin to the satisfaction of a dyed-in-the-wool golfer upon discovering that she can play a bit of tennis as well. When I asked the Chief Justice why she was so satisfied with *BCE*, she said it was because "there was very little law on the subject. There was very little written about it."[8] When I told Al Hudec this, he commented, "Well, I find that a bit of an odd answer. She is right that there is very little Canadian law on the topic, but it's an area covered on a daily basis by the Delaware Courts, and there is certainly a lot of academic literature around the topic."[9] (Many corporate matters, including mergers and acquisitions, are litigated in the courts of the U.S. state of Delaware, under whose laws a large number of American companies are incorporated.)

The Supreme Court had moved decisively and with unprecedented speed. Was it right to do so? Most thought the court had to give leave, notwithstanding the five-to-nothing decision of the court of appeal. After all, the hubbub created by the decision below presumably meant that the legal issues were important. Because of the takeover deal's timetable, granting leave to appeal would be meaningless unless the court was ready to dispose of the matter on its merits by the end of June. Hats off to the Supreme Court, many said; it understands the real world. One senior corporate lawyer emailed me, "They did everything that could have been asked of them in responding under impossible time lines, and then getting it right." Another way of looking at it is that judges who didn't know much about corporate law gave a final answer to a crucial and complex question without having had enough time to consider the matter carefully, and they did it to meet the timetable of leveraged buyout artists and hedge fund managers.

At the end of it all, a supreme irony! At the last minute, the much-delayed BCE takeover—finally set to close on December 11, 2008—crashed and burned. The company was unable to meet a solvency test found in the June 2007 takeover agreement. This failure allowed the buyer, the Ontario Teachers' Pension Plan, and the banks financing the transaction, to walk away from the deal. The solvency test required BCE to have assets that exceeded liabilities, which, because of the market collapse in the autumn of 2008, it no longer had. The solvency test was inserted into the definitive agreement to give BCE a legal defence against any possible action by aggrieved bondholders, the very same bondholders who lost before the Supreme Court. Despite the Supreme Court's expeditious judgment, the bondholders—in a sense—won the day.[10]

Delivery of the court's written reasons on December 19, 2008, a week or so after the transaction had failed, was obviously anti-climactic. The reasons, for what they were worth, were unanimous. The court found that BCE directors had not acted in an oppressive manner contrary to the Canada Business Corporations Act (CBCA), the statute which lays down the rules for a transaction of this type.[11] The court said that the debenture holders had failed to establish a reasonable expectation that the investment grade of the debentures would be maintained. They had established a reasonable expectation that the debenture holders' interests would be considered, but that expectation was fulfilled.[12]

The Supreme Court then considered whether the transaction should have been approved as fair and reasonable, a CBCA requirement. For an arrangement to be fair and reasonable, it must have a valid business purpose, and the objections of those whose legal rights are being arranged must be resolved in a fair and balanced way. The court found that the BCE transaction met this test.

Corporate lawyers who earlier in the year had been delighted at the Supreme Court's overruling of the Quebec Court of Appeal, and at the speed at which the court had done so, were not so impressed by the reasons in the case. One emailed me: "I am so accustomed to reading Delaware Chancery Court decisions, which are so rich in providing practical advice on deal processes, that I find the SCC approach very different—much more traditionally legal in its approach—more careful to be 'nuanced' in the approach and leave lots of discretion to decide another way in a different set of circumstances.... I didn't think it was that well written: smelled a bit like a research paper from a clerk rather than the pen of a sophisticated senior jurist."

When the so-called "ABCP case" came up in 2008, the courtroom drama and fun of *BCE* was over and the judges were working on the reasons, almost certainly finding them heavy going and hard work. Nonetheless, it was a surprise when, on September 19, the Supreme Court refused leave to appeal from the Ontario Court of Appeal's decision in the ABCP litigation ("ABCP" is short for asset-backed commercial paper).[13] Court watchers who had thought that the justices, having tasted the red meat of a big commercial case in *BCE*, would want more, were wrong. Apparently the judges had had enough of complex and confusing corporate matters, at least for the time being.

In August 2007, a liquidity crisis threatened the Canadian

asset-backed commercial paper market. ("Commercial paper" refers to a short-term promissory note, evidencing a debt and promising to repay it. "Asset-backed" means that assets are pledged to the lender as protection against non-payment, assets that are intended to produce cash for redemption needed when the note matures.) In 2007, many maturing Canadian notes could not be redeemed by holders, since the assets behind them turned out to be inappropriately long-term (and sometimes dubious) and could not generate the cash required.

The major participants in the Canadian ABCP market agreed to attempt a restructuring. A committee put forward a restructuring plan that converted the existing notes into new, long-term notes that would trade freely. An Ontario judge sanctioned the plan on June 5, 2008, but some holders of ABCP notes were against the scheme. They had many arguments for their opposition, but the key one was that, under the Companies' Creditors Arrangement Act (CCAA),[14] the court (so they said) could not sanction a plan that called for creditors to give releases to third parties, such as dealers who sold the ABCP notes, against whom they might have claims for relief—claims, for example, for negligence or conflict of interest. Such releases were proposed because several key participants would not participate in the restructuring without them. The Ontario Court of Appeal rejected the argument and unanimously upheld the restructuring plan.

There was general surprise that the Supreme Court refused leave to appeal from the Ontario Court of Appeal's decision. One lawyer commented, "ABCP brought together a half-dozen issues on the leading edge of insolvency law." Another said, "My guess would have been that the Supreme Court would hear the appeal." A third said, "This was the classic situation for granting leave." A fourth commented, "If you ask me, the Supreme Court was intimidated by the scope of the issues and the very short time frame." Had the judges learned something from their *BCE* experience? Kevin McElcheran, a lawyer who represented five large banks in the case, had a different take. He noted that in *BCE* the transaction could not proceed unless the Supreme Court granted leave, whereas in ABCP denying leave would best facilitate the transaction.[15] So, according to McElcheran, the court was just helping the business community a second time.

The ABCP problem was finally resolved early in 2009, no thanks to the Supreme Court, when a judge approved a final arrangement to replace the asset-backed commercial paper with new bonds.

———

Money and the Constitution may intersect. And it's not always rich investors in esoteric securities who are the actors in the money drama. They may be ordinary people—people, for example, who rely on employment insurance and pay EI premiums.

In December 2008, a seven-judge panel of the Supreme Court (McLachlin, Binnie, LeBel, Deschamps, Fish, Abella, and Rothstein) decided unanimously that the federal government had turned employment insurance premiums for the years 2002, 2003, and 2005 into an unconstitutional tax.[16] The premiums had been collected illegally. LeBel gave the court's judgment. He began: "The debate, which was originally political in nature and will no doubt always be partly political, has moved into the judicial realm."[17]

In 2002, 2003, and 2005, Parliament made the Governor in Council (i.e., the cabinet) responsible for setting the applicable premium rate, without stating that it was delegating taxing authority. There were no criteria for setting the premiums. Rates were within the cabinet's discretion. But the Constitution Act, 1867,[18] says that there should be no taxation without representation. The delegation of taxing authority is only constitutional if the

legislation provides expressly and unambiguously for the delegation. That hadn't happened. The premiums, the court found, had
therefore been set illegally.

The appellants argued that vast surpluses (over $50 billion)
illegally built up in the employment insurance fund should be
returned to the employers and workers who had paid premiums.
The federal government, they said, had misappropriated employment insurance monies. Premiums had been illegally diverted
from their intended purposes and allocated to deficit reduction,
which had great political appeal to the Chrétien government.
The Supreme Court did not explicitly deal with the fate of these
funds, accumulated over several years. It simply declared that the
employers' and employees' premiums for 2002, 2003, and 2005
were collected unlawfully. The declaration was suspended for
twelve months to allow the government to sort out the mess. One
editorial commented, "The court gave Ottawa a year to act, but
didn't suggest how to fix a situation whose financial implications
are staggering."[19] The government answer to the problem, cynical
in the eyes of some, was a provision in the 2009 budget retro-
actively authorizing the illegal premiums.

Canadian tax guru Vern Krishna called the 2009 *Lipson* decision[20]
"the most significant tax decision in 70 years."[21] The split amongst
the Supreme Court judges in the case revealed a philosophical
divide over taxation, the majority favouring the government,
the minority favouring the taxpayer. The two judges who knew
most about tax, Binnie and Rothstein, dissented from the pro-
government majority and favoured the taxpayer, although they
disagreed with each other and were quite bad-tempered about the
whole thing.

Earl Lipson wanted to save on income tax. His professional advisors had an idea that (they thought) would allow him to deduct interest on his residential mortgage from his taxable income. In April 1994, Earl and his wife Jordanna signed an agreement to buy a house in Toronto for $750,000. The closing was on September 1. The day before the closing, Jordanna borrowed $562,500 from the Bank of Montreal to buy shares in a family corporation. Earl agreed to repay the loan the next day. Jordanna paid the borrowed money directly to her husband, who transferred the family corporation shares to her. Earl and Jordanna then together obtained a mortgage from the Bank of Montreal for $562,500. They used the mortgage loan funds to repay the share loan. Earl, relying on the interplay of complex provisions of the Income Tax Act,[22] claimed interest on the house mortgage as a deduction from his income. After all, simply put, the mortgage proceeds had been used for business purposes.

The minister of national revenue disallowed the mortgage interest deductions, on the grounds that the series of transactions amounted to abusive tax avoidance. An appeal from the reassessment to the Tax Court of Canada, and from there to the Federal Court of Appeal, was unsuccessful. In April 2008, the parties ended up in the Supreme Court. Judgment was handed down on January 8, 2009. The appeal was dismissed again, but it was a close run thing, four to three. Members of the badly split court were not above taking petulant swipes at each other in their judgments. For example, Rothstein on Binnie: "Binnie J.'s reliance on an overly broad foundation to base his opinion distorts the actual site of legal conflict. This leads to an unhelpful legal analysis ..."[23]

LeBel gave judgment for the majority (which included Fish, Abella, and Charron). He favoured the government side, writing that the Lipson transactions constituted abusive tax avoidance under the general anti-avoidance rule, generally referred to as

GAAR, found in the Income Tax Act.[24] Binnie gave dissenting reasons for himself and Deschamps. These two were on the taxpayer's side. They saw nothing wrong in a taxpayer rearranging his capital (borrowed or non-borrowed) to save money on taxes. Rothstein would have allowed the appeal as well but for an entirely different reason (referred to cuttingly by Binnie as "a sort of deus ex machina to dispose of the appeals on a basis not advanced by any of the parties").[25] He thought the GAAR did not apply because there was a specific anti-avoidance rule that pre-empted its application.

Paying taxes is about as close to government as most people get (unless they have a run-in with the police). Ultimately, the Supreme Court will tell you what you have to pay, and what you can keep for yourself.

As the economy came close to collapse in 2008–09, company pension plans were on many people's minds. Workers at Nortel Networks Corporation, which filed for protection under the Companies' Creditors Arrangement Act in January 2009, were appalled to discover their pension plans were underfunded. It was even worse to discover that under the CCAA they were just unsecured creditors for the shortfall. Big commercial lenders, who had taken Nortel assets to secure their loans, were ahead of them in line and would be paid first. The pensioners might not be paid at all. Passions ran high.

The Nortel pensioners quickly turned their problem into a political issue. Former employees of other businesses in similar straits joined in the uproar. Newspapers, radio, and television paid attention. There were many questions. What happened if a pension plan was underfunded, particularly if the company went bankrupt? What about a plan with a surplus: how could that surplus be used?

Some of these political and policy questions bled into the judicial arena and arrived at the Supreme Court.

Every newspaper reader knows about Nortel, but the pension issue came to the Supreme Court from a relatively obscure source. Kerry (Canada) Inc. is the Canadian subsidiary of the Kerry Group, a large international food manufacturing company. Kerry (Canada) and its corporate predecessors have had an employee pension plan since 1954, with funds held by a trustee under a trust agreement. In 2001, the plan had been in a surplus position for several years. Beginning in 1985, third-party plan expenses for actuarial, investment management, and audit services were paid from plan funds and, because of the surplus, Kerry also started taking contribution holidays from its funding obligations.

Before 2000, the Kerry plan was a defined benefit (DB) pension plan, the type of plan that right from the start guarantees an employee specific benefits on retirement, for example, a certain dollar amount to be paid every month. In 2000, a defined contribution (DC) component of the plan was introduced. In a DC plan, the employer guarantees not the benefit that will be received eventually but the amount of contribution it will make for each employee. The benefits on retirement are determined by these contributions and any earnings from their investment. A specific monthly pension payment is not guaranteed, and the monthly amount will not be known until the employee retires. Since no benefits are guaranteed, DC plans do not have surpluses or deficits. The best way to think about the difference between a defined benefit plan and a defined contribution plan is this: in the former, the employer has the investment risk; in the latter, the risk belongs to the employee.

The DB component of the Kerry pension plan continued for existing employees but was closed to new employees: they became members of the separate DC component. Kerry announced its intention to take contribution holidays from its obligations to DC members by using the surplus accumulated in the DB component. Former employees of the company, who were DB plan beneficiaries, objected. They argued that company contribution holidays while the DB plan was in a surplus position were improper, and that the surplus in the DB plan could not be used to fund the employer's contribution obligations to the separate DC plan component. They also argued that plan expenses should be paid by the company, not from trust funds. Decisions in lower courts, including a unanimous Ontario Court of Appeal, favoured the company.

The Supreme Court of Canada heard the case on November 18, 2008, and gave judgment on August 7, 2009.[26] Justice Rothstein gave reasons for the five-judge majority (himself, Binnie, Deschamps, Abella, and Charron). Justices LeBel and Fish dissented in part. On the question of plan expenses, Rothstein found nothing in plan documents, expressly or implicitly, or in statutory or common law authority, that required the company to pay expenses out of its own pocket. Rothstein had no trouble with contribution holidays within the DB component: "The Company's contributions are determined by actuarial calculations. Nothing … prevents the Company from taking a contribution holiday where the actuary certifies that no contributions are necessary to provide the required retirement income to members."[27] Most importantly, Rothstein found that using DB funds for a DC holiday was fine. There was one plan and one trust, albeit with two components. Surplus DB funds applied to DC accounts simply moved funds within the trust. Nothing in law, or in plan documents, prevented this from being done.

LeBel gave his and Fish's dissenting reasons. He began by observing, "The issues raised in this appeal affect the millions of Canadians who are members of occupational pension plans."[28] LeBel and Fish did not agree that the DB surplus could be used to fund a DC contribution. LeBel said that when the DC plan was created in 2000, the company's employees ceased to be members of a single plan. The employees in the DC plan were not beneficiaries of the DB trust. He gave a careful analysis of the policy considerations and economic realities underlying contribution holidays, issues ignored by the majority. In considering the attributes of a DB plan, LeBel wrote:

> Many employees believe that surplus should be maintained to serve as a "cushion" against future market failings or employer insolvency ... Indeed, there is a very real risk that contribution holidays could affect the stability of pension plans. According to the report of the Ontario Expert Commission on Pensions, some employers have taken contribution holidays when the results of their last triennial valuation permitted them, despite the fact that the plans were under-funded at the time the holidays were taken. Research conducted on federally regulated pension plans and cited in the Commission report revealed that "45% of under-funded plans would not have been under-funded had they [the employers] not taken contribution holidays" ...[29]

It would be interesting to know how many defined benefit plans which in the past have generated a surplus used by the employer to take a contribution holiday are now, as a result of the recent recession, underfunded. Simon Archer, on the Osgoode Hall blog that chronicles the Supreme Court, noted, "This use of surplus permits sponsors to run DB plans as 'profit centres', using investment income to reduce cash contributions to the plan (or to a DC plan). One 2005 study of federal plans found that, but for contribution holidays, that sample of plans surveyed would have been fully-funded."[30]

And so the Supreme Court sometimes turns away from Charter matters and criminal cases and looks at money-related issues that drive the country's economy. Its record in doing so is uncertain. In *BCE*, it acted very quickly and was apparently proud that it did so, but some think it blundered through ignorance and that the reasons it delivered were weak. The court ran from the ABCP litigation; ruled that some collected employment insurance premiums amounted to an unconstitutional tax, but didn't instruct the government on how to resolve the resulting huge financial mess; split badly on the scope of the general anti-avoidance rule in taxation; and, faced with a mounting pension crisis across the country, controversially favoured corporations and their lenders rather than workers, ignoring the underlying issues.

PART II

PART II

———⟨◆⟩———

EIGHT

Pretty Sweet Work

Het ow do you become a Supreme Court judge, one of the most
powerful people in the land?[1]

Early in April 2008, Supreme Court Justice Michel Bastarache
announced he would soon resign. No one seemed very interested
in why Bastarache was leaving the court fifteen years before he
reached the mandatory retirement age of seventy-five. He had
recently undergone heart surgery for a blocked artery, but many
people have bypass surgery and resume demanding careers.

Bastarache took on some big jobs after he left the court, jobs
that required a lot of energy and commitment—for example,
heading a high-profile Quebec public inquiry into allegations of
influence peddling in the appointment of provincial court judges.
His health didn't seem to be an issue. An Ottawa insider told me
what he thought was the real story behind Bastarache's resignation
from the Supreme Court: "There was a lot of conflict on the court.
He couldn't stand it anymore. He had to get out." Bastarache
himself has let it be known that he wasn't happy at the court and

found its environment unpleasant, full of bad personal relationships. But nobody on the outside cared much about all that when
he announced his resignation. What they did care about was who
would fill the vacancy. Feverish speculation and intense jockeying
for advantage began immediately. A seat on the Supreme Court is
a big prize.

Section 6 of the Supreme Court Act[2] requires that three justices
come from Quebec. There is nothing in the statute about the
home provinces of the other six. A weak convention has developed, driven by obvious political considerations, that three must
come from Ontario, two from the Western provinces, and one
from Atlantic Canada. Bastarache occupied the seat reserved by
custom for the Atlantic provinces (he is from New Brunswick).
Following his resignation announcement, many senior judges,
lawyers, and law professors from those provinces must have gazed
into a full-length mirror and dreamed how they would look in the
bright scarlet robes that Supreme Court judges wear on ceremonial occasions. As for politicians from Eastern Canada, they got
busy urging Supreme Court representation for their respective
provinces.

None were louder than Newfoundlanders, aggrieved that no one
from the Rock had ever been appointed to the Supreme Court.
Newfoundland's justice minister, Jerome Kennedy, issued a statement that thundered, "Everyday the Supreme Court of Canada
passes judgments which affect the lives of Newfoundlanders and
Labradorians and I believe a serious oversight has occurred by not
allowing our province a voice in these decisions."[3] Later Kennedy
said, "We stand really at a crossroads in terms of our relationship with Canada."[4] It took Russell Wangersky, the editor of *The
Telegram* (St. John's) and an esteemed author, to ask the obvious
question: "What is a judge from this province supposed to do on
the Supreme Court that a judge from another province wouldn't?"[5]

The Canadian Bar Association, representing about a third of the country's lawyers, pompously announced that it required "a seat at the table" at any public hearings held to screen a replacement for Bastarache.[6] This was not the first time the CBA had tried to muscle in on the appointment process. In February 2006, its president wrote to the prime minister offering the association's "assistance" with the process of choosing Supreme Court judges. There is no public record of a response by the prime minister. Perhaps he felt that the CBA's assistance was unnecessary. Bernard Amyot, CBA president when Bastarache resigned, warned that in any public interview of a proposed replacement, "criticism of past judgments, questions on issues that might come before the court, on personal beliefs or preferences that intrude on the candidate's privacy or dignity would be inappropriate."[7] By contrast, when U.S. Chief Justice John Roberts Jr. appeared before the Senate committee considering his nomination in 2005, the committee chairman, Arlen Specter, began the proceedings by saying, "Senators have the right to ask whatever question they choose."[8]

The grinding of axes went on. Court watchers blogged away tirelessly, offering their lists of worthy candidates. Commentators who dislike the Charter of Rights and Freedoms demanded that someone with a strong commitment to the division of powers (read: the primacy of Parliament) be appointed. Human rights advocates, leery of legislators who might be swayed by majority opinion, railed against the old-fashioned notion of parliamentary sovereignty. Newspaper editorialists and op-ed pundits gave their two cents' worth. Other voices chimed in: a woman should be appointed (that would mean a female majority on the court); there should be a judge from the First Nations—etcetera, etcetera.[9]

Bilingualism became an issue. In May 2008, John Major, a unilingual retired Supreme Court of Canada judge from Alberta known for plain speaking, publicly observed that the translation services at the court were excellent and the ability to speak both official languages should not be a prime component of the job description.[10] Privately, Major has said that all that matters is ability, and that ability should even trump the conventional geographic representation. Another retired Supreme Court judge, this one a francophone, had a very different view: I was told, "Judges should be bilingual. I am adamant on that." A second francophone retiree expressed the same opinion, and added: "Several judges who say they're bilingual aren't really. They certainly can't understand technical legal French. There should be proper testing, as they have in Belgium."

Major's public comments on bilingualism ignited a firestorm. An editorial in Montreal's *The Gazette* quickly offered, "Knowing both languages ... is the best way to connect the two distinct cultures" but "the ultimate priority should always be skill as a jurist, not skill as a linguist."[11] Liberal MP Denis Coderre wasn't having any of that, and tabled a private member's bill amending the Official Languages Act to require Supreme Court judges to be bilingual. The *National Post* called Coderre's bill a "bad idea," Coderre himself an "anglo-baiter," and conjured up the image of subjecting a Supreme Court candidate "to a literacy test in some backroom, with a proctor lurking over him, stopwatch in hand, as he attempted to navigate the imparfait du subjonctif ..."[12] Quebec's National Assembly voted unanimously to demand that only bilingual judges be appointed to the Supreme Court: This is not a request, it is a demand, said Premier Jean Charest.[13] *The Globe and Mail* weighed in with an editorial entitled "Jurists, rather than linguists," offering the odd observation that "the court is not known for an ability in aboriginal languages, yet it has made several ground-breaking rulings in support of aboriginal rights."[14] In the same newspaper, Gordon Gibson called the Coderre proposal mean-spirited and foolish: "Nuts to him; shame on him, I say."[15]

André Pratte of *La Presse* said of Gibson's views, "These kinds of comments remind one of the hysteria surrounding bilingual labels on cereal boxes in the 1960s."[16] The Commissioner of Official Languages, Graham Fraser, felt obliged to get involved. He wrote, again in *The Globe and Mail,* "Those whose understanding of the legal world in Canada is limited to what has been written or said in only one language are less competent, as judges, than those who understand the Canadian legal tradition as a whole."[17]

Newfoundland and Labrador Justice Minister Jerome Kennedy, still all riled up, had his peculiar say. Speaking of Chief Justice J. Derek Green of the Supreme Court of Newfoundland and Labrador (Trial Division), Mr. Kennedy said, "If he were appointed to the SCC today, I'm sure he could be bilingual by the time it came to take his seat. He is that bright."[18] Kennedy's kind comments about Green were particularly ironic. In 2003, Green had complained to the Law Society of Newfoundland and Labrador about remarks Kennedy, then a high-profile criminal defence lawyer, had made at a conference. Kennedy had said that some trial judges didn't know what they were doing: "Part of it is as a result of political appointments. Part of this is as a result of intentional or unintentional biases."[19] A law society disciplinary panel dismissed the complaint. By 2008, Jerome Kennedy apparently had a different point of view on the appointment of judges.

With Jerome Kennedy's tortured fulminations, the debate over bilingualism at the Supreme Court of Canada seemed more or less over, at least for the time being (it was to resurface with a vengeance later[20]). Summer came, and with the return of warm weather Canadians seemed to lose interest in the Supreme Court vacancy. A few law professors blogged on, but no one paid much attention. There was a renewed flicker of interest when Chief Justice Beverley McLachlin said at the Canadian Bar Association convention in August 2008 that Michel Bastarache had considerable experience in corporate and commercial law, and that it would be nice to maintain some balance on the court.[21] Was she attempting to influence the new appointment? Some said yes, and that it was improper.

Thus, the process of selecting a new Supreme Court of Canada judge unfolded—a strange brew of personal ambition, geographic imperatives, political posturing, language policy, catcalls from the sidelines, cries from special interest groups, and competing judicial philosophies.

Most lawyers would really like to be a judge, any kind of judge. To be a justice of the Supreme Court of Canada is the pinnacle of legal ambition (although Justice Bertha Wilson once said being a Supreme Court judge was "not so much the peak of a legal career as the ultimate form of public service"[22]). But not everyone dreams the dream. It was rumoured that several Quebec lawyers made clear that they were not interested in filling Claire L'Heureux-Dubé's shoes when she retired in 2002, mostly because they did not want to move to Ottawa, in their eyes a small, parochial, and English-dominated city. L'Heureux-Dubé, famously exuberant and convivial, has said that when she came to Ottawa in 1987 she at first lived a monk-like existence, and missed being able to call up her French-speaking friends late at night to see if they would like to order in a pizza.[23]

One thing's for sure: successful lawyers don't want to be judges because of the money. A Supreme Court judge makes less than a junior Bay Street lawyer, or a successful big-city real-estate agent. Every four years, the Judicial Compensation and Benefits Commission, established in 1999 under the Judges Act,[24] reviews and make recommendations to the minister of justice about the compensation and benefits of federally appointed judges. This process reflects a constitutional requirement that, to preserve the independence of the judiciary, judges' compensation must be determined independently of the executive and legislative branches. The Supreme Court itself laid down this rule in the 1997 case of *Reference Re Remuneration of Judges*,[25] a case that law professor Adam Dodek of the University of Ottawa has written created "a code of judicial remuneration" because of the detailed policy design it offered,[26] and which led directly to the creation of the Judicial Compensation and Benefits Commission.

The Judicial Compensation and Benefits Commission last reported on May 30, 2008.[27] If the Commission's recommendations had been accepted, the Chief Justice's salary would have been raised from $278,400 to $349,800, and that of the other justices would have increased from $257,800 to $323,800. But the recommendations were not accepted. In February 2009, Rob Nicholson, the minister of justice, said, "During this period of global economic uncertainty, it is vital the Government keeps its sight fixed on sound fiscal management ... In the Government's view, the public reasonably expects judges to be subject to similar restraint as that implemented for the federal public administration broadly..."[28] Under the 2009 federal budget, annual wage increases for the federal public administration were limited to 2.3 percent in 2007–08 and 1.5 percent for the following three years, and judges were no exception.

U.S. federal judges have long claimed they are underpaid (they make about the same amount as their Canadian counterparts). Chief Justice John Roberts Jr., in his 2006 *Year-End Report on the Federal Judiciary*,[29] said that the pay problem had reached the level of a "constitutional crisis." But, as Adam Liptak pointed out in *The New York Times*,[30] many who have considered the issue carefully have a different point of view. In a 2008 article in the *Boston University*

Law Review, lawyer and economist Scott Baker concluded, "Low pay does not impact voting patterns, citation practices, the speed of controversial case disposition, or opinion quality."[31] A 2007 empirical study of U.S. high court judges provided little evidence that raising salaries would improve judicial performance, and concluded, "The case for a pay raise has not been made."[32] Liptak came down on the side of the naysayers. He wrote of the United States, "Being a judge is pretty sweet work and the job is in high demand. It comes with status, power, good working conditions, no clients, the ability to affect policy and the satisfaction of doing justice." There's also a good pension and excellent job security. Canadian judges have the same advantages. What's not to like? Although ... one is reminded of a story told about William O. Douglas, appointed to the U.S. Supreme Court by President Roosevelt in 1939.

> Summoned one day in March 1939 to the Oval Office, he was greeted by the president, who told him, "I have a new job for you. It's a mean job, a dirty job, a thankless job ...
>
> "It's a job you'll detest ...
>
> "This job is something like being in jail ..."[33]

The Supreme Court Act gives the executive branch the power to appoint Supreme Court judges.[34] That means the prime minister decides. Any accompanying brouhaha means little or nothing. In 2003, when Morris Fish was appointed to the court, *The Globe and Mail* editorialized: "What a peculiar nation Canada is. It grants its Supreme Court judges enormous power to scrutinize, strike down, even rewrite the laws passed by democratically elected legislators. Yet it allows its prime minister to appoint those judges after a secretive process, without any opportunity for public discussion."[35]

Chief Justice McLachlin has been reported as saying that, as far as she is concerned, the current appointment process is just fine. In 2004, the *Edmonton Journal* reported that, in a meeting with its editorial board, McLachlin said one person should carry the responsibility of selecting judges for the top court. "The more you diffuse the decision, the more you diffuse the power—you diffuse the responsibility and you open the door for compromised candidates."[36] She went even further the following year, in an interview with Kirk Makin of *The Globe and Mail* marking her fifth year as Chief Justice. "I think there is a very simple trade-off here ... The more you question candidates on the merits of cases, the more you're going to impair the appearance of impartiality ..."[37] Not all her colleagues agree. When Ian Binnie was appointed in 1998, he robustly observed that "the prospect of being questioned about his experience, credentials and beliefs by some form of parliamentary committee would not have fazed him. 'I agree that Supreme Court judges are accountable just like anybody else for their opinions ... They certainly wield a lot of authority.'"[38]

Until the appointment of Marshall Rothstein in 2006, something called a "protocol of consultation" was said to be part of the selection process. This seems to have meant that the prime minister consulted with anyone he felt like—not much of a protocol, you might think. "The consultation, if that's what you want to call it, was all driven by politics, pure and simple," someone involved in the 2004 appointment of Justices Charron and Abella told me. But political sensitivity developed over this cut-and-dried, very private process, with both journalists and legal academics criticizing it vociferously. Prime Minister Paul Martin was sensitive to the criticism. On the day his government was sworn in, December 12, 2003, he told Irwin Cotler, the new minister of justice, that reform of the judicial appointments process was important,[39] and announced that "the government will specifically consult the

Standing Committee on Justice and Human Rights on how best to implement prior review of appointments of Supreme Court of Canada Judges."[40] This led Cotler to take the modest step of appearing before a parliamentary committee a few months later to "discuss" the appointments of Abella and Charron.[41] The candidates did not appear themselves. Vic Toews and Peter MacKay, opposition MPs at the time, respectively described the 2004 hearing as a "rubber stamp" and "window dressing."[42] Stephen Harper was said not to be impressed by the so-called hearing.

In April 2005, moving forward in mini-steps, Cotler announced a "reformed" process of picking Supreme Court judges, involving a new advisory committee.[43] This committee would consist of one nominee from each political party, one retired judge, and, from the region where the vacancy arose, one nominee of the provincial attorneys general, one nominee of the provincial law societies, and two individuals who were neither judges nor lawyers. A new advisory committee would be struck each time there was a Supreme Court vacancy to be filled. The minister of justice would give the committee a list of five to eight candidates, and the committee would pick three from this list (and not rank them). Observers were not impressed by these proposals. Jacob Ziegel, a well-known retired law professor, commented that the advisory committee "would simply act as a rubber stamp for the government's pre-selected list of candidates," and said that what was striking about these proposals was "the government's neurotic obsession with perpetuating executive paternalism into the 21st century."[44]

In August 2005, Justice John Major announced that he would leave the court at the end of the year. No doubt Paul Martin and Irwin Cotler looked forward to making their third Supreme Court appointment. Implementing his reformed process, Cotler duly appointed an advisory committee and gave it a list of six names. The committee did its job, small as that job was, and, as instructed, returned three unranked names to Cotler. The process was supposed to be secret, but it was well known that the names were Marshall Rothstein of the Federal Court of Appeal, Constance Hunt of the Alberta Court of Appeal, and Peter MacKinnon, president of the University of Saskatchewan.

In January 2006, Stephen Harper won a federal election. He stayed with his predecessor's short list, perhaps because it contained one name that particularly appealed to him. His choice for the court, announced on February 23, 2006, was Marshall Rothstein. But Harper wanted to go a step beyond Cotler's reformed process. He wanted Rothstein publicly interviewed by a parliamentary committee.

On February 27, 2006, a mere four days after Harper announced that Rothstein was his choice, the nominee appeared before an ad hoc parliamentary committee (ad hoc, because Parliament was not in session). Committee members had obviously had little or no opportunity to do things you might expect of them—for example, read judgments written by Rothstein while he was a member of the Federal Court of Appeal (although they had been supplied with copies), or cogitate over his qualifications, or at least find out something, anything, about him. The committee was chaired by Vic Toews, now justice minister, who had once been a student of Rothstein's at the University of Manitoba law faculty. Irwin Cotler was a committee member. Before the hearing began, Toews asked Rothstein if he was nervous. "You bet!" said Rothstein. "Me too!" said Toews.[45]

Professor Peter Hogg of Osgoode Hall Law School began the proceedings by lecturing the assembled members of Parliament about what they should and should not do. Said Hogg, "There are some questions that he [Rothstein] cannot be expected to answer." What were those questions? The very ones, of course, that most people wanted asked and answered. Said Hogg, "He cannot express views on cases or issues that could come before the Court. He cannot tell you how he would decide a hypothetical case … he cannot tell you what his views are on controversial issues …"[46] After the hearing and his appointment, Rothstein received about forty requests for an interview from journalists. He refused them all. "I didn't give interviews then, and I don't give them now. It's prudential."

John Major, the judge who was replaced by Rothstein, commented on CBC *Newsworld* that the Rothstein hearing was ridiculous, and that Professor Hogg was a grandstander and a glad-hander.[47] Luiza Ch. Savage, writing in *Maclean's,* called the hearing "polite, but pointless."[48] Andrew Coyne's blog described the process as one "that could have no bearing on the actual outcome" and commented: "Now we know that Mr. Justice Marshall Rothstein likes long walks by the beach, hates insincere people, and his favourite Beatle is Paul, what lessons can we learn from Monday's toe-in-the-water exercise in democratic accountability? Just this: that Canada's political culture remains as exquisitely constipated as ever."[49] But Chief Justice Beverley McLachlin saw it from a different point of view. It "was very respectfully done,'' she commented.[50]

With the appointment of Marshall Rothstein in 2006, Supreme Court watchers heaved a sigh of relief. No vacancy was now expected until 2013, when Justice Morris Fish would reach the retirement age of seventy-five. Then came Justice Bastarache's surprise resignation. On May 28, 2008, Justice Minister Rob Nicholson announced yet another process for choosing the new judge.[51] To identify a pool of qualified candidates, Nicholson would consult with the attorneys general of the Atlantic provinces as well as with leading members of the legal community. A list of candidates then compiled by Nicholson (presumably, as he saw fit, although no doubt in consultation with the prime minister) would be reviewed in secret by a selection panel composed of five members of Parliament—two from the government caucus and one from each of the opposition parties. The panel's job was to provide an unranked secret short list of three candidates to the prime minister. The person chosen from the list by the prime minister would appear at a public hearing of a parliamentary committee. The committee would not have veto power. Minister of Public Works and Government Services Christian Paradis and Secretary of State for Small Business and Tourism Diane Ablonczy were appointed the government representatives on the panel. Dominic LeBlanc was there for the Liberals; Joe Comartin, for the NDP; and Réal Ménard represented the Bloc Québécois.

Before the first meeting of the panel, on August 12, Joe Comartin and Réal Ménard vociferously objected to cabinet ministers representing the government on the panel. Comartin was quoted by Canadian Press as saying, "This committee, as envisioned, was to provide parliamentary and independent advice to the prime minister. If it's cabinet people on it, the suspicion has to be that they're not there providing independent advice, they're just there as mouthpieces for the Prime Minister's office." Justice Minister Rob Nicholson wasn't impressed with this line of argument. "The selection of a Supreme Court judge is the prime minister's prerogative," he said dismissively,[52] and that was the end of that.

At the August 12 meeting, after six hours of bad-tempered wrangling, the opposition party members fell into line with the government. "We're working with the people who were named but we think we made our point," Ménard told the CBC. Ablonczy became panel chair and the panel's members all signed a confidentiality agreement making her sole spokesman. By the end of

September, the panel was to give the three-name short list to the prime minister, who would make his choice. The chosen candidate, like Rothstein, would appear at a public hearing of an ad hoc parliamentary committee that would have no veto power and could only ask polite questions.

At the beginning of September, two panel teleconferences were cancelled because the non-government members were not available. On September 5, two days before he called an election, Harper publicly announced that Thomas Cromwell was his choice and would go through the formal appointment process, such as it was, presumably including an appearance before a parliamentary committee. Forget about the advisory panel; Harper said it was holding up the selection process. Panel member Dominic LeBlanc, an MP from New Brunswick, was particularly miffed. He insisted that meetings had been scheduled for that very week. LeBlanc said wistfully, "I was going to have the committee at my house in Grande-Digue for a lobster dinner."[53]

Tom Cromwell was left in limbo, waiting for the election results. If the government changed, maybe someone else would be chosen to fill the empty seat. Perhaps Cromwell prepared for a public appearance before a parliamentary committee. If he did, he was wasting his time. Harper, re-elected on October 14, called Parliament into session on November 18, but prorogued it on December 4. There was no time or inclination for a parliamentary committee to go through the empty formalities of quizzing someone the prime minister had picked to be a Supreme Court judge. On December 22, Harper announced that Tom Cromwell was the new judge. Cromwell, wearing ceremonial robes of bright scarlet trimmed with white mink, was sworn in on January 5, 2009.

So much for Irwin Cotler's reformed (and itself imperfect) selection process. Goodbye to membership on the selection panel of a retired judge, nominees of provincial attorneys general, a nominee of the provincial law societies, and two individuals who were neither lawyers nor judges. So much for a seat at the table for the Canadian Bar Association. The Conservative government obviously believed that picking a Supreme Court of Canada judge is a job for the politicians, pure and simple.

In the United States, Supreme Court justices are nominated by the president and must be confirmed by the Senate following public hearings by the Judiciary Committee, where members feel free to ask any question they like. Regular public hearings of judicial nominees began after the U.S. Supreme Court's 1954 anti-segregation decision in *Brown v. Board of Education;*[54] that decision infuriated Southern Democrats, who then insisted on public grilling of prospective members of the court. These hearings can be brutal, as anyone old enough to remember the 1991 Clarence Thomas confirmation process will know. Thomas's own comment then on his Senate confirmation hearings was, "This is a circus. It's a national disgrace."[55] Brutal, perhaps, but very valuable in the eyes of most commentators. In 1987, Robert Bork, nominated by Ronald Reagan, was quizzed by the Senate Judiciary Committee for five days, only to be rejected. Linda Greenhouse, who covered the Supreme Court for *The New York Times* for many years, has written that the debate over the Bork nomination was "fair and profound," and became "a national referendum on the modern course of constitutional law."[56] American legal analyst Jeffrey Toobin, commenting on the appearance of Sonia Sotomayor before the Senate Judiciary Committee, noted that since the Bork hearing, Supreme Court nominees have taken to heart its lesson of the less said the better, but all the same, "The tableau of the first Hispanic nominee to the Court ... was a satisfying one for those who care about a diverse and inclusive society."[57] With the Charter of Rights and Freedoms, Canada moved much closer to the American constitutional model by empowering the judicial branch, with the difference that Canada does not check that branch or the executive branch by requiring that the legislature approve senior judicial appointments.

Over the last forty years or so, seven nominations have either been rejected by the U.S. Senate or withdrawn by the president when it became clear that rejection was likely (Fortas, Thornberry, Haynsworth, Carswell, Bork, Ginsburg, and Miers). Robust as the U.S. appointment process is, it has been authoritatively described as inadequate. In *The Next Justice: Repairing the Supreme Court Appointments Process,*[58] Christopher Eisgruber, provost of Princeton University, former law professor at New York University, and former law clerk to U.S. Supreme Court Justice John Paul Stevens, argues that Americans need "a better way to talk about Supreme Court appointments, and they need it now, before any president nominates the court's next justice."[59] The U.S. appointment process, says Eisgruber, is broken. In particular, in spite of gruelling hours of questioning in Senate confirmation hearings, the public learns little about the nominees and their judicial philosophies. Eisgruber writes that a judge's judicial philosophy will express a view "about when courts should impose their own, controversial interpretation of the Constitution."[60] We should assess judges and Supreme Court nominees, writes Eisgruber, based on their judicial philosophies. *The New York Times* has weighed in on this subject: an editorial in April 2008 said, "Senators should examine a nominee's entire legal career" and the Senate "needs to upgrade the confirmation process."[61]

When the prime minister of Canada picks a Supreme Court of Canada judge, he chooses someone who, in the long haul of history, may turn out to be more important than he is. Paul Martin was prime minister for two years and a bit. Afterwards, he spent time on his farm in the Eastern Townships, looking after a herd of sheep. Meanwhile, the two Supreme Court judges Martin had appointed, Rosalie Abella and Louise Charron, were busy writing judgments in Ottawa. They will be doing so for many years to come if they remain on the court until the mandatory retirement age of seventy-five (Justice Abella was born in 1946; Justice Charron, in 1951). The Canadian people are stuck with Abella and Charron, for better or worse, for a long time. Unlike Paul Martin, they cannot be voted out of office. Journalists pointed out in 2010 that three judges—LeBel, Fish, and Binnie—were within five years of the mandatory retirement age of seventy-five, and others would soon be able to retire on a full judicial pension.[62] Whoever is prime minister over the next three or four years will have the chance to remake the court.

As for Tom Cromwell, he will likely be on the court until 2027, when he turns seventy-five. What about Stephen Harper, who appointed Cromwell? Where he'll be in 2027 is anyone's guess.

NINE

The Chief

Three justices lead the current court. Chief Justice Beverley McLachlin, because of her office, is one of them. McLachlin's position gives her a limited formal power, mostly arising from her right to choose which judge will write the majority opinion in a particular case. (She has said more than once that she has "very little power."[1]) Inside the court, formal eminence also gives her informal influence. As for the world outside, the chief justice has a bully pulpit, for she is the court's official spokesperson. (She also acts as deputy governor general.)

Ian Binnie is a leader, not by formal position but because of brains, experience, and an independent streak. He is considered by many to be the smartest judge on the court and has the credibility that comes from a long and diverse career as a practising lawyer. Binnie oozes self-confidence and experience and speaks and writes with clarity and humour. The third of the triumvirate, Rosalie Abella, is a leader because of her passion and energy; she always commands attention, no matter what the circumstances. In the next chapter, I discuss Binnie and Abella. In this one, I describe "The Chief."

I interviewed Chief Justice McLachlin in her chambers in June 2010. Her octagonal office may be the most beautiful room in Ottawa. "It has excellent feng shui," she told me. McLachlin, sixty-six years old when I spoke to her, is invariably elegant in appearance and dress. In conversation, she is cautious and prudential, even wary, presumably anxious to say nothing that might be inappropriate or controversial. To me, she seems remote, controlled, careful to a fault. Her occasional laughter might almost be scripted. Perhaps these characteristics come from the burdens of office.

A day or two before I went Ottawa to speak with the chief justice, I mentioned my impending trip to someone in the small Nova Scotia fishing village where I live during the summer. "What do you think I should ask her?" I said. There was a moment's reflection, and then came the answer: "Ask her if she believes in God." And so, I asked Beverley McLachlin if she believed in God. "Yes. Or, at least, I believe there is some supreme mystical being. I'm not religious myself. But I respect those who are." A very careful answer, this, but an interesting one from someone who has made the journey from small-town religious fundamentalism to deciding that the time has come for same-sex marriage.

Beverley McLachlin was born in Pincher Creek, Alberta, on September 7, 1943, the first of Ernest and Eleanora Gietz's five children.[2] Her parents were fundamentalist Christians; McLachlin has described them as "fervent believers"[3] and her father as "protestant-evangelical."[4] She is reported as saying that her parents were of "high moral value."[5] As a child, she attended a Pentecostal church in Pincher Creek. The Gietzes had a ranch southwest of town and ran a sawmill. They took in paying guests. In a 2004 interview at New York University, McLachlin described her family as large, busy, and happy.[6]

Pincher Creek is a town of about 3,600, east of the Rocky Mountains, a hundred miles or so south of Calgary, near the Montana border, in ranching country. It's a typical small Canadian community. It's not prosperous; it doesn't have a piece of the Alberta oil and gas boom, and relies mostly on tourism for its limited economic well-being. The population has declined over the last few years but not much else has changed. The median income of the town is below that of the province.[7] One blogger on a CBC 2008 election site wrote, "It is basically red neck Alberta for lack of a better term ... it is basically farmers, people who have left Calgary to comminute [sic] into the city, and a whole whack of people who just want to be left alone."[8] A story in the *Toronto Star* quoted a local rancher, Stan Fisher, who described Pincher Creek as the "real Alberta. Raise horses and rodeo is all we do."[9]

The town is in the federal riding of Macleod. The member of Parliament is a Conservative, Ted Menzies, who farms near Claresholm. The riding has voted for the Conservative Party and its predecessors for as long as anyone can remember. After the 2004 election, when he first won his seat, he said, "This is Conservative country ... No Liberal is likely to ever represent this riding."[10] In the 2006 election, Menzies won 75 percent of the vote; in 2008, he got 77 percent. In the 2006 campaign, he was reported as saying, "We are a fiercely independent group of miners, loggers and farmers who like to keep our tax money to ourselves and spend it where we see fit."[11]

McLachlin has often described herself as a "farm girl" and speaks of a deep affection for Pincher Creek: "You had this sense of privilege that you were living in this very special place, even though it was remote and not very important."[12] She has said that she thinks of her hometown every day.[13] She often goes back there to spend time at a cottage owned by one of her brothers. A painting by Robert McInnes called *Pincher Creek,* showing wheatfields and a farmhouse, hangs in her Supreme Court office.

McLachlin thinks there has always been a lot more to Pincher Creek than rodeos and wind. "There was always a strong emphasis put on literacy, reading and respect for learning ... This really made a big difference in my life in a very concrete sense.... Even though we were living in a small community we were living in a large world thanks to the library."[14] In the 2004 NYU interview, McLachlin said that her small-town, old-fashioned background had a considerable effect on her work as a judge:

> I think I have a very strong sense of a connection between people and place. Understanding that is important to the law. Much of the law has to do with where people want to be, what kind of culture they want to have the right to further, geographically, culturally and so on. I think that is very important. I also think that my background has helped to ground me in a common sense practicality because when you are from that type of background you have to make things work, you have responsibilities from an early age. In some ways when I got to the university I was very naive, I didn't understand much about city life. But I did understand about the importance of getting along with people, the importance of respecting people, the importance of doing your honest best at whatever responsibility was given to you.

After finishing high school, Beverley McLachlin followed a conventional path. There was little to suggest future eminence. She went to Edmonton in 1960 to study philosophy at the University of Alberta, with the vague and traditional idea (for that time) of becoming a teacher. In 1964, she spent the summer in

Algeria, as a member of the annual World University Service of Canada seminar, which every year takes outstanding university students for a summer's study in a foreign country; this is one of the few things in her resumé that suggests a taste for adventure. Another summer, she worked as a newspaper reporter, assigned to the women's pages.

In 1965, B.A. in hand, she enrolled in the University of Alberta law school. In 1967, she married Rory McLachlin, a biologist and environmental consultant. He smoked his own salmon, made his own wine, and cut his own firewood.[15] In 1968, she graduated at the top of her class (a class of sixty-five, with only a handful of women), and was awarded the Horace Harvey Gold Medal. "She was a first class student," Wilbur Bowker, dean of law at the time, told a reporter years later.[16]

McLachlin was called to the Alberta bar in 1969. For two years, she practised law with Wood, Moir, Hyde and Ross, a small Edmonton law firm that no longer exists. This seems like an odd choice; a gold medallist, even a woman gold medallist in those days, would have been accepted as a junior lawyer by any of the big establishment firms. After two years, McLachlin and her husband moved to the small city of Fort St. John in northeastern British Columbia, where Rory farmed. There, she was called to the bar of British Columbia, and practised with Thomas, Herdy, Mitchell and Company, another small firm that has since disappeared. Again, she stayed for only two years.

In 1972, McLachlin moved to Vancouver and joined the large establishment law firm of Bull, Housser and Tupper. At Bull, Housser she was mentored by W.J. Wallace, a well-known litigator, who later became a judge of the British Columbia Court of Appeal. Wallace had very positive memories of her. He remembered a lunch with colleagues in the Cavalier Room at Vancouver's Georgia Hotel. "In those days, after lunch you lit up a cigar ... She asked if she could smoke and lit up a cigarillo. I think it was the only time I saw her smoke, but she showed she wasn't going to be intimidated."[17]

Once more, Beverley McLachlin moved on quickly. In 1975, she joined the law faculty of the University of British Columbia as an associate professor, teaching evidence, civil litigation, and creditors' remedies. Being a woman likely played some role in her UBC appointment. Justice Ruth Bader Ginsburg of the U.S. Supreme Court was appointed to the law faculty of Columbia University in the early 1970s. Ginsburg has commented: "That was 1972, every law school was looking for its woman."[18]

In 1976, McLachlin's son Angus was born. Her husband, Rory, was very helpful. "He put his career on the back burner and put mine first ... Rory did a lot of the child-rearing. Every time Angus had to go to emergency, it always seems it was Rory with him. It liberated me to do other things."[19]

In April 1981, her spectacular judicial career began. McLachlin was appointed to the Vancouver County Court at the age of thirty-seven. She has speculated that being a woman played a role. McLachlin was at the county court for only a few months. This was when she began to learn French, a sensible thing to do for an anglophone aspiring to higher office. In September 1981, she was appointed to the Supreme Court of British Columbia. "I think I got carried along in this huge *crise de conscience*—'we have no women judges, what are we going to do about it?' And there was one that looked not too bad so they pushed me up very quickly."[20] Four years later, she was elevated to the B.C. Court of Appeal. Three years after that, in September 1988, Brian Mulroney called to offer her the job of chief justice of the province's Supreme Court. She was out at a reception when the call came, and Angus, now twelve years old, took a message. Three days later, her husband, Rory, died of throat cancer.

Her relentless climb to great judicial power quickly continued. In March 1989, Brian Mulroney offered her the "western seat" on the Supreme Court of Canada, just vacated by Bill McIntyre (who was from British Columbia). She was the third woman to be appointed to the highest court. When she was sworn in, the president of the Law Society of British Columbia said that she'd made it through the court system faster than most cases. At the swearing-in ceremony, Justice Bertha Wilson leaned over to McLachlin and whispered, "Three down, six to go."[21] "We are very proud of her," said her aunt, Tina Gietz, back in Pincher Creek (McLachlin's mother died in 1972, and her father in 1977); "She has always been well liked wherever she goes and is quite a capable woman, with both feet on the ground all the time."[22] Kirk Makin of *The Globe and Mail* commented, "Legal observers ... think that she will add smoothness to the uneven chemistry of the Supreme Court."[23] French was still a bit of a problem, but McLachlin was working away at it. Her office told a reporter in 2010: "At the time of her appointment to the Supreme Court of Canada she had good reading French, and moderate oral French."[24]

At the end of 1999, Prime Minister Chrétien called to offer McLachlin the job of chief justice of Canada. She accepted immediately. The first woman to hold the position, she was sworn in on January 7, 2000. In announcing her appointment, Chrétien said, "It was a great opportunity to have, for the first time, a woman as chief justice of Canada."[25] Peter Russell, a long-time commentator on the Supreme Court, has said, "I think Chrétien, like Mulroney, loved the political spin factor, being able to say something like he names the first woman chief justice."[26] Some of McLachlin's friends had thought for a long time that she wanted the job badly. Some had regarded her efforts to master French as "a sign of a careerist's ambition." A former law clerk told me that McLachlin "worked very hard to become chief justice." McLachlin's appointment was widely hailed, particularly by the legal community. She was described as "the ideal person for the job," wise, energetic, sophisticated, bright, practical, loyal, unfailingly polite, someone whose "warmth and sense of humour are awesome," clear-thinking, open-minded, a methodical and prolific workhorse.[27] She was even described as "photogenic," undoubtedly the first chief justice to receive this compliment.

It is said that Frank Iacobucci was bitter that he had not been given the top job. He considered himself better qualified than McLachlin, and many agreed. He regarded himself, with some justification, as the intellectual leader of the court. His credentials as a Canadian are impeccable—he is of Italian origin, son of a steelworker. He is from Vancouver. He had worked hard to get the position, sometimes even—as another Supreme Court judge put it—working subtly to undermine McLachlin's position. But, thought Iacobucci, Chrétien could not resist appointing a woman and—another strike against him—he was unfairly considered as being in the Mulroney camp. Iacobucci resigned from the court in 2004 "to spend more time with his family." Since then, he has had a distinguished career as, among other things, acting president of the University of Toronto, although friends say he misses being a judge.

———

McLachlin's first decade on the Supreme Court defied easy characterization. Several of her more important judgments appealed to those on the right—the 1995 *RJR-MacDonald* case, for example, where she held that a federal ban on tobacco advertising was an infringement of the right to self-expression.[28] But many of her judgments were attractive to the left—the 1998 *Vriend* decision,[29] for instance, in which she agreed that the 1982 Charter of Rights and Freedoms required Alberta human rights legislation to protect gay rights. She was not afraid to dissent; in her first decade she agreed with the majority less than half the time. Some considered her a judge for all seasons, not rooted in any particular view of the law, but most agreed she had poise, common sense, and an impressive work ethic.

A former McLachlin clerk who talked to me pointed to her lone dissent, as a junior judge in a full nine-member panel, in the 1991 case of *R. v. Barnes*,[30] this, it was suggested, was early evidence of her independence of mind and strength of purpose. She's certainly not without courage. In the 1990 *Keegstra* case,[31] on appeal from her home province of Alberta, McLachlin was one of three dissenting judges; she considered that Criminal Code provisions, which made promoting hatred against an identifiable group (in this case, Jews) a crime, were unconstitutional as contrary to freedom of expression. "That was a brave thing to do for an ambitious woman," I was told.

Was there a subtle tactical ability deployed in aid of ambition? One of her former law clerks said that, once it was suspected that Tony Lamer would soon be resigning as chief justice, McLachlin was careful not to be closely identified any more with judgments that might prove overly controversial. In *R. v. Ewanchuk*,[32] for example, the infamous 1999 "no means no" sexual assault case, in which a seventeen-year-old Edmonton woman, out of fear, appeared to allow sexual advances, she did not join the five judges who agreed with John Major's majority opinion rejecting "implied consent" as a defence to sexual assault. Nor did she throw in her lot (as Charles Gonthier did) with Claire L'Heureux-Dubé's very aggressive concurring reasons which severely criticized the Alberta Court of Appeal for relying on "inappropriate myths and stereotypes." Instead, McLachlin gave an antiseptic one-paragraph concurring judgment.

What effect has she had on Charter cases since becoming chief justice? Benjamin Alarie and Andrew Green, of the University of Toronto's law faculty, have done a quantitative analysis of 105 claims under the Charter that have been decided by the court over the last ten years.[33] They conclude that McLachlin's voting pattern shows that she fosters cooperation and tries to bring other justices to a common position. Consensus, and not any particular theory or principle, is what seems to count for the chief justice. A former law clerk commented to me that she seeks "consensus above all," and "will cobble together just about anything to achieve agreement." Her own voting pattern, say Alarie and Green, is squarely in the middle. But, a recent study by two other law professors confirms McLachlin's tendency to dissent; it shows that overall she has been the greatest dissenter of the current court, although she has dissented far less since becoming chief justice.[34]

In criminal law, there is a clear trend for the court to favour the Crown and the police, rather than the accused, a trend promoted by the chief justice. Queen's University law professor Donald Stuart, a criminal law expert, argued at a June 2009 CBA conference that a law-and-order bias has crept into recent Supreme Court Charter decisions.[35] McLachlin gave the majority reasons (with Justice Charron) in the 2009 criminal law case of R. v. Grant,[36] which (with its three companion cases) has been described as the most important criminal law decision in years. Her approach offered striking affirmation of the bias identified by Professor Stuart; in three of the four Grant cases, the court ruled that evidence the police had obtained illegally was admissible. If there were any doubt where the chief justice stood after this, it was dispelled by the 2010 Sinclair case, which gave a very narrow view of a detainee's Charter right to legal counsel during police interrogation; McLachlin and Charron wrote for the majority in that case.

What of the freedoms of association, expression, and religion?

McLachlin is generally given good marks for clarity and progressive thinking on these issues, but her grades may not be completely deserved. In the 2005 *Labaye* case, for example, she wrote the judgment for a seven-judge majority which found the operation of a commercial sex club did not involve acts of indecency (which would have made it a crime). This met with the approval of civil libertarians. But McLachlin's reasons were murky and unconvincing, and there was a compelling and clear dissent by Justices LeBel and Bastarache. In the 2009 case of *Alberta v. Hutterian Brethren of Wilson Colony,* a much-criticized decision, McLachlin gave the majority judgment which was casual about religious freedom; there was a powerful dissent by Justices Abella, LeBel, and Fish.

Another favourite question: How does being a woman influence her decisions? That debate began in 1990, when McLachlin had been sitting on the court for less than two years. In *Hess,*[37] a case about statutory rape, she dissented (along with Justice Gonthier) from the majority judgment given by the feminist judge Bertha Wilson. This was *lèse-majesté;* the dissent has been characterized as "a direct challenge, not just to Wilson but to feminist orthodoxy."[38] The appellants in *Hess* had been criminally charged with sexual intercourse with a female under the age of fourteen. The Criminal Code said that belief by an accused that a female was older than fourteen (so-called "mental innocence") was not a defence. Was this contrary to the Charter of Rights and Freedoms? Wilson said it was, because it infringed the Charter section 7 right to liberty. In the course of Wilson's judgment—and this is where the trouble began—she also considered whether the Criminal Code provision infringed section 15(1) of the Charter, which provides that every individual is equal before the law. The appellants argued that it did infringe, because the section provided that only men could be charged. Wilson disagreed, stating, "There are certain biological realities that one cannot ignore and that may legitimately shape the definition of particular offences."[39]

McLachlin took exception to the Wilson analysis. She said of the Criminal Code provision: "It makes distinctions on the enumerated ground of sex. It burdens men as it does not burden women. It offers protection to young females which it does not offer to young males. It is discriminatory." On the broader question, McLachlin found that, although the provision was contrary to section 7 of the Charter, it was rescued by section 1, which provides that Charter rights are subject to reasonable limits that can be demonstrably justified in a free and democratic society. The particular result in *Hess* was broadly unimportant (new trials were ordered for the appellants). What counted more was an apparent philosophical divide between two women on the court. Bertha Wilson saw women as a disadvantaged group requiring especial protection. Beverley McLachlin began from the position that men and women were equal.

In January 1991, Bertha Wilson retired. She was replaced by Frank Iacobucci. Almost immediately, the court was faced with *Seaboyer*,[40] the infamous rape-shield case. Seaboyer was charged with sexual assault. The judge at the preliminary inquiry refused to allow Seaboyer's lawyer to cross-examine the woman about her previous sexual conduct. Seaboyer argued that cross-examination should be permitted, since other acts of sexual intercourse may have caused bruises that were put into evidence against him. The technical issue was whether the Criminal Code "rape-shield" provisions infringed the principles of fundamental justice or the right to a fair trial found in sections 7 and 11(d) of the Charter. These provisions restricted the right of the defence, in a trial for a sexual offence, to cross-examine and present evidence of a complainant's sexual conduct on previous occasions.

McLachlin gave the reasons for a seven-member majority. The impugned provisions were struck down as unconstitutional.

McLachlin said that a law that excludes relevant evidence without a good reason for doing so runs afoul of fundamental conceptions of justice.[41] Claire L'Heureux-Dubé gave lengthy, wide-ranging, and palpably angry dissenting reasons (dissenting in part) for herself and Charles Gonthier. The reasons contained much discussion of "the stereotypes and myths about rape." She said: "Perhaps more than any other crime, the fear and constant reality of sexual assault affects how women conduct their lives and how they define their relationship with the larger society."[42] Prominent feminists accused McLachlin of encouraging rape. "Women's groups responded with an almost visceral revulsion."[43]

Since *Seaboyer,* McLachlin seems to have won over at least part of the feminist camp. Sean Fine wrote in 1995 that she was working her way toward a new feminism: "What she is trying to do is refashion the relationship between those often conflicting partners, liberty and equality."[44] Even so, as late as 1999 when she was appointed chief justice, she was hailed by many on the right, who still appreciated what was seen as her rejection, in the *Hess* and *Seaboyer* cases, of special treatment for women.

As the Chief Justice grew into her job, she acquired a new appreciation of her own power and the power of the court. In a 2005 speech given in New Zealand, McLachlin said that there are times when the court must enforce norms that "transcend the law and executive action." These norms may not be written down, in which case the judges must conjure them up:

The law involves rules of different orders. The highest is the order of fundamental constitutional principles. These are the rules that guide all other law-making and the exercise of executive power by the state. More and more in our democratic states, we try to set these out in writing. But when we do not, or when, as is inevitable, the written text is unclear or incomplete, recourse must be had to unwritten sources. The task of the judge, confronted with conflict between a constitutional principle of the highest order on the one hand, and an ordinary law or executive act on the other, is to interpret and apply the law as a whole—including relevant unwritten constitutional principles.[45]

In other words, sometimes the highest applicable laws are not written anywhere, and must be summoned up, from wherever, by a judge.

McLachlin also developed a keen sense of her position. One former law clerk to one of McLachlin's predecessors as chief justice, a lawyer who has since often appeared before the Supreme Court, told me that McLachlin "is on a power trip. She forgets she is just one of nine judges." Another clerk said, "She loves her prerogatives as chief justice, like being deputy governor general, and the RCMP protection, and the limos."

In 1992, McLachlin married lawyer Frank McArdle, who is best known for running an annual conference for Canadian lawyers in Cambridge, England. McArdle has been described as "a cheerful, semi-retired extrovert, who's completely supportive of her success."[46] He proposed to McLachlin over an airplane public-address system on a flight to England. (This would not have been to everyone's taste; perhaps it is what cheerful extroverts do.) She has said, "I benefited greatly from the fact that I have been married to two wonderful men (at different times)."[47] McArdle was divorced from his first wife, who died in 2009.

McLachlin and McArdle live in Rockcliffe, the premier residential area of Ottawa. "She has embraced Ottawa," someone told me.

McLachlin gets up at about 6:30, and every morning takes her dog for a walk in a nearby park. She likes to cook, knit, cross-country ski, play the piano, and listen to opera, particularly Mozart. Once she wrote fiction (her mother apparently wanted to be a writer): it is said she has two unpublished novels in the bottom drawer of her desk, a mystery with a woman lawyer as the central character, and a historical fiction set in Alberta. She reads Alice Munro and Margaret Atwood, and Fred Stenson, a celebrated writer of historical fiction who was also born in Pincher Creek. When I interviewed her in June 2010, she told me she was reading a biography of Cicero, and had just finished Stieg Larsson's *The Girl with a Dragon Tattoo* ("I read it on a trip," she said, with a slightly apologetic air). McLachlin's son Angus is a musician in Montreal. In Pincher Creek, a street has been renamed Beverley McLachlin Drive. Beverley and Frank own a cottage in the Gatineau. She's a grandmother. "I'm very grounded," the Chief Justice told me. "I do my own shopping. I'm quite anonymous." She goes to many diplomatic and other parties, and is frequently mentioned in the society pages of Ottawa newspapers.

There's no such thing as a quintessential Canadian. If there were, she might be Beverley McLachlin. No elite background here: She is from a small town, the child of deeply religious parents, and was educated well but not in foreign or unusual schools and universities. She's never been divorced but had experience as a single mother after her first husband died. She has no strange hobbies or interests (mainstream all the way). She's even-handed and even-tempered, and probably smarter, more self-confident, perhaps more ambitious, and certainly luckier, professionally, than most.

In Chapter 1, I quoted Richard Posner, himself an eminent judge: "Empirical scholars have found that many judicial decisions ... are strongly influenced by a judge's political preferences or by other extralegal factors, such as the judge's personal characteristics and personal and professional experiences, which may shape his political preferences or operate directly on his response to a case."[48] In a 2005 interview to mark her fifth year in office, McLachlin said of her job, "I think that people are coming to understand better and better ... that it is not a political role; that it is not a partisan role.... The law is an organic thing. As society changes, it has to grow. Sometimes when we address these situations, people say: 'Oh, the court is being very activist.' But that is part of our role."[49] This seems like what Ronald Dworkin has called, in the U.S. context, "the opaque platitude that a good judge decides as the law requires."[50]

Five years after being made Chief Justice, in 2005, McLachlin still attracted the kind of lavish praise that was heaped upon her when she was first appointed. Various law professors, vociferous as ever, called her "a warm individual in step with her times," "a gifted writer," "very good at presenting the Supreme Court as a modern, 'cooler' institution," "very open-minded, down to earth and not stuffy at all," "fiercely free-thinking, while respectful of legal tradition," and—the ultimate Canadian accolade—"the law's Wayne Gretzky." Similar encomiums were lavished on her when she celebrated her tenth anniversary as The Chief. Writing in the *Ottawa Citizen* in 2010, Andrew Cohen proposed McLachlin for the job of governor general.[51]

Although tough, McLachlin strikes people as low-key and friendly, and spends considerable time consulting her judges: "I try to get around and talk to everybody ... Not with any particular message, just to keep channels open. My door is open, and justices pop in just for a chat. That's the kind of thing that promotes open dialogue. It's all about dialogue and discussion here."[52] In an interview, she said, "My job is not to have an agenda. My job is to contribute to an atmosphere where everyone feels free to discuss whatever they want to discuss."[53] Another Supreme Court judge told me, "McLachlin can't stand conflict. Her mantra is 'compromise, compromise, compromise.' And she hates it when people criticize the court." Retired Supreme Court Justice John Major has said, "She has presented the best public face of the Supreme Court to the public of any of the chief justices of my time."[54] Justice Rothstein told me, "She's the administrative and intellectual leader. She's incredible." Justice LeBel has been lavish in his praise, referring to McLachlin's astute management skills and her ability to tone down challenges and clashes within the court. He says she is good at "bringing people to reason, going around to see people on occasion, suggesting changes in reasons [for judgment] that will perhaps not change anything to the substance, but avoid hurting someone."[55]

But there remain dissenters from the general view. Some ask why Justice Michel Bastarache left the court fifteen years early, apparently because he could no longer tolerate personality clashes. Others find the Chief Justice uninspiring. "No presence at all," one Ottawa insider told me. "I was at a dinner speech she made, and it was very boring. People started chatting with each other before she had finished." A senior federal bureaucrat described a forty-minute after-dinner speech McLachlin gave at the Canadian War Museum. "People were texting each other during the speech, things like, can we seize one of these tanks and break out of here?" There's a consensus that the Chief Justice is a dull and pedestrian speaker. One very senior federal politician, perhaps overreacting to that, told me "Beverley McLachlin has never had an original idea in her life." Someone referred me to an article in *The New York Times* about Elena Kagan, written by the influential commentator David

Brooks; Kagan sounds just like McLachlin, I was told. Brooks describes Kagan as smart, deft, friendly, prudential, deliberate, and cautious. She is one of a cohort that has "a professional and strategic attitude toward life ... prudential rather than poetic."[56] I read these lines to McLachlin, and asked her if they described her. She replied, "I read poetry." I asked, "Who is your favourite poet?" "Yeats," she said.[57]

In her 2005 interview with Kirk Makin, Chief Justice McLachlin said: "In my life, I have always taken things one step at a time. I've never made long-range plans. I never dreamed that I would be a judge. I never dreamed that I'd be on the Supreme Court of Canada. I never dreamed that I'd be Chief Justice."[58] It could be true. In a 2009 television interview, when asked if being a judge meant she was cut off from normal life, she replied, "I've been a judge so long that normal life for me is acting like a judge."[59]

TEN

Leaders of the Court

Ian Binnie is the most senior Supreme Court justice after Chief Justice McLachlin (seniority depends on date of appointment). The two have worked side by side for more than a decade. One insider told me that, for a time at least, Binnie was a favourite of McLachlin. Yet their backgrounds and temperaments are quite different.

The Chief Justice had an unexceptional background until she started her rapid ascent through the judicial ranks—childhood in a small town, law school in Alberta, sketchy and limited exposure to legal practice. She is known for common sense, hard work, and caution, and for having a big dollop of ambition. Binnie is a big-city guy, who was born in Montreal and has lived most of his adult life in Toronto. He had an elite education at McGill, Cambridge University in England, and the University of Toronto. Before becoming a judge, he practised law with a major firm on Bay Street and was one of Canada's best-known and most respected litigators. He looks like a Bay Street lawyer of his generation;

he's tall and thin, and, with patrician casualness, generally wears nondescript blue suits and old-fashioned glasses with large lenses. In his public utterances at least, unlike McLachlin, he is not always careful. Shortly after he was appointed, *Maclean's* referred to him as "Mr. Malaprop."[1]

It's Binnie who "runs things" at the court, according to a very senior Ottawa politician and court watcher. A journalist who writes extensively about the court told me the same thing. An eminent Toronto litigator described him as "brilliant." Another senior counsel told me that Binnie had "carefully positioned" himself for a Supreme Court appointment and had "a well-developed sense of self-worth"; this lawyer commented that Binnie keeps to himself and is not very interested in the opinions of others. For example, I was told, "He doesn't give a damn about the opinions of his law clerks. A law clerk's job is to summarize documents and do research." A former Binnie law clerk whom I interviewed differed somewhat, saying Binnie's clerks "felt close" to him: "He mentored us, he was a teacher. And he is super smart." One of Binnie's fellow judges told me, with a hint of disdain, that Binnie thinks of himself as "an intellectual, as the philosopher of the court." A former colleague had a different take: "He's very smart, but has no philosophy. There's no theory. All he cares about is results."

Binnie has shown himself to be courageous, principled, and independently minded. He is not afraid to take an unpopular minority view—for example, in the *Chaoulli* case, where he repudiated judicial involvement in the debate about private health care insurance; in *A.C.*, where he was prepared to let a fifteen-year-old refuse lifesaving medical treatment; in *Amselem*, in which he refused to let a claim to religious freedom trump an inconsistent private agreement entered into by the claimant; in *Grant*, where he criticized a "claimant-centred" approach to the psychology of relations between citizens and the police; and in *Lipson*, where he spoke out in favour of the taxpayer rather than the government. One thing is for sure: Binnie is the court's best writer, clear and concise, with a good turn of phrase, and a wry sense of humour.

He got the call from Justice Minister Anne McLellan on January 8, 1998, offering the seat on the Supreme Court made vacant by the sudden death of his friend John Sopinka a few weeks before. Binnie was no blushing bride. "You don't think twice about accepting that appointment," Binnie told a reporter. "You grab it."[2] He has said, disingenuously in some people's eyes, that he wasn't expecting the job, and was "startled" and "astonished" when first sounded out about it; he described the phone call from McLellan as an "out-of-body experience."[3] In another account, Binnie has said that he was first sounded out in December 1997 but didn't take the inquiry seriously.[4]

Some observers found Binnie's appointment surprising. Many thought that Prime Minister Chrétien would likely appoint a woman (in 1998 there were only two women on the court, Beverley McLachlin and Claire L'Heureux-Dubé, and there was pressure for more). Some said that Binnie was a beneficiary of the acrimonious competition between Rosie Abella and John Laskin for Sopinka's seat; the struggle was so intense, with so many partisans of each in the legal community, that neither could be safely appointed, leaving the way open for a third choice. (Abella was eventually appointed to the court in 2004.)

In an editorial, *The Globe and Mail* criticized not the appointment itself but the way it was done: "A closed secretive process. No official candidates. No public discussion. Zero public knowledge. Just several weeks of backroom manoeuvring followed by an announcement."[5] Binnie and his wife celebrated with champagne and take-out chicken on the evening of the announcement.

When he was appointed, Binnie was a high-flying Bay Street corporate lawyer and partner of the elite Toronto-based law firm

McCarthy Tétrault. He was born in Montreal in 1939, the son of a lawyer. In 1960, he graduated from McGill with a B.A.; then went to Cambridge University in England to study law; and finished his formal education at the University of Toronto law school, graduating in 1965. That same year, he married Susan Strickland. They have four children (one a Rhodes Scholar, another a doctor). From 1982 to 1986, Binnie was federal associate deputy minister of justice, giving advice to the government on constitutional matters. He was privy to early versions of the Charter of Rights and Freedoms. In a 2009 interview, Binnie said: "There wasn't any expectation from the government that the Charter will become such a popular icon, such a cultural identification of Canadians with their rights. I am very glad that the Charter had the impact it had, but I don't think it was envisaged even by Trudeau to achieve the centrality to Canadian culture it now has."[6] Some think it was no accident that he was appointed to the court just a month before it was due to hear the reference on Quebec secession, the most important case ever. He has stated categorically he was never asked his views about the reference before he was offered the Supreme Court job.[7]

When Binnie was put on the court, everyone agreed he was pretty smart. That seemed like a good thing. But negative comments floated around. He had limited trial experience (although, it was noted, he had argued twenty-six cases before the Supreme Court). He had no experience as a judge[8] (offset, said many, by his "experience in the trenches"). He knew little about criminal law, which takes up a good part of the court's docket. And Binnie's elite background bothered some lawyers. One said, "He's never acted for the little guy, so I don't think he understands the problems of the little people." It didn't help when Binnie, asked what he did in his spare time, replied, "I play squash and ski, the usual kind of things."[9]

The Ontario Attorney General at the time, Charles Harnick, struck a reassuring note: "His easy-going nature and gentle disposition ... and his absolute lack of pretension suggest Mr. Justice Binnie would be just as comfortable looking out onto the wheat fields of the Prairies or the whitecaps of the Maritimes as he is in the towers of corporate Canada."[10] One of Binnie's Supreme Court colleagues, with some affection, told me a slightly different story: "He likes to play at being an Englishman. He wears cardigans with holes in at the elbows." This judge agreed about Binnie's lack of pretension. "On airplanes, he always travels coach. Once he went to a judicial conference in Hawaii and stayed at a $25-a-night hotel."

Much has been made of Binnie's sense of humour and his skill at public speaking. One Toronto litigator said, "He is very puckish at times. He ... has a very amusing way of seeing things."[11] A former partner of Binnie's said, "There's no situation, no predicament which he cannot lighten with a quip or an amusing insight."[12] Some of his fabled humour was on display when he was sworn in, on February 2, 1998. The *Ottawa Citizen* reported: "Judge Binnie had the ordinarily solemn chamber in stitches when he noted that when the current Supreme Court justices were told of his appointment last month, Judge John Major's reaction was, 'Tell Binnie now he won't have to shout at us any more.' 'Some of the cordiality may therefore be due to the fact now I will be on the inside shouting out rather than on the outside shouting in,' the new judge said to raucous laughter.'"[13] (It doesn't take much to get people laughing on these kinds of occasions, and, of course, lawyers always laugh at judges' jokes.)

It was not long before Binnie's "wit" got him into trouble. On March 7, 1998, just a few weeks after he had been sworn in, he gave a speech to about two hundred people attending a dinner given by the Osgoode Hall Law School Inn (branch) of Phi Delta Phi, a legal fraternity. Kirk Makin described what happened in *The Globe and Mail:* "Judge Binnie made jocular reference to an instruction found in a booklet laying out some fraternity initiation rituals. 'The use of the fraternity flag, wigs, candles and dramatic lighting will vary depending on the setting, character and tradition of the Inn,' he quoted the pamphlet as saying. Judge Binnie then remarked that upon seeing the instruction, he had wondered whether he would be attending some kind of 'faggoty dressup party.'"[14] His "jocular" comment left a room full of law students "shocked and silent." Was the judge biased against gays? Binnie later said he wasn't, apologized for his remark in a letter to the dean of the law school, and had another apology posted on the Osgoode bulletin board. Svend Robinson, a gay activist who was then a member of Parliament, was reported as saying, "The matter should send a loud warning to Judge Binnie that he has departed his former life as a private lawyer with a reputation for delivering thigh-slapping, irreverent speeches. 'This will be a strong lesson in how the world of the Supreme Court is very different than the world of McCarthy's ...'"[15] One of his former Supreme Court fellow judges said about it dismissively: "Oh, Binnie just loves to debate. He comes at speeches as if they're a debate. Sometimes he goes too far, but that's just Binnie. Everyone should just get over it."

Binnie has remained irrepressible despite this early embarrassment in his judicial career. He has become almost a fixture on the humorous lecture circuit. In 2002, for example, at the annual Leacock Debate in Toronto, he debated the proposition "All Good Things Come to an End" with Kim Campbell (he was against the motion). In 2004, at the Legal Archives 2004 Historical Dinners in Calgary and Edmonton, he gave a speech entitled "Legal Humour: titillating, ghastly, or just plain oxymoronic?" In November 2008, at the annual Hastings County Law Association banquet, by all reports he had them rolling in the aisles. The local newspaper reported, "If the lawyers and judges present were expecting a legal dissertation ... they got a lot of laughs instead."

———————

Binnie displayed a more serious side just a few months after his "faggoty dressup party" gaffe. In a November 1998 speech to the Criminal Lawyers' Association, the first John Sopinka Advocacy Lecture, he gave valuable insight into pleading before the Supreme Court and into the court's decision-making process. It was a measured and revealing speech, but once more Justice Binnie found himself in hot water. Kirk Makin of *The Globe and Mail* went on the attack, based on Binnie's description of the conference that judges have immediately after hearing a case: "The Supreme Court decides the outcome of its cases within minutes or hours of hearing them—not after the weeks and months of sober debate that most observers believe is the norm ..."[16] Binnie wrote a letter to the newspaper's editor. "Kirk Makin misunderstood ... The 'weeks and months of sober debate' that Mr. Makin mentions takes place while the court's reasons are being written and rewritten and—not infrequently—the opinions of individual judges are modified."[17]

There was to be more trouble between Binnie and the media. In August 2001, Binnie "mocked journalists during a 30-minute speech, accusing them of superficial and biased reporting.... The media, he asserted, is more in the business of entertaining than informing."[18] Binnie went after the *National Post* in particular. Observers speculated that he was still upset over the severe and sustained criticism of his judgment in the 1999 *Donald Marshall* case[19] (the same Donald Marshall who spent eleven years in prison for a murder he did not commit).

In the *Marshall* case, Binnie, giving judgment for the majority (McLachlin and Gonthier dissented), found that East Coast Aboriginal peoples had a treaty right to fish without a licence, even in the off-season. This led to violent confrontations in the Maritimes between native and non-native fishermen. The court faced a wave of "unprecedented anger."[20] In an editorial, *The Globe and Mail* said, "The spectre of the Supreme Court functioning illegitimately to create an unintended right based on vague and quasi-historical interpretations is certainly raised by this judgment ... It is the spectre of a court wrenched from the fabric of democratic life, operating according to internally rationalized norms beyond effective social redress."[21] The *National Post* reported on its front page that a historian who had been an expert witness in the case believed Binnie seriously distorted his testimony when he quoted it in his judgment.[22]

Two months later, in dismissing a motion for a rehearing and a stay made by the West Nova Fishermen's Coalition, the Supreme Court, in a unanimous judgment (the panel included Beverley McLachlin, who had just succeeded Antonio Lamer as chief justice, and Charles Gonthier, both of whom had dissented in the earlier judgment) clarified its earlier decision. It made clear that there were considerable limitations on the treaty right. In particular, it stressed the federal government's ability to regulate the fishery, and that its earlier judgment related only to the fishery and did not extend to other resources.[23] "The Supreme Court blinked," said the *National Post* in an editorial. "The court's antics in the Marshall case bear an uncanny resemblance to when a political party floats a 'trial balloon' to the press and then reverses course after public criticism."[24] Jeffrey Simpson, in *The Globe and Mail*, wrote:

The justices have rallied together and fired a series of shots at just about everyone but themselves ... This judgment is an astonishing and probably unprecedented performance. Everybody else—aboriginals, non-aboriginals, governments, commentators—got things mixed up; the court, according to the justices, was right all along.

But that cannot logically be. How could the two previous dissenters now join their colleagues in a judgment that fundamentally endorses the wisdom of the ruling against which they dissented? Conversely, how could the majority now join the two dissenters who said the original ruling was wrong?[25]

Columnist Lorne Gunter said of the court, "It unleashed a wave of destruction and outrage with its Sept. 17 decision ... and then a month later pulled off one of the biggest flip-flops in Canadian judicial history ... [It is] a frivolous, capricious court that is making the law up as it goes along."[26]

No wonder Ian Binnie was upset. The authors of one book commented, in Binnie's defence, "Poor understanding by journalists of a complex and sometimes ambiguous decision may have contributed to the mayhem in the Atlantic fisheries in the fall of 1999."[27] But the author of another book produced a sustained and damning indictment of Binnie and the entire court. Alex Cameron is a constitutional litigator in Nova Scotia. In *Power Without Law*,[28] Cameron writes that the first *Marshall* decision "exhibits a worrisome inattention to historical and legal principle. In fact, the evidence ... and the constitutional law relevant to it are contrary to the decision rendered by the majority."[29] Cameron says of the second *Marshall* decision, "The judges added to the confusion that their original decision had caused. They had gone well beyond their proper judicial role, responding to an application that was wholly without merit, not by dismissing it out of hand but by significantly rewriting the decision they had rendered."[30]

Later, things seemed to settle down a little for Justice Binnie. In

February 2003, Kirk Makin wrote, "Five years after being yanked straight from the ranks of litigators, Judge Binnie has arrived."[31] Makin described Binnie as "the court's most streetwise jurist."

But Makin wrote too soon. Several months later in 2003, controversy would again swirl around Binnie's head. In December 2002, he had given reasons for a unanimous decision in an Indian lands claim case.[32] Two First Nations bands on the east coast of Vancouver Island, the Wewaikai and the Wewaykum, claimed each other's reserve lands; the court dismissed the claims of each. In February 2003, the chief of the Wewaykum band made a freedom of information request to the Department of Justice, seeking copies of all records concerning the bands' claims that made reference to Binnie. The department found a number of memoranda showing that in late 1985 and early 1986, when Binnie was an associate deputy minister, he had received information concerning the Wewaykum claim and had attended a meeting where the claim was discussed. On May 26, the Crown filed a motion with the court seeking directions as to any steps that should be taken in light of this information. Binnie recused himself from any further proceedings and filed a statement saying that he had no recollection of personal involvement in the case. In a memorandum, the Crown said that it did not consider there was any reasonable apprehension of bias. The bands sought an order setting aside the court's judgment, arguing that there was a reasonable apprehension of bias (not actual bias) so far as Binnie was concerned.

The court heard argument on June 23, and gave its unanimous forty-seven-page judgment (without Binnie participating) on September 26.[33] It found no reasonable apprehension of bias. It noted particularly that Binnie's supervisory role regarding the land claims dated back over fifteen years. A reasonable person would consider that factor, and it made bias or its apprehension improbable. Was this a tempest in a teapot?[34] Perhaps, but it was a tempest that embarrassed the Supreme Court, and embarrassed Binnie, who just a year before had written the reasons in *R. v. Neil*,[35] the seminal conflict-of-interest case. Interestingly, lawyers who represent Aboriginal bands tell me that they consider Binnie "good" on their cases, and the key Supreme Court justice for them. "He gets it real fast," one said.

In April 2004, Binnie was at the podium again, this time at McGill University law school. He said that the Charter of Rights and Freedoms was the glue of Canadian culture and identity, and quoted approvingly "the Canadian political philosopher Michael Ignatieff: 'rights, not roots; values, not origins' hold the country together.'"[36] In February 2007, he was back at McGill, this time debating U.S. Supreme Court Justice Antonin Scalia. Binnie extolled the virtues of judicial activism; Scalia attacked Binnie "for believing that unelected judges are qualified to act as social engineers who possess a greater level of expertise in deciding morally laden issues than doctors, engineers, the U.S. Founding Fathers or 'Joe Six-Pack.'"[37] A version of Binnie's presentation, emphasizing that judges should be interpreting the Canadian Constitution in light of the country's experience, was later published.[38] "The history of Charter negotiations demonstrates that in many cases, the framers had only the most general idea of the scope of the rights they were entrenching in the Constitution ... and so they chose very open textured language, which they then delegated to the courts to refine and develop." Binnie added, "Judges could and should move cautiously and incrementally."

In August 2008, he was speaking to the Canadian Bar Association annual meeting. This time his subject was "the corporate conscience of Canada," and his message was that Canadian businesses should pay attention to human rights abuses in Third World countries where they do business. He touched on the same theme from a global point of view in an article published by the

American Bar Association in 2009. Binnie wrote: "Corporate
entities … have no body to imprison, no soul to damn and no
conscience to trouble."[39] In 2010, Binnie became even more
adventurous in his public appearances. On March 4, he took the
role of a judge in a play called *Shakespeare in Court* at the faculty
of law of the University of Western Ontario. On March 31, he
was addressing the Empire Club in Toronto. His topic: "Is There
Nobody Smarter than a Toronto Lawyer?" At the Empire Club, he
spoke to people he identified as "beefy lawyers in the audience." In
a funny speech, he said the Charter was supposed to have been a
gift to the little guy fighting city hall, but that Bay Street lawyers
had grabbed it with both hands to make money from corporate
clients, proving that indeed they were very smart.

Clever, tough, a bit devil-may-care, a dominant force on the
court, a judge with guts and humour. Is there anybody smarter
than Ian Binnie?

Justice Rosalie Silberman Abella seems different from the rest.
"[A] cross between Celine Dion and Ruth Bader Ginsburg," wrote
Dahlia Lithwick in *Slate*.[40] She is by far the most public of the
justices, including the chief justice. She gives speeches all the time,
expressing views on many subjects (we know that she considers
the United Nations ineffective, for example[41]). In 2003 (before
she was appointed to the Supreme Court), she was a judge of
the Giller Prize, Canada's pre-eminent award for literary fiction.
She is often seen at parties in Toronto and Ottawa. She has lots
of friends from diverse backgrounds, many well known, rich and
powerful. Some of them got together and gave $1 million for the
creation of a new moot courtroom at the University of Toronto
named after her.[42] The Osgoode Hall Law School blog named her

"Judge of the Year" for 2009, saying (tongue in cheek?) "Abella contributed greatly to diversity of judicial opinion ..."[43] In 2010, *Canadian Lawyer* magazine named her one of the top 25 influential Canadian lawyers; Beverley McLachlin made the list (ranked #1), but no other Supreme Court judge did.[44] Abella is a celebrity judge, the only one Canada has.

Abella is bold, uncompromising, and outspoken in her beliefs, beliefs that cover a lot of intellectual territory and often upset people, mostly those on the political right. To boot, she is likeable and accessible; she is probably the only judge of the Supreme Court ever to have been described publicly as "cuddly." It is hard not to fall into Abella's orbit. Still fairly junior on the Supreme Court, she is a powerful presence there, a presence—if gossip be believed— not always appreciated, sometimes even resented, by her shyer and more conventional colleagues. Five years after she arrived at the court, veteran justice reporter Kirk Makin concluded that she "has emerged as a tower of strength in her favoured fields—family law, employment law, youth criminal justice and human rights," and that "the growing number of majority judgments that she writes has stifled any suggestion that Judge Abella aspires to be a squeaky wheel."[45] And she is not afraid to show the passion that sets her apart—for example, in the *Wilson Colony* case about driver's licence photographs for Hutterites, where she dissented in strong terms.

Most people call her "Rosie" (even those who've never met her). When Abella was appointed chair of the Ontario Labour Relations Board in 1984 (at thirty-eight, she had already been a family court judge for nine years; she was the first female Jewish judge to be appointed in Ontario), there was an outpouring of praise. The deputy minister of labour said she brought to the board a creative mind, a sensitivity to resolving conflicts, and a high intelligence. A former vice-chair of the board described her as extraordinarily capable and intellectually honest. *The Globe and Mail* said she was personable and dynamic.[46] Two-and-a-half years later, Stevie Cameron wrote in *The Globe* that "only 40, with so much still before her, Rosie Abella has already affected Canada's history."[47] This was a reference to Abella's one-woman royal commission on employment equity, which led to the federal Employment Equity Act of 1986. Cameron continued: "Judge Abella, a pre-Raphaelite sprite with tumbling hair, an elfin creature in a red dress with red stockings and red shoes, dances into rooms and hugs her friends. She has 1,000 best friends ..." She quoted Peter Herrndorf, now president of the National Arts Centre, who said of Abella, "She's brilliant, compassionate and lovable. She's incredibly cuddly, but she also has a very, very tough mind." Cameron wrote that Abella's ambition was to contribute to the intellectual process of the country; "colleagues say that someday she will be on the Supreme Court of Canada."

Abella was born in a displaced persons camp near Stuttgart, Germany, on July 1, 1946. Her parents, Jacob and Fanny Silberman, both Polish, were Holocaust survivors. Her brother, Julius, died in Treblinka concentration camp at the age of two, before she was born. The family came to Canada in 1950 on an American troop ship, the U.S.S. *General Stuart Heintzelman,* landing at Pier 21 in Halifax (now Canada's national immigration museum). Jacob Silberman had originally been a lawyer in Germany, having graduated from Jagiellonian University in Krakow in 1934, but he sold insurance in Canada after a stint as an underwear cutter. Fanny eventually sold real estate.

As a child, Abella was an avid reader and an excellent piano student. She is still a book lover: "I'm addicted to reading books. I don't golf, I don't ski, and I don't watch TV."[48] In 1968, she married Irving Abella, a professor of Canadian history at York University. In 1970, she graduated from the University of Toronto law school (her father, Jacob, died of liver cancer one month before she graduated; her mother, in 2010[49]). Abella was called to the bar of Ontario in 1972. She practised law for four years and then began her rise through the judicial ranks with an appointment in 1976 to the Family Division of the Ontario Provincial Court.

There's a lot of information about what Rosalie Abella thinks, more than about the opinions of any other Supreme Court judge. Partly, that's because Abella's extraordinary personality attracts great interest, and partly it's because she gives a lot of speeches.

Consider, for example, what she said in a lecture at the 1989 inaugural conference of Queen's University School of Public Policy.[50] Abella was chair of the Ontario Law Reform Commission at the time. She said that judges have always been involved in public policy formation, basing their decisions partly on their values and on opinions about what would be acceptable or desirable for society. The Charter, she said, had allowed public policy to come out of the judicial closet. But, Abella asked, was it undemocratic for the unelected to make policy? A partial answer to this question, said Abella, an answer she has often given, is that the unelected are far more likely to protect minority rights than the elected. "The legislature which relies on majority support cannot be expected to risk political self-destruction by promulgating minority causes. The courts risk nothing." A leading lawyer for Aboriginal tribes that I spoke to vehemently agreed with this point of view. "If you happen to be a member of a minority, like an Aboriginal," he said, "you're much better, since the Charter, relying on the Supreme Court than on Parliament. If you rely on Parliament, you'll get screwed." The former Lord Chief Justice of England and Wales, the late Tom Bingham, has written, "It is unpopular minorities whom charters and bills of rights exist to protect. In almost any society, the majority (which usually includes the rich and the powerful) can look after itself."[51]

In a speech two-and-a-half years later at the University of British Columbia, using the colourful imagery she favours, Abella emphasized the contribution to public policy of many diverse participants. *The Vancouver Sun* reported: "'Pure Mozart' is the way Judge Rosie Abella describes the interrelationship of the judiciary, lawyers, politicians, academia and the public. 'At times lyrical, at times profoundly moving and complex, but always in perfect harmony, moving toward a cause.' Two other words describe the relationship, she said: 'Ella Fitzgerald.'"[52] Judicial neutrality, said Abella in the Vancouver speech, doesn't mean that judges don't have prior conceptions about social values and certain instincts, emotions, and habits.

The Vancouver speech did not have the media on the list of contributors to public policy. That omission was fixed in Abella's 1997 address to the Canadian Club of Toronto.[53] She emphasized how the media's reaction to a court case helps formulate public policy. Then she identified four myths about the judiciary. The first is that judges should not make law; to that, Abella replied, "Almost every time judges interpret, they make law and, implicitly, weigh competing values." The second is that the courts are biased; Abella commented, "Weighing values and taking public policy into account does not impair judicial neutrality or impartiality." The third myth is that the courts are politicized; "If it is clearly appropriate for courts to deal with the interpretation of rights, one wonders why they are deemed to be 'politicised' only when they interpret them expansively." The final myth is that the courts should pay more attention to public opinion; Abella replied, "Courts deciding cases are entitled scrupulously to regard public opinion as the responsibility of the legislature and generally as immaterial to judicial determination."

One of Abella's most pointed speeches was given to benchers of the Law Society of Upper Canada on October 14, 1999. It was reported by Tracey Tyler of the *Toronto Star:* "The public is fed up as never before with a legal system that has become too complicated and costly and is run by lawyers focused on wealth, one of Ontario's top judges says. The public's disaffection stems in part from a waning professionalism among lawyers, says Madam Justice Rosalie Abella of the Ontario Court of Appeal. Many have been caught up in clinging to riches accumulated in the 1980s, she suggested.... Economic pressures and a misplaced preoccupation with rules and legal process have caused the profession to lose sight of the ideals of justice and the public interest, she argued."[54] These views won her few friends in the legal profession, which is notoriously sensitive to criticism, particularly coming from its own.

It is often said that Rosie Abella is a feminist and often this is not meant as a compliment.[55] The label is sometimes applied because she has spoken out many times about employment equity for women.[56] Sometimes the "feminist" epithet is applied for other reasons. A typical controversy surrounded the 1995 Ontario Court of Appeal decision in *MacGyver v. Richards,*[57] in which Abella gave the main judgment for a panel of three judges (Abella was appointed to the Court of Appeal in 1992 and remained there until she moved to the Supreme Court in 2004). In *MacGyver,* the court enlarged the power after divorce of a custodial parent, in particular giving that parent a "mobility right"—the right in most cases to move with a child despite objections from the non-custodial parent. Abella said: "When ... a court has been asked to decide what is in a child's best interests and a choice must be made between the responsible wishes and needs of the parent with custody and the parent with access, it seems to me manifestly unfair to treat these wishes and needs as being on an equal footing."[58]

The decision was widely and emotionally attacked. A series of articles in *The Globe and Mail*, by reporter Sean Fine, was highly critical of Abella's judgment.[59] The first article quoted something she wrote in 1981: "Is there a role for the court as the conscience of the community, giving expression to ideas as a means of educating and directing society's thoughts?"[60] Abella's answer was that, when it came to family law, the courts and the legislatures are partners. The second *Globe* article, more than 2500 words long, described Abella as an "ardent advocate for equality."[61] A number of lawyers critical of her judgment in *MacGyver* were quoted, many as saying that the consequence of the decision was unsettled law that would lead to more custody battles. These criticisms prompted a counter-attack by Michele Landsberg in the *Toronto Star*.[62] Landsberg wrote that part of Sean Fine's criticism was "personal, trivializing Abella and diminishing her stature.... he goes out of his way to mention that Abella's parents were Holocaust survivors and that her father, a lawyer, had to work as an underwear cutter when he arrived in Canada. What is the possible relevance?" One might have expected that to be the end of this particular controversy, but high feeling lingered on. When Abella was named to the Supreme Court in 2004, an article in the Kitchener newspaper *The Record* said her nomination "should frighten everyone who cares about children."[63] The article was written by a man active in a support group for divorced fathers with children from the broken marriage.

Just the possibility of Abella's appointment to the Supreme Court got people agitated. In November 1997, when Justice John Sopinka suddenly died, Jeffrey Simpson wrote that the race to replace Sopinka was between Abella and John Laskin (Laskin was another Ontario Court of Appeal judge).[64] Lobbying was rampant, he said. "Phone calls, letters and personal representations have been flooding Ottawa, with Judge Abella the lightning rod for the majority of the representations, both pro and con." A few weeks later, Simpson announced that Ian Binnie was now at the top of the list.[65] What had happened to Abella and Laskin? Simpson wrote, "The Abella and Laskin reputations both took some hits, many unjustified, as supporters of one praised their own favourite and, in passing or directly, ran down the other." Another commentator said, "The Toronto legal establishment began a whisper campaign against her."[66]

In 1999, Abella was passed over again, this time in favour of Louise Arbour. Journalist Michael Valpy quickly proposed, in the most exuberant terms, that Abella be appointed governor general. "Once, twice, maybe three times in history, someone comes along who is so perfect for the job as representative of the constitutional sovereign and erstwhile personification of the nation that foreheads are slapped amid cries of 'Of course!' and 'My God, yes!'"[67] Abella, meanwhile, not in the least subdued by being passed over, continued to promote her aggressive views of the judicial function. In an April 2000 speech to an Osgoode Hall Law School conference, she returned to her theme that the courts are the best place to protect minority rights and that the work of the courts in doing so supports democracy rather than impairs it. She vigorously attacked critics of Supreme Court Charter decisions. "While their articulated target was the Supreme Court of Canada, their real target was the way the Charter was transforming their traditional expectations and entitlements."[68] *The Globe and Mail* thought she had overstepped the mark. An editorial said the question was the degree to which judges should rewrite laws from the bench: "Judge Abella holds legislatures in low repute compared with the courts, which, she implies, answer to higher goods and are capable of more visionary action."[69]

Rosie Abella finally made it to the Supreme Court of Canada in August 2004. In June of that year, Louise Arbour and Frank Iacobucci, both from Ontario, left the court (Arbour was appointed in 1999 and resigned at age fifty-seven; Iacobucci was appointed in 1991 and was sixty-seven when he retired from the bench). The empty Ontario seats were filled by Abella and Louise Charron. Even that time around, Abella was seen as something of a long shot. One friend told her that she didn't have a chance. There were two strikes against her, he said; she was a woman and she was Jewish, and both groups were already well represented. Some insiders say that, contrary to what most people think, Irwin Cotler, the justice minister at the time, had not been keen on appointing Abella. Cotler had been president of the Canadian Jewish Congress, as had Irving Abella, Rosie's husband. Cotler, I was told, was concerned that the whole thing would look too cozy. Appointing Abella didn't seem like good politics.

Abella's appointment, predictably enough, attracted great attention. It went far beyond the normal routine praise of a new judge offered up by the legal establishment. *The Globe and Mail* columnist Michael Valpy was again quick off the mark, with some more feverish prose: "She's charismatic Rosie to the world. She can work a room like a penny-stock promoter, charm a crowd in a football stadium. She radiates sunshine. She hugs, she bubbles, she laughs, she incandescently smiles. She's a darling on the Toronto arts world, an it-guest at every haut-monde Toronto party."[70] Andrew Coyne, over at the *National Post,* felt differently: "Ms. Abella is so far out of the mainstream, even among liberal jurists, that her appointment can only be seen as a deliberate provocation.... it is not only her views that make Ms. Abella such a wrongheaded choice. It is the way she expresses them, and the evident contempt she has for people of opposing views."[71] Two days later, an article by David Asper, then chairman of the *National Post,* called Coyne's attack unfair and one that reflected "a fundamental misunderstanding of the judicial process."[72] Meanwhile, the Canada Family Action Coalition and Real Women of Canada denounced the appointment of both Abella and Louise Charron. After all, in 1998 Abella had written an Ontario Court of Appeal judgment that said "spouse" in the Income Tax Act included same-sex partners,[73] and Charron had decided in 1996 that same-sex partners could seek alimony.[74] Others suggested that appointing both judges just before the same-sex reference was to be heard by the court was stacking the deck.

"They. Are. Women." Thus spoke Chief Justice Beverley McLachlin on Monday, October 4, 2004, as she publicly welcomed Rosalie Abella and Louise Charron to the Supreme Court of Canada. There were now four female judges on the court. "In one generation, a journey that started in a displaced persons camp in Germany ended in the Supreme Court of Canada," said Abella, struggling to maintain her composure. The *Toronto Star* reported the reaction to Abella's speech: "Across the courtroom there were gasps and sniffles as people wiped their eyes. Justice Minister Irwin Cotler, Ontario Attorney-General Michael Bryant, Ontario Chief Justice Roy McMurtry all admitted they were moved to tears."[75] McLachlin described Abella's arrival: "She has generously distributed greetings, kisses and bear hugs, and only slowed down last week, when she injured her knee while putting up her favourite picture of Fred Astaire."[76] As Abella and Charron were welcomed, about two dozen demonstrated outside the building, saying the new judges were biased against fathers' rights.

Abella remains feisty and independent. In the November 2009 case of *Plourde v. Wal-Mart Canada Corporation,*[77] the Supreme Court decided six to three that Wal-Mart did not violate workers' rights to organize a collective bargaining unit when it closed a branch in Jonquière following failure to reach a collective agreement. Writing for the minority (herself, LeBel, and Cromwell), Abella aggressively and thoroughly chastised her colleagues for not understanding and for misapplying Quebec's labour code, describing the approach of her colleagues as "a marked and arbitrary departure from the philosophical underpinnings, objectives and general scope of the *Labour Code.*"[78]

In May 2010, in *R. v. National Post,*[79] the court ruled eight to one that journalists do not have an absolute constitutional right to protect their sources; the rights they do have, said the majority, may be outweighed by a law enforcement interest in obtaining information. Abella was alone in dissent. She said: "In this case, the state seeks to obtain evidence that is of only questionable assistance in connection with a crime of moderate seriousness. It is information that could, theoretically, identify a journalist's confidential source, a person who may not even be in a position to provide information of any utility whatever to the investigation. When both sides of the scales are weighed in this light, there is, in my view, no contest. I would refuse to order disclosure and quash both the search warrant and assistance order."[80]

The following month, June 2010, the court upheld, eight to one, the right of an accused under the Criminal Code to obtain an automatic media blackout on evidence submitted during a bail hearing.[81] Once again, Abella was the lone voice of dissent. She said: "To maintain public trust in the justice system, the public must be able to see the judicial process at work. The public's ability to engage in meaningful discussion about *what* a judge decides, depends primarily on knowing *why* the particular decision is made."[82]

It has been reported in the *University of Toronto Magazine* that Abella has a picture of Louis Armstrong and Billie Holiday hanging in her chambers.[83] Also hanging there is her father's law degree. By all accounts, she loves her job. When Roy McMurtry retired as Ontario chief justice in 2007, there was talk that Abella wanted the job so that she could get out of Ottawa and return to Toronto (Justice Warren Winkler was appointed to succeed McMurtry). Not so, her friends say: she's staying put, loved by most, but watched warily by the legal profession, by those who believe in Parliament's supremacy, and by those out there on the right wing.

ELEVEN

Middle of the Pack

The telephone call came on Wednesday, December 22, 1999. Anne McLellan, the federal justice minister, was on the line. Would Louis LeBel, a judge of the Quebec Court of Appeal for fifteen years, accept an appointment to the Supreme Court of Canada? The seat had been made vacant by the resignation of Antonio Lamer and had to be filled by a Quebecker to maintain that province's three-seat quota. Yes, of course LeBel would accept.

The Globe and Mail reported the next day, "Supreme Court pundits were left gasping as Prime Minister Jean Chrétien bypassed a clutch of so-called favourites ..."[1] The appointment, said the *National Post,* "stunned the legal community ..."[2] But LeBel himself was not all that surprised. He had heard rumours about his possible appointment as early as September.

The pundits and legal community quickly recovered their sang-froid and began the usual ritual of heaping praise on the appointee. LeBel was described as mannerly, intelligent, and knowledgeable; low-key, charming, and polite; a patient scholar; a very learned jurist; a very dedicated, soft-spoken, and intelligent man; hard-working and collegial; a brilliant legal mind; a very nice, gentle person.[3]

Kirk Makin of *The Globe and Mail* reported, "Like Judge Binnie, Judge LeBel may owe his appointment in large measure to intense lobbying that took place behind the scenes ..."[4] Some influential Quebeckers wanted a Jew or an anglophone to fill Lamer's seat—Morris Fish of the Quebec Court of Appeal seemed the obvious choice, meeting both criteria. Liberal Party stalwarts wanted Michel Robert, also a Quebec Court of Appeal judge, with a strong Liberal background. Criminal lawyers wanted a criminal lawyer—Morris Fish again, or Michel Proulx, yet another Court of Appeal judge—to replace the expertise of the departing Tony Lamer. "In bypassing them all and appointing a dark horse," wrote Makin, "Mr. Chrétien may have shrewdly lessened the recriminations that were bound to issue from any of the offended factions and lobbies."

The LeBel appointment was particularly upsetting to Quebec anglophones, who had not had one of their own on the Supreme Court since the retirement of Douglas Abbott in 1973 and felt a historical entitlement. It was disappointing to the Jewish community; there had not been a Jewish judge on the Supreme Court since Bora Laskin died in 1984. Appointing Morris Fish would have satisfied both constituencies. But, as Montreal lawyer Simon Potter noted, "naming an Anglophone to the Supreme Court could be an added irritant only days after Mr. Chrétien introduced legislation ... setting the ground rules for Québec separation."[5] The appointment calculus, as always, was heavily political.

In some eyes, there was an important negative note about Louis LeBel. Many were still troubled by his judgment in the 1989 case of *Daigle v. Tremblay.*[6] The Quebec Court of Appeal, with LeBel as part of the majority, had upheld an injunction preventing Chantal

Daigle from aborting her twenty-one-week-old fetus. Daigle's ex-boyfriend had obtained the injunction from a trial judge a week earlier. In his judgment, LeBel said that Quebec's Charter of Rights protected the fetus as a human being with a right to life. LeBel also said that the Quebec Civil Code recognized the fetus as a partial juridical person (a "juridical person" is someone who is not a natural person but who has standing in law—the most common example is a corporation). And he said that the prospective father had the necessary legal interest to request an injunction.

Clayton Ruby, a well-known Toronto lawyer, commented shortly after the *Daigle* decision that the Quebec Court of Appeal decision was based on "the language of Christian fundamentalism."[7] Montreal criminal lawyer Pierre Poupart said, "Judges will find laws to justify their faith."[8] Ten thousand women took to the streets of Montreal to support Chantal Daigle. Two weeks after the Quebec Court of Appeal's decision, the Supreme Court, sitting in a panel of nine, unanimously overruled it.[9] (By then, Daigle had obtained an abortion in the United States.) The Supreme Court specifically and comprehensively repudiated LeBel's legal reasoning. A fetus, it said, is not included within the term "human being" in the Quebec Charter, and therefore does not enjoy the right to life conferred by section 1 of the Charter. Nor does the Quebec Civil Code recognize that the fetus is a juridical person. As for the argument about the father's legal interest, the court said that the argument had no jurisprudential basis. Others outside the court went further; they were suspicious about the influence of LeBel's Catholic faith.

When LeBel was appointed to the Supreme Court, Henri Grondin, his former law partner, who had known LeBel since nursery school, said, "He's a very religious judge ... He was against the abortion because, he told me, 'I cannot, as a Christian, support that.'"[10] A reporter asked LeBel in a telephone interview what he thought of abortion, and he replied, "I don't have to answer that question."[11] To another reporter, he said that Supreme Court jurisprudence—presumably he was particularly thinking of the Supreme Court's judgment in *Daigle*—"is part of the law of the land, and I am bound by what has been decided."[12] To yet another, he said, "My personal view would be irrelevant."[13]

By the time he was formally welcomed to the court, on February 14, 2000, Justice LeBel had indicated in an interview that he had changed his mind about the judiciary's role when it came to abortion. "Abortion is a very complex issue," he said, "and I have grown to doubt very much the ability of the law to govern such a question ... How can you really apply such a law?"[14] Ten days later, Justice LeBel, walking along Ottawa's Wellington Street on his way to the court, slipped on a patch of ice and broke his leg. Overall, it was not a good start to his new job.

Louis LeBel was born in Quebec City in 1939. Both his father and grandfather were lawyers. His childhood home was full of books. He has a passion for music, theatre, art, literature, swimming, and growing roses. LeBel graduated from Quebec City's Collège des Jésuites in 1958. He earned a first law degree from Laval University in 1961; a graduate law degree from Laval in 1965; and an LL.M. from the University of Toronto in 1966 (LeBel credits his Toronto degree with making him fully bilingual). He practised law in Quebec City until he was appointed to the Court of Appeal in 1984. LeBel is married with three children. His wife, Louise Poudrier, is a retired Laval University law professor. He is considered a centrist and morally conservative, moderate and pragmatic, someone who believes in judicial restraint and tends to defer to politicians. He is lanky and fit, refined and well dressed, charming and soft-spoken, with a quiet but distinct sense of humour.

Before becoming a judge, LeBel had been an active member of both the provincial and federal Liberal parties. A few weeks after his appointment, veteran Quebec journalist Lysiane Gagnon, in a broadside attack, pointed out that LeBel helped draft a constitutional proposal promoted by Claude Ryan when he was leader of the Quebec Liberal Party: "This proposal pompously called for a massive political restructuring of the whole of Canada, an unrealistic scheme that was quickly shelved by all political groups ..."[15] Gagnon was also upset about LeBel's role in what she called his "stomach-turning" *Daigle* judgment.

Shortly before taking his seat, LeBel said in an interview that one of his objectives as a Supreme Court judge was to help bridge a communication gap "that is leaving Canadians puzzled about the meaning of decisions on some of the most pressing issues of the day."[16] Since then, communication gap or no, LeBel has not said much publicly. One exception is a candid speech deploring problems of access to justice, delivered at a Université de Montréal conference on June 18, 2009.

The *Daigle* decision was still reverberating fifteen years later. In 2004, political columnist Chantal Hébert, writing about the selection process for Supreme Court justices, wrote: "If there had been a parliamentary review process in place along the lines of that which is on trial on Parliament Hill today, would LeBel's role in the Daigle case have come up for scrutiny when he was appointed to the Supreme Court in 2000? The answer to that question is most certainly yes."[17] Hébert said that in the *Daigle* case the Supreme Court conveyed bluntly "the sense that a fellow judge may have let his personal views supersede his legal thinking."

In the meantime, LeBel has been largely true to his reputation as a morally conservative centrist. In the eyes of many, he consistently shows good sense and good judgment. He was in the minority in the *Amselem* case, agreeing that freedom of religion is not absolute. In *Labaye*, again in the minority, he rejected a laissez-faire attitude toward sex in a public place, holding that such behaviour offended community tolerance. In *Kerry,* this time giving reasons for the majority, he applied the income tax general anti-avoidance rule, generally referred to as GAAR, in the face of strong dissenting reasons from Ian Binnie. When he was asked what gave him the greatest satisfaction in his judicial career, LeBel's answer was surprising. He picked out not the great Charter cases but his work in administrative law, and in the esoteric and unfashionable field of private international law.[18]

LeBel is not afraid to offend powerful pockets of opinion in his home province. In the October 2009 case of *Nguyen v. Quebec,*[19] a unanimous seven-judge panel of the Supreme Court struck down Quebec's Bill 104, which amended the Charter of the French language known as Bill 101 and blocked thousands of children from attending English-language schools. LeBel wrote for the court, setting forth what *The Globe and Mail* in an editorial called "an artful, admirable … compromise."[20] Bill 104 had removed the Bill 101 right of children whose parents were not educated in English in Canada to attend a public English school after spending one year in a private English institution. It was considered a particular blow by the province's immigrant community. LeBel said Bill 104 was contrary to section 23 of the federal Charter of Rights, which establishes the general framework for the minority-language educational rights of Canadian citizens, and was not justified by section 1 of the Charter. The ruling was suspended for one year to give the Quebec National Assembly time to address the issue, firmly sending the controversy back into the political arena.

Pauline Marois, leader of the provincial Parti Québécois, said of the decision: "The Supreme Court, a court appointed by another nation, once again hacks to pieces one of the fundamental instruments of the Quebec nation."[21] Christine St-Pierre, the Liberal minister of culture, was quoted as saying she was "shocked and disappointed" by the ruling.[22] Mario Beaulieu, president of the

Société Saint-Jean-Baptiste, commented, "It is unacceptable that the future of French in Quebec should be at the mercy of federal institutions controlled by English Canada ..."[23] It didn't seem to matter to these critics that the judge who crafted the judgment was from Quebec. Quebec's Liberal government announced in the summer of 2010 that it would "respect" the Supreme Court's decision, but that new legislation would require a child not otherwise eligible for an English school to attend a private English institution for three years (not one year as before) to acquire such eligibility; this, argued the government, would adequately respect minority-language educational rights. The new law was passed by the Quebec National Assembly on October 19, after an all-night debate, just three days before the Supreme Court one-year deadline expired. Benoît Charette, a Parti Québécois member of the National Assembly, said, "It is sad to see this government on its knees before the Supreme Court."[24]

Some think LeBel is underestimated. He may not be a flamboyant star with a big public persona, like Binnie or Abella, but he is nothing if not thoughtful. One of his former Supreme Court colleagues told me: "LeBel is the intellectual leader of the court. He has a gut for justice. He has the 'outrage thing.' He's the only one who's got it. Even Rosie doesn't have it, not really. LeBel gets angry when the little guy is wrongly treated." A good example is his dissenting judgment (with Morris Fish) in the 2010 *Sinclair* case dealing with the right to counsel during police interrogation; he strongly repudiated the view of the majority, expressed in a judgment by Chief Justice McLachlin and Justice Charron, arguing that the majority's conclusion eroded the basic principles of Canadian criminal law, particularly the protection against self-incrimination and the presumption of innocence.

LeBel's own verdict on his judicial career is curiously ambiguous: "I found that the life in the Supreme Court of Canada, if not always easy, is interesting and, in the end, I feel a good life."[25] In an interview, he told me that judges are not just technicians, that what they do can have a dramatic effect on the life of an individual, that a judge is always pursuing an elusive notion of justice. I asked him if he slept well at night. "I sleep only about five hours," he said, "but, for me, that is enough."[26]

When Louise Charron was appointed to the Supreme Court in 2004, she was, of course, overshadowed by Rosie Abella, who was appointed at the same time. Who could compete with Rosie? She had been a media darling for years. Very few people had ever heard of Charron. Yet, a senior litigator who regularly appears before the Supreme Court told me that he thought Charron was the ablest lawyer on the court.

Louise Charron, a Franco-Ontarian, was born in Sturgeon Falls, a small and bilingual northern Ontario logging town between Sudbury and North Bay. She is the daughter of a bank manager (the family house was attached to the bank) and the youngest of four children. She is married (a second marriage) to a retired policeman and has a son and two stepsons. Charron has a law degree from the University of Ottawa and was called to the bar in 1977. She is bilingual and has been an assistant Crown attorney, a law professor, and a member of the Ontario Court of Appeal. Her first judicial appointment, to the Ottawa district court, was in 1988. She was "dumbfounded" by her appointment.[27] Another district court judge commented at the time on Charron's appointment, "The girls are just coming into the right age for it."[28] No doubt, he came to regret this remark.

When Charron was appointed to the Supreme Court, the newspapers reported on her in the usual complimentary and bland way. She has "a pleasant personality," we were told, and a good sense of humour; she is "down to earth" and "loads of fun"; she is "a quiet, reserved woman"; she enjoys yoga and painting; she is thought to be conservative on matters of criminal law but progressive on social issues; she is a "soft-spoken, no-nonsense jurist"; she is "a top-notch legal mind, a prodigious worker and an even-handed jurist unburdened with ideological baggage"; she is "a good team player with a quiet, dry sense of humour"; she is "low-profile"; she is "not seen as being either a law-and-order type or a big judicial activist"; she "lives largely outside the social circles of the Toronto legal establishment." One oddly discordant note was struck: she has been called a "radical feminist."[29]

Charron was sworn in with Abella on Monday, October 4, 2004. She inherited the formal robes that had once belonged to Bertha Wilson, the first woman judge on the Supreme Court, and been worn by Louise Arbour, her immediate predecessor. Charron seems well liked and respected in a quiet sort of way but is seldom in or near the forefront. She takes a particular interest in criminal law matters; most notably, she joined with McLachlin in giving the majority reasons in the important 2009 *Grant* cases and in the 2010 *Sinclair* case. Both these judgments show a strong law-and-order bias and favour the police rather than the accused, pitting her against LeBel, Fish, and Abella, the court's dyed-in-the-wool libertarians.

In 2010, atypically, Charron created a bit of a stir. One newspaper began a story: "The speech that Supreme Court of Canada Justice Louise Charron decided not to give at a recent symposium on women in the legal profession might have sent shock waves through the ranks of Bay Street lawyers."[30] The text of the speech, prepared by a former Charron law clerk now teaching at the University of Ottawa, formed part of the conference materials. It said that one reason women left legal practice was the priority of profit, which made firms unwilling to allow shorter hours and flexible work schedules. Perhaps Charron decided not to give the speech when she realized that the "radical feminist" tag might be revived.

———

Marshall Rothstein and I crossed paths in the early 1960s when we were both students at the University of Manitoba. He was the quintessential Big Man on Campus; former president of the students' union, active in the Conservative Club, a member of the Jewish fraternity Sigma Alpha Mu (members were known as "Sammies"), a law student, and a wearer of three-piece suits. "Vote for the Marshall" was his election slogan when he was running for student union president, and it was painted on the university water tower. "Eccentric," one friend from those days recalled, "and he didn't seem to have many close friends." "A nerd," said another Winnipeg contemporary. As I remember, there was an endearing shambolic quality to Rothstein; he drove an old sedan full of ancient, discarded newspapers and other junk, nothing slick about it at all, walked with a weird gait, and had a goofy sense of humour. During the summers, he had a job as a waiter on transcontinental trains. Many years later, this summer job was offered as evidence that Rothstein understood the working man, but, as I remember, in those days jobs on the trains were highly prized by students; they were gold, everyone wanted one.

There has been nothing glitzy about Rothstein's life. He was born in Winnipeg in 1940, into a middle-class Jewish family, the only child of Max, an accountant and businessman originally from Poland, and Lillian, a schoolteacher, who had come to Canada from Russia. He didn't go away to a fancy law school and, unlike many of his contemporaries, didn't leave Winnipeg for greener pastures once he graduated. Rothstein got his law degree from the University of Manitoba law school in 1966. A few weeks later, he married Sheila Dorfman, a doctor. They have four living children—a son died from cancer at age ten. Sheila is well known for her thrift.[31] She is also known for her spunk. Once, on duty at the hospital and pregnant, she delivered a patient's baby and then went to the room next door and had her own. After graduating, Rothstein joined a well-known downtown Winnipeg law firm, and buckled down, practising transportation law. He worked as a junior for the eminent Arthur Mauro. He's always been known as a very hard worker, often spending seven days a week in his office. Marshall Rothstein was all set for a prosperous and satisfying life and career.

In June 1992, the Mulroney government appointed Rothstein a judge of the Federal Court trial division. In 1999, he moved up to the Federal Court of Appeal, put there by the Jean Chrétien government. And then, in February 2006, he took the prairie seat on the Supreme Court of Canada, replacing John Major. It is often said that, in the process of becoming a Supreme Court judge, Rothstein made history. This is because, after Rothstein was "nominated" by Stephen Harper, he was publicly interviewed, and then approved, by an ad hoc parliamentary committee; he remains the only sitting Supreme Court justice who has had this experience. Most observers consider that the parliamentary committee interview and approval were inconsequential, if not farcical. One account reported: "It was a toasting rather than a roasting ... as a love-in of MPs gently prodded the next Supreme Court appointee to see if he had the right stuff to join the gods of Canadian law.... Rothstein hadn't even opened his mouth for the first-ever questioning of a potential justice's credentials when fawning praise for his 'pleasant ... engaging ... highly respected' character, glowing tributes to his 'brilliant' judgments, 'clear' writing and accolades for his prodigious production of written verdicts were gushing forth from the political fan club seated around a horseshoe table before him."[32] Or, as George Jonas wrote, "We've done something 'American' this week—held a televised hearing for a nominee to the Supreme Court—yet managed to avoid the trap of becoming Americans by the diabolically cunning method of making our hearing meaningless."[33] It's a good bet that at least some of the MPs praising Rothstein's brilliant and clear judgments had never read one.

In his interview by the parliamentary committee, Rothstein played effectively to the conservative gallery. "The important thing," he was reported as saying by Terry O'Neill of Montreal's *The Gazette,* "is that judges, when applying the Charter, have to have recognition that the statute that they're dealing with was passed by a democratically elected legislature … and therefore, they have to approach the matter with some restraint."[34] If Rothstein were truly restrained, commented O'Neill, this would put him at odds with Rosie Abella, and perhaps with Beverley McLachlin as well. Some time later, Conservative commentator L. Ian MacDonald observed, "Rothstein is temperamentally the least inclined member of this court to drink the Charter Kool-Aid …"[35] In an interview, I read him this comment and asked for a reaction. He just smiled.

The parliamentary committee asked virtually nothing about intellectual property law, a telling omission given Rothstein's prominence in that field. His best-known intellectual property judgment was the Federal Court of Appeal decision known as the "Harvard mouse" case.[36] In that case, Rothstein held that so-called "higher life forms" could be patented. He was subsequently overruled by the Supreme Court in a decision that Rothstein publicly criticized several times before his appointment to the court. Well-known intellectual property lawyer Michael Geist commented that the parliamentary committee's near-silence on intellectual property matters was "a mistake ... since Judge Rothstein's lengthy record on patent, copyright and trademark matters suggests that he may well challenge the status quo at Canada's highest court."[37] It was easier for a member of the committee to ask the nominee about his favourite rock-and-roll band (the Beatles) than to ask serious questions about complex legal issues.

When Rothstein was named to the Supreme Court by the prime minister, the usual sycophantic plaudits poured in from the legal profession. Rothstein was "hard-working," "fair-minded, intellectually demanding, 'bloody bright'"; he had "an intense work ethic and the capacity to absorb the details of even the most complex cases," not to mention "tremendous energy"; when working on a case, he was "like a homing missile onto the important legal issue."[38] It was noted that he would bring an understanding of the Federal Court, replacing the expertise of Frank Iacobucci (who had been chief justice of the Federal Court before his appointment to the Supreme Court), an expertise lost when Iacobucci retired in 2004. Rothstein's own sardonic view of things? "It's a lot of work at the Supreme Court. When I was appointed I got a small raise, but my hourly rate went down!"[39]

There was bad feeling in Saskatchewan over the Rothstein appointment. Lawyers in that province felt it was their turn to have someone take the Prairie seat on the Supreme Court. They thought the best man for the job was obvious: Saskatchewan lawyer Denis Pelletier, also of the Federal Court of Appeal, who was highly regarded—and bilingual, unlike Rothstein. But for some reason, the Saskatchewan candidate put on the short list by the government (by Justice Minister Irwin Cotler, before Stephen Harper won the 2006 election) was Peter MacKinnon, president of the University of Saskatchewan. "MacKinnon was a non-starter," a close observer of the process told me. Perhaps he was put up as a straw man. Meanwhile, Aboriginals were angry that the chance to appoint one of their own to the Supreme Court had been missed, particularly because they felt there was an outstanding candidate available, Justice Murray Sinclair of the Manitoba Court of Queen's Bench. Justice Sinclair later became chair of the Truth and Reconciliation Commission of Canada.

Interesting information about the new judge came from a profile of Rothstein's wife, Sheila, by journalist Julie Smyth. In this piece, Sheila, we are told, is a petite redhead, "part of the top tier of Ottawa society." She and her husband live in an "elegant" twenty-eighth-floor condominium; they have "sensual art" above their night table; the apartment is filled with other art, modern and impressionist works from Quebec for her, classic scenes of grain elevators and prairie landscapes for him. The profile went on to say that Dr. Rothstein works in a walk-in clinic; she is an atheist and an internet junkie; she and Marshall take pains to stay physically fit and love to play Scrabble together.[40] Another writer notes that Rothstein likes to cook and often prepares dinner for the two of them, and for small dinner parties. His specialty is salmon covered in a mixture of Italian salad dressing and apricot jam.[41]

Rothstein does not speak French. Whether Supreme Court judges should be bilingual has been a big issue in recent years, and was much debated before the appointment of Tom Cromwell (who is bilingual). In Rothstein's case, the issue won't go away. In June 2009, journalist Richard Cleroux wrote, "The other day Supreme Court Chief Justice Beverley McLachlin interrupted a lawyer rattling along at high speed in French. 'Would you please slow down a bit because Justice Marshall Rothstein may have trouble grasping what you are saying,' she said."[42] Continued Cleroux: "Rothstein promised to learn French, but at age 69, learning another language is not easy. The Supreme Court justices have not gone public with their complaints, but reports leaking out reveal Rothstein's English-only has been a problem for the

MIDDLE OF THE PACK 199

bench ..." Rothstein told me he finds the whole issue "irritating, embarrassing and depressing."

A law professor who is a close student of the Supreme Court told me, "Rothstein is solid but not popular with the academy." I was taken aback. Why was he not popular with professors? The answer: "Because he is perceived to be conservative. He was appointed by Harper. He is from the West. He is from the Federal Court. He is a unilingual anglophone. More strikes against him than Jack Major who was civil libertarian on criminal stuff ..."

At bottom, Marshall Rothstein, by his own account, is like everyone else. He tells this story: "Last week I opened a can of tuna fish, and threw the empty can in the garbage. Next morning, my wife sent me an e-mail in the office: 'Rules: One, wrap all fish products before putting in garbage; Two, close blinds in living room. Sun bleaches couches; Three, put toilet seat DOWN.' We are ordinary people."[43]

TWELVE

Bringing Up the Rear

Marie Deschamps, Morris Fish, and Tom Cromwell so far have had less impact than the other six Supreme Court judges. Deschamps has written interesting reasons in important cases (notably *Chaoulli*), and has been described as a "fearless and original thinker,"[1] but many observers think her career on the Supreme Court overall has been lacklustre. Morris Fish was sixty-five when he was finally appointed a Supreme Court judge (after being passed over twice), and some think that he ran out of intellectual steam early on. Yet, in 2009 Fish wrote more opinions (nineteen) than anyone else, and also more dissents (nine); a newspaper article even called him "The Great Dissenter,"[2] and many admire him for his strong defence of the rights of the criminally accused. Cromwell has only been around since 2009 but has got off to a fine start (although some are disturbed by his strong law-and-order bias in criminal cases). There's good reason to think that, as time goes by, Cromwell will become increasingly influential and important. Some have already picked him as the next chief justice. For the moment, but maybe not for long, he's bringing up the rear with Deschamps and Fish.

———◆———

Jean Chrétien himself made the call to Marie Deschamps, from his Lac des Piles vacation cottage near Shawinigan.[3] It was Thursday, August 8, 2002. Deschamps, then a judge of the Quebec Court of Appeal, had just finished a morning ten-kilometre run when she was told the prime minister was on the line.

Chrétien offered Deschamps the Supreme Court seat recently vacated by the formidable Claire L'Heureux-Dubé. She accepted immediately. "I like working, and it's a very good challenge," she told a reporter later.[4] Montreal's *The Gazette* quoted her: "Every jurist wants to be involved in the most important cases and the largest societal debates, and the place where those debates take place is the Supreme Court."[5] Another interviewer described Deschamps as "joyful" at her appointment.[6] Chrétien must have been pleased too. He had now appointed a majority of the Supreme Court justices. The court was now the Chrétien court. Perhaps that is why he made the call to Deschamps personally, to mark the occasion.

The experts, though, had a question. Who on earth is Marie Deschamps? "This is right out of the blue," said one court watcher. "I don't know enough about Justice Deschamps or her decisions," he said. "I don't think I could make an intelligent comment."[7] Another pundit "expressed disappointment at Deschamps's nomination, saying that she was not the most qualified candidate among those in line for the job."[8] A law professor said he knew nothing about Deschamps. Norman Spector, one-time chief of staff to Prime Minister Mulroney, wrote, "Her name had been on no one's list …"[9] Deschamps herself was reported as saying that she couldn't think of one of her judgments that would be known to the public.[10]

Montreal's *The Gazette* reported, "Prime Minister Jean Chrétien has once again confounded the legal pundits, handpicking a little-known Quebec appellate judge ahead of more heralded candidates to fill a vacancy on the Supreme Court."[11] Some said that Chrétien was obliged to appoint a woman to replace L'Heureux-Dubé. Otherwise, he would be severely criticized for letting the female contingent drop by one. Some were mightily annoyed that, once more, a Quebec vacancy had not been filled by an anglophone, leaving the province's linguistic minority still unrepresented on the country's highest court.

After they wondered who she was, the professional commentators got into gear and delivered the usual flattery. Deschamps was: a tireless worker who quickly mastered even the most intricate and complex cases; someone with a collegial style; a solid workhorse; tough and inquisitive; tough but fair; very universal (whatever that means); strong-minded; a person of great integrity and resolve; not a scaredy cat; in possession of ample intelligence, and the will and stamina to survive; not worried about being popular; a thoughtful and solid generalist.[12] But, somewhat unusually, there were, and remain, naysayers. A careful observer of the court told me that Deschamps is "very limited. She's not an intellectual. She doesn't go back to first principles. She's not at all like the woman she replaced, L'Heureux-Dubé. I can't understand why she was picked."

Marie Deschamps was forty-nine when she was appointed to the Supreme Court. She had been on the Quebec Court of Appeal for ten years. Before that, Deschamps had been a trial judge for two years, and before that she practised commercial and corporate law with a well-known Montreal firm. She comes from an upper-middle-class background. Her father was president of the Olympics Installation Board and served as Quebec's delegate-general to Paris and Brussels. She is a fitness buff, aspiring to run marathons. She swims, skis, plays tennis, and snowboards. Exercise is important, she says. She is known as an art aficionado and collector.

Deschamps has lived for a long time with Paul Gobeil, an influential Liberal, a provincial cabinet minister in the 1980s, and a prominent Quebec businessman who has been chairman of the Export Development Corporation, a federal Crown corporation. They have two children. She commutes from Ottawa to Montreal regularly to be with her family. At the time of her appointment, Deschamps expected gossip about Gobeil's Liberal connections. She said: "Anyone can comment in any way they want and I cannot prevent anyone from thinking what they want, but the fact is I don't think he had anything to do with this."[13] *The Globe and Mail* editorialized: "Her appointment raises the question of whether Liberal Party connections are helpful for prospective jurists.... she is not accountable for her spouse's activities. But because she is the third of Mr. Chrétien's five appointments to the country's top court with Liberal Party connections—Mr. Justice Louis LeBel and Mr. Justice Michel Bastarache were the others—one becomes a little curious. Is Mr. Chrétien more comfortable keeping the court within the family?"[14]

Deschamps was sworn in on September 30, 2002. In her remarks at the ceremony, she commented on the heavy responsibilities she was assuming as "chief justice of the Supreme Court." Amid laughter, she immediately corrected herself. Less than two years later, veteran legal reporter Janice Tibbetts was describing Deschamps as "the great dissenter," arguing that she was emerging as one of the Supreme Court's "most fearless and original thinkers," taking the place of Claire L'Heureux-Dubé in more ways than one.[15] Tibbetts noted that Deschamps, in her first eighteen months on the court, had written more dissenting or separate opinions than any other judge. These included judgments in the "spanking case,"[16] in which she dissented and held that section 43 of the Criminal Code, which purported to justify the use of reasonable force by parents and teachers, was contrary to the Charter; the *Caine* case,[17] in which, dissenting, she held that the provisions of the Narcotic Control Act prohibiting the possession of marijuana and providing for imprisonment were disproportionate to the societal problems at issue and therefore arbitrary and contrary to the Charter; and *Miglin v. Miglin*,[18] in which, dissenting yet again, Deschamps took a broad view of the circumstances in which a separation agreement might be modified, saying that excessive deference to such agreements by the courts is an undesirable policy.

A year after the 2004 Tibbetts article, and a day after the *Chaoulli* decision, the *National Post* was describing Deschamps as "a plain-spoken, independent judge not afraid to stand out from the crowd."[19] A lawyer who appeared before the court in *Chaoulli* told me that Deschamps's decision in that case "showed a lot of courage" and that counsel had not been expecting the outcome and were "dumbfounded."

Most recently, Deschamps asserted her independence in the 2009 *Grant* criminal law cases. In *Grant* itself, although she agreed with the majority that the gun uncovered illegally by the police should be admitted into evidence, she rejected the majority's emphasis on Grant's state of mind in deciding whether he had been detained by a police officer. The Osgoode Hall Law School blog about the Supreme Court picked her opinion in *Grant* as 2009's "Concurring Opinion of the Year."[20] In *Harrison*, one of the so-called *Grant* "companion cases," Deschamps was the sole dissenter, angrily reaffirming the views she expressed in *Grant*. A former law clerk told me that Deschamps has the Quebec francophone obsession with collective rights, rather than individual rights; this might help explain her relative lack of concern in the *Grant* cases for the rights of the accused. And it may also explain her dissent in *Amselem,* where the judges in the minority rejected the majority view that freedom of religion was absolute. In 2009, Deschamps wrote four unanimous or majority judgments, and nine concurrences (agreeing with another judge's disposition of the case, but giving her own reasons) and dissents, further emphasizing that she is her own woman (and perhaps annoying Chief Justice McLachlin, who much prefers unanimity to concurrence and dissent).

In the first part of 2010, Deschamps reinforced her reputation for independence by dissenting (joined by Charron and Rothstein) in the high-profile *Morelli* case.[21] This decision overturned a conviction for possessing computer-based child pornography, on the basis that the Information to Obtain a Search Warrant (a document used in the process of securing a warrant) was carelessly drafted, materially misleading, and factually incomplete. As a result, the search and seizure that followed was contrary to section 8 of the Charter. Deschamps, by contrast, thought the evidence was adequate for a warrant to issue. Her analysis received considerable and biting criticism in the majority judgment of Morris Fish, who, in describing her argument, used phrases like "neither the logical nor legal relevance of these considerations is apparent to me."[22]

There's ambivalence and uncertainty about Marie Deschamps's role on the Supreme Court. Is she a great dissenter, a fearless and original thinker, or something less than that? Deschamps doesn't reach the mandatory retirement age until 2027. We have lots of time to find out.

Morris Fish went to Baron Byng High School on Montreal's St. Urbain Street. The school (and the street) was made famous by writer Mordecai Richler. In his novel *The Apprenticeship of Duddy*

Kravitz,[23] the central character—Duddy—went to Fletcher's Field High School, a thinly disguised Baron Byng. Richler himself was a student at Baron Byng from 1944 to 1948, a few years before Fish went there, and recalled, "We were a rough-and-ready lot. The sons and daughters of pants pressers, sewing-machine operators, scrap metal dealers, taxi drivers, keepers of street-corner news-agent kiosks, plumbers, shoe-repair mavens, and grocery store proprietors."[24]

At the start of the new millennium, the Supreme Court of Canada had neither an anglophone Quebecker nor a Jew sitting as judge. The last anglophone justice from Quebec had been Doug Abbott, a former federal minister of finance appointed by Louis St. Laurent in 1954; Abbott retired in 1973. The first Jew ever to sit on the Supreme Court, Bora Laskin, was appointed in 1970 by Pierre Trudeau and died as chief justice in 1984. Since Abbott retired, there had, from time to time, been rumblings about the need to have another anglophone Quebecker on the court. In the past, the convention had been to keep one seat for an anglophone Quebec justice but that tradition had fallen by the wayside, with the "reserved" spot filled by a francophone for over thirty years. Many also wanted another Jewish appointment.

In 1999, following the resignation of Chief Justice Antonio Lamer from the court, savvy journalist Lysiane Gagnon picked Morris Fish as the person most likely to be appointed to the vacant seat.[25] Fish, an anglophone and a Jew, was a judge of the Quebec Court of Appeal. L. Ian MacDonald, once Prime Minister Mulroney's chief speechwriter, wrote that the appointment of Fish would be a "welcome signal."[26] (A signal of what and to whom he did not say.) But, as we have seen, the appointment went to Louis LeBel, to the surprise of many.

A few months later, in September 2000, Brian Mulroney gave a speech to the Quebec chapter of the Canadian Jewish Congress.

He urged Jean Chrétien to appoint Fish to the Supreme Court. The *National Post* reported the former prime minister as saying, "Morris Fish has been one of Canada's outstanding criminal lawyers and civil libertarians. When I named him to the Quebec Court of Appeal, I thought of him as Supreme Court material and I still do … It has been nearly 50 years since a member of Quebec's English-speaking community has been appointed to the Supreme Court and no member of the Quebec Jewish community has ever sat on the Supreme Court. The time is right and I hope that the time is coming soon."[27] An editorial in *The Globe and Mail* described Mulroney's endorsement of Fish as "the kiss of death."[28]

The next opportunity to appoint a Quebec judge came soon, in the summer of 2002, with the retirement of Claire L'Heureux-Dubé. Kirk Makin wrote, "The stars may have finally aligned for Judge Fish …"[29] But Jean Chrétien ignored Brian Mulroney's endorsement, and the alignment of the stars, and appointed Marie Deschamps instead, surprising just about everybody. Was Fish to be always the bridesmaid but never the bride? Some commentators noted with concern that there were now five francophones on the court—Gonthier, LeBel, and Deschamps, from Quebec; Bastarache, from New Brunswick; and Arbour, from Ontario. And Binnie, born in Montreal and a McGill graduate, was a sort-of Quebecker in the eyes of some.

A year later, Justice Charles Gonthier retired. On July 31, 2003, the appointment of Morris Fish to the Supreme Court was announced. "Finally!" said Montreal lawyer Gérard Dugré.[30] "Third time lucky," wrote Ian MacDonald.[31] One newspaper account, using obvious code words, said Chrétien was being praised for bringing "cultural diversity" to the Supreme Court.[32] The usual expressions of approval, perhaps more enthusiastic and genuine than usual (Fish has always been well liked), began to flow in. Fish was described as brilliant, open-minded, sympathetic to

society's most vulnerable members, exhibiting fairness and understanding, very analytical, inquisitive, curious, pleasant, a perfect
gentleman, a phenomenal human being, someone able to write
beautifully in both English and French, someone with his feet
on the ground. "He's a mensch on the bench," said lawyer Max
Bernard, a member of the Quebec executive of the Canadian
Jewish Congress.[33] (*Mensch* is a Yiddish word used to describe a
person of integrity and honour.) Chief Justice McLachlin used the
same expression at Fish's formal swearing in on October 15, 2003.
But Morris Fish has a more modest appraisal of his talents. He told
a reporter, "I'm one of those people who rises easily to mediocrity.
It's getting beyond it that is the obstacle."[34]

Born in 1938, the son of Aaron Fish and Zlata Grober, Fish is
married to Judith Hinks, a special education teacher. Before she
moved to Ottawa to be with her husband (later she moved back
to Montreal), Hinks worked with pediatric patients in the psychi-
atric department of Montreal's Jewish General Hospital.[35] Fish and
Hinks have two daughters.

Fish was appointed to the Quebec Court of Appeal in 1989.
Before that, he had been a criminal defence lawyer, specializing in
white-collar crime. He served as special counsel to various committees and commissions of inquiry, including the famous Cliche
Commission of the 1970s that investigated the role of organized
crime in Quebec's construction industry; one member of the
Cliche Commission was Brian Mulroney, then a largely unknown
Montreal lawyer. Fish is a graduate of McGill law school and the
University of Paris. It is reported that his hobbies include photog-
raphy, tennis, gardening, and painting. A senior litigator told
me that Fish is a shy man, who keeps to himself. When Dahlia
Lithwick made her comment that "men with fantastic hair" sit on
the court, she must have meant Fish; he has an unruly mop of
white hair.

When Fish was appointed, many newspaper articles mentioned his "literary flair." This seems to be a reference to the writing he did as a part-time journalist during his university years. Fish edited the campus newspaper, the *McGill Daily.* He had a part-time job as a reporter for Montreal's now-defunct *Star* newspaper. One of his *Star* co-workers in those early days was Peter Desbarats, now a distinguished journalist. Desbarats has written about Fish at the *Star:* "On Friday afternoons, when classes were finished for the week, he would descend from the McGill campus to the *Star* office near Old Montreal and pick up his assignments for the evening. He finished at midnight. Then he might stop on his way home at The Montreal Men's Press Club (no female members allowed) just as the evening's action was hitting its stride. After a drink or two, and long before the press club closed its doors at 6 A.M. for a six-hour respite, Morris would head for home and a few hours of sleep before he started his Saturday eight-hour shift at 6 A.M."[36]

The literary flair is still in evidence. A young and gifted criminal defence lawyer told me he always makes a particular point of reading judgments by Fish. "He writes so well, his judgments are so good," said my friend. At the time of his appointment, commentators noted Fish's "passion" for the Charter of Rights and Freedoms. His appointment came just days after the Government of Canada referred the highly sensitive question of same-sex marriage to the Supreme Court. Ian MacDonald commented that this reference "pits the supremacy of Parliament against the emerging culture of judge-made law. Who rules supreme in this land, the legislature or the judiciary?"[37] Many waited to see how Morris Fish would answer this question. He had no discernible effect on the outcome.

But the Charter passion is certainly there. Nowhere was it more eloquently evident than in his *Cornell* dissent, where he fulminated against aggressive police practices. And it was apparent again in his majority judgment in *Morelli,* where he took a similar dim view of police behaviour (and displayed an impressive understanding of the world of computers and the internet),[38] and was highly critical of his colleague Justice Deschamps.

———

Thomas Cromwell is the new kid in the classroom. He's been on the court since the beginning of 2009. He won't have to retire until 2027.

When Cromwell was nominated (at age fifty-six), almost everyone agreed that he was a fine choice. He was born in Kingston, Ontario. His father, Ed Cromwell, owned Cromwell Appliances on Brock Street. Tom Cromwell graduated from Queen's University, earning a music degree in 1973 and a law degree in 1976. He went to Exeter College of Oxford University (which made him an honorary fellow after his appointment to the Supreme Court) and graduated with the notoriously difficult Bachelor of Civil Law degree. From 1984 until 1997, Cromwell taught at Dalhousie law school, taking a three-year leave of absence to be executive legal officer for then Supreme Court Chief Justice Antonio Lamer (the executive legal officer helps the chief justice with his administrative responsibilities and handles media relations). He was appointed to the Nova Scotia Court of Appeal in 1997. He's bilingual.

The legal profession, as usual, hailed Cromwell's appointment. The widely read legal blog Slaw.ca applauded ten good things Cromwell would bring to the court. They included his musical skill (he plays the piano) and his Oxford qualifications, the latter offsetting Supreme Court Justice Ian Binnie's degree from rival Cambridge. More to the point are some of the other items listed: Cromwell's passion for court reform, his interest in law reform, and his practical approach to legal reasoning.

People say nice things about Tom Cromwell. They say he's

courteous but firm. He's thought to be non-ideological, a centrist. "He was the overwhelming choice of people who … made recommendations to me," said Justice Minister Rob Nicholson, when he announced the nomination. A former president of the Canadian Bar Association said approvingly, "He's the kind of guy who'd bag his own groceries."

Cromwell's first judgment as a Supreme Court justice suggested considerable backbone. In *R. v. Van,*[39] he gave clear, well-written, and forceful dissenting reasons for a court split five to four. Duc Van sought a new trial on the grounds that his trial for attempted murder had been improperly influenced by a police witness who had described him in his testimony as guilty, and that the trial judge had made a serious mistake in failing to warn the jury not to take the policeman's hearsay and opinion evidence into consideration. The majority (McLachlin, LeBel, Deschamps, Abella, and Rothstein, with LeBel giving the reasons) thought the witness's improperly expressed opinion and the judge's failure to warn were harmless. No prejudice had been caused to the accused and the verdict would have been the same absent the error. The minority (Binnie, Fish, and Charron, in addition to Cromwell) disagreed. Said the new judge: "The case, as left to the jury, in effect pitted the opinion of an experienced and respected police officer against the testimony of the accused in a way not permitted by law. The key question at trial was whether there was a reasonable doubt on all of the evidence. In my opinion, it cannot be said in that context that it was a harmless error to leave the officer's opinion to the jury without telling them they should give it absolutely no weight."[40]

He was dissenting again, this time on the side of the police, in the touchy criminal law case of *R. v. Burke*. He gave the majority reasons in *R. v. Cornell*, again deciding in favour of the police and fuelling an embryonic reputation for being a law-and-order judge (*Burke* and *Cornell* are discussed in Chapter 6). Cromwell led a five-to-four majority in the 2010 *Tercon Contractors* decision, a traditional contract interpretation case of the kind beloved by Oxford law graduates.[41] The issue in *Tercon* was whether a sweeping exclusion of liability clause in a contract was enforceable in the face of a very serious breach of that contract by the party seeking to rely on the clause, a breach that substantially deprived the victim of everything he had contracted for. Cromwell for the majority, in a clear and compelling judgment, said it was not enforceable. And he wrote for a unanimous court in a 2010 negligence case, *Fullowka v. Pinkerton's of Canada*[42] (the Giant Mine case). He appears to be a judge of strong and independent opinions, particularly interested in the traditional private law subjects of contract and tort, which may now receive more sophisticated attention than in recent times.

Perhaps quiet by nature, Cromwell has so far largely remained in the shadows. His is not a flamboyant personality, unlike his American counterpart Sonia Sotomayor (appointed about the same time as Cromwell), who is already writing her memoirs. In her first session at the U.S. Supreme Court, Sotomayor, described by *The New Yorker* magazine as the court's "most exuberant rookie interrogator since Scalia,"[43] spoke thirty-three times, more than any other justice. "Like a transfer student who picks a fight on the first day of school, Sotomayor seemed to be showing that she was not to be taken ... for a pushover, a token, or a slouch. She would not be cowed by the pomp of the setting—the velvet draperies, the spittoons—nor would she be inhibited by the Court's finicky codes of seniority and decorum."[44]

Cromwell, by contrast, plays it close to the vest. He's not "exuberant." He doesn't ask a lot of questions from the bench. He's not picking any fights for the sake of it. He's meditative. When he received an honorary degree from Queen's in 2010, he told the graduating law class that lawyers could learn a lot from the composer Johann Sebastian Bach. "His enormous talent," said Cromwell of Bach, "did not stop him from seeking out mentors, from voraciously studying the works of other composers and, perhaps most importantly, from continuous self-improvement and self-criticism."[45]

THIRTEEN

Working Together
in the Tower of Song

"There's not much to gossip about," a retired Supreme Court judge told me, as I poked away at him, hoping to provoke a little indiscretion. "There's not a lot of political intrigue at the court. In fact, there isn't any. A civilized collegiality prevails. Everyone is very friendly. You don't have much to write about if you're interested in gossip." A sitting judge said much the same thing. "It's not like the United States Supreme Court," I was told. "We all get along very well."

But, a third judge, now retired, told a different story: "Judges are loners. They're all divas. There's no real collegiality. They don't discuss anything with each other. Everyone is only interested in his own glory." A fourth, another retiree, agreed about the lack of collegiality. One problem, he said, was that several judges didn't really live in Ottawa. They took every opportunity to go back to their hometown.[1] "When we weren't hearing cases, and I was working in my office, I was often there by myself. There was no one to talk to." He added, after a moment's quiet reflection, looking out of the window, "It was pretty lonely, I can tell you."

———

The official story is of judges working happily together. How could it be otherwise? Chief Justice Beverley McLachlin told a reporter in 2009, "Our goal is to try to reduce to a minimum the number of things we differ on."[2] Consensus is one of the chief justice's most important goals.

But no group of nine intelligent and opinionated people, grappling with difficult issues, sometimes divided by philosophy and sensibility, will sing in harmony. You don't get to be a Supreme Court justice unless you're tough, smart, and bloody-minded. To people like this, dissent is sometimes more attractive than agreement. A dissenting judgment, one judge told me proudly, is the law of tomorrow. McLachlin herself has said that the right to dissent is "highly prized and respected." Dissent, she said, contains "seeds for future developments."[3] Dissent, maybe, but all agree we shouldn't have U.S. Supreme Court–style dissent, not in Canada. In the U.S. Supreme Court, dissent can be the "nuclear option,"[4] a weapon used when "bargaining and accommodation among ideologically proximate justices has broken down irreparably,"[5] with angry and sarcastic judgments being read from the bench.

That's not to say that, in the Supreme Court of Canada, personal relationships don't go wrong. It is no secret that the first women appointed to the court, Bertha Wilson and Claire L'Heureux-Dubé, felt unwelcome, excluded from an "old boys' club," and severely resented their treatment. Wilson felt it particularly in the *Morgentaler* case. Several judges, men and women, chafed under Tony Lamer's regime as chief justice (1990–2000); he was considered something of a bully, a tendency exacerbated by his fondness for alcohol. Lamer is said to have told more than one colleague, at post-hearing conferences, to "shut up." One judge wouldn't speak to Lamer for several years, and two others are supposed to have left the court early because of their antipathy toward him. L'Heureux-Dubé couldn't abide Lamer, and she and John Major barely spoke to each other: one of their colleagues said, "This made meetings very difficult." One retired judge told me that things got "very bad" with Lamer. It is rumoured that a committee appointed by the other judges went to him and told him he should resign.

Personal likes and dislikes may be fuelled by ambition. When it looked as if Beverley McLachlin was the leading candidate to succeed Lamer as chief justice, rivals attempted to undermine her position (so a retired justice told me). But McLachlin, sometimes perceived as cold and calculating, proved adept at manoeuvring to her advantage and outmatched them. Lamer, while backing McLachlin, was, for a time at least, assuring one of her competitors of his support.

Jan Crawford Greenburg, an astute observer of the Supreme Court of the United States, has written: "The justices labor in solitude, separated from their peers. But they still define themselves very much in relation to one another. Those dynamics can be as much personal as professional, and they can attract or repel."[6] The same is true of the Canadian Supreme Court.[7] A retired judge told me, "You see the same people all the time, the other eight, constantly. Some you like, some not so much. There's quite a cultural mix too, different kinds of people from all across the country. We speak different languages in more ways than one."

———

Four of the nine judges are women, and the chief justice is one of them. This is a gender composition unmatched by any other senior court in the world. Does it have any effect? Chief Justice Beverley McLachlin generally (although not always) says it does not; others say differently. Donald Songer's book *The Transformation of the Supreme Court of Canada* argues, based on close analysis of cases, that women judges on the Supreme Court of Canada have a very particular view of the law.[8] Judicial conflict, Songer maintains, is often structured by gender. His data suggest, for example, that women judges are more likely than male judges to support the prosecution in criminal cases, claimants in civil liberties cases, and the economic underdog.

Chief Justice McLachlin has often rejected this kind of analysis. She has referred to the court as "gender neutral."[9] But, Ruth Bader Ginsburg, her sister Supreme Court judge to the south, seems to give weight to gender. In July 2009, *The New York Times* published legal journalist Emily Bazelon's interview of Ginsburg, then the only woman on the United States Supreme Court.[10] Bazelon reported that Ginsburg was wearing "an elegant cream-colored suit, matching pumps and turquoise earrings ..." (I have been unable to find any description in *The New York Times* of how male Supreme Court judges dress.) There was this exchange between the two:

JUSTICE GINSBURG: ... I think the idea in the 1950s and '60s was that if it was a woman's voice, you could tune out, because she wasn't going to say anything significant. There's much less of that. But it still exists, and it's not a special experience that I've had. I've talked to other women in high places, and they've had the same experience.

Q: I wonder if that would change if there were more women who were part of the mix on the court?

JUSTICE GINSBURG: I think it undoubtedly would. You can imagine in Canada, where McLachlin is the chief, I think they

must have a different way of hearing a woman's voice if she is
the leader.

Be you man or woman, being a Supreme Court judge is a
strange job. You might think it an unnatural life. When I was a law
clerk in the late 1960s, I would often see three of the judges who
were friends—Spence, Ritchie, and Judson—wandering down
Wellington Street together, on their way from the court to have
lunch at the old Rideau Club (the club's building burned down in
1979). They looked forlorn, their overcoats flapping in the winter
wind, three old men together. In those days, judges felt that the
only safe people to talk to were each other. It was a monkish, schol-
arly existence. Some of this atmosphere still prevails, although not
nearly to the same degree.

These days the judges don't have to go out for lunch. They have
their own dining room overlooking the Gatineau Hills, and a chef,
Oliver Bartsch, who used to work for Prime Minister Stephen
Harper, and, before that, the governor general. Chef Bartsch has
said that the judges particularly like fish, and he "has also tried out
North African, Thai and Indian flavours, as well as quintessential
Canadian fare."[11]

Most of the work still has to be done alone, a well-fed judge
reading and writing at his desk, perhaps late into the night. But
now, unlike before, Supreme Court judges feel free to roam the
world and give speeches on all manner of things, to judge literary
contests, to act in plays. Abella and Binnie, in particular, do it all
the time. There are dangers in this freedom. Greenburg again,
writing about the United States: "The legal conferences and
embassy parties and European trips and flattery from academics
and powerful editorial pages can lead all but the most firmly rooted
justices to drift away from their moorings."[12] When I worked at
the Supreme Court of Canada, judges gave their law clerks the

invitations to embassy parties that poured in. Those judges had no taste for the high life, but we clerks welcomed the free liquor and canapés, the assumed importance and the frisson of glamour. Many foreign diplomats, confused about who exactly we were, went home with strange tales about the extraordinary youth of Canada's senior judges. Now, judges are less likely to give party invitations away.

A retired Supreme Court justice told me: "The court is not a place of high excitement. Look at where the building is. Why did they put it there, so far from everything? You have to walk half a mile to buy a newspaper. So you stay in the building. And the judges' offices are a long way from each other. It's easier to call another judge on the phone, than visit." Another, a Quebecker, said: "I felt very isolated at the court. It's not a normal life. It's particularly difficult if you're a French-Canadian. French-Canadians are not happy as Supreme Court judges. We have a completely different way of looking at things. When I arrived there, I thought, 'This is a prison, a cemetery.'"

It is well known that several Quebeckers have turned down Supreme Court appointments, not wishing to leave their home province to live in Ottawa, not willing to inhabit "a prison, a cemetery." This is a sentiment not just held by those from Quebec. Writing of an earlier time, when Bora Laskin was appointed to the court (in 1970) after several other Toronto lawyers had made it plain they were not interested in the job, Philip Girard has noted, "As with many of Toronto's best counsel, the disadvantages of a move to Ottawa outweighed any prestige to be gained by serving on Canada's highest court."[13] But not everyone, not even every Quebecker, shares this point of view. Louis LeBel, appointed in 1999, decided right at the beginning to buy a house in Ottawa and to become part of the local community. "We bought at the height of the Ottawa high-tech boom," he told me with a rueful smile.

"But we wanted to move to Ottawa in the right way." LeBel told me that he did not find life as a Supreme Court judge as closed and monastic as he had feared. "There is more contact with the outside world than I had as a judge on the Quebec Court of Appeal."

So there they are, these nine judges, installed in their beautiful offices, each with a fireplace, eyeing each other warily, waiting to hear and decide cases, perhaps your case. How do you appeal to the Supreme Court of Canada? How does a case get before the judges, and how do they handle it once they get it?

When I practised law, a client would sometimes come into my office, outraged by something that had happened, slam his fist on the table, and say, "I'll take it all the way to the Supreme Court if I have to!" I would explain that it would take years to do that, likely cost him a fortune even if he won (a big part of the fortune would go to legal fees), and that the result was unpredictable even if we thought his case was ironclad. I would quote the English judge Lord Edmund-Davies, "Litigation is not an activity that has contributed markedly to the happiness of mankind." Often, my advice, and that of Lord Edmund-Davies, would be ignored. Some years later, perhaps, the client would have lost in a provincial court of appeal or the Federal Court of Appeal, but still not be ready to give up. On to the Supreme Court, expense and uncertainty be damned.

The Supreme Court Act says an appeal lies where the court "is of the opinion that any question involved therein is, by reason of its public importance or the importance of any issue of law or any issue of mixed law and fact involved in that question, one that ought to be decided by the Supreme Court ..."[14] There are two important things in this ponderous formula. One is that you can only appeal if you are given permission to do so by the court (in the lingo, "if leave is granted"). There are some very limited exceptions to this requirement in criminal cases, notably that an appeal may be brought without leave if one judge in the court of appeal below dissented on a point of law. The other important thing in the statutory formula is that somewhere there must be "public importance," which is a useful phrase because it can mean anything to anyone.

An application for leave to appeal to the Supreme Court must be in writing. It must include the judgments of the courts below and give the applicant's argument. Normally the court will decide whether to grant leave based on the written application, although it may order an oral hearing (this is rarely done). The application is filed with the court registrar, and a lawyer in the registrar's office prepares a short summary, with a recommendation whether leave should be granted or not, which is sent to every judge along with a copy of the original documents. A panel of three judges has the job of making a recommendation on any given leave application. Each judge sits on one of these panels, whose membership rotates from time to time. In some cases, but not all, the judges on a panel will chat with each other about the applications before them. A judge spends about half a day a week considering leave applications. Unlike at the U.S. Supreme Court, law clerks at the Canadian court have little or nothing to do with deciding who gets leave to appeal. In the United States, law clerks are in the front line in considering petitions and have been described as "The Junior Court."[15]

Panel recommendations about leaves to appeal are considered at monthly meetings of all nine judges. In most cases, disposal of an application is quick and easy, because the answer is no. If all members of a panel have decided to deny leave, a "dismissal memo" will have been sent in advance of the meeting to the other judges, and the application won't even be discussed when they gather unless someone raises a problem or asks a question. Five hundred to six hundred leave applications are received in a typical year and considerably fewer than 20 percent of them are successful.[16] The number of successful leave applications has been declining dramatically recently; it is now down to about 10 percent, resulting, of course, in far fewer judgments as well. One lawyer who appears before the court has commented, "The court is less accessible than it has been at any time in its modern history since 1975." Another observed, "There are areas of law that the court could have, should have, granted leave in, and did not."[17]

A retired judge told me, "Applications for leave fall into three categories. There are the 'no-brainers,' cases that are clearly important and should be heard. There are the 'no-hopers,' those that are frivolous, etcetera. And then there's the rest, that we have to think about—that's about half of the applications we receive." A panel recommendation is normally decisive, but sometimes there will be a general discussion at the monthly meeting. A judge not on the panel may have strong views, and the panel recommendation might not be followed. The process for a leave application, from start to finish, generally takes about three months.

It's easy to think that the leave to appeal process is mechanical and doesn't matter much. It might seem like an administrative detail. But one retired judge told me that "applications for leave are the most important things of all. What is important is justice. Law has nothing to do with it. Supreme Court judges are in the business of justice, which is not the same as law. If you don't grant leave when you should, justice has been denied. Others of my colleagues felt the same way about this. It wasn't only me." Another judge said exactly the same thing. After all, if your application for leave is denied, there's nowhere else to go. It's the end of the road. Chief Justice Beverley McLachlin says she takes the leave to appeal process very seriously. "We all work on them diligently and come to the conferences fully prepared to discuss the applications."[18]

If an application for leave is granted, the parties must then file full appeal documents. The key document is the "factum." This, so the Supreme Court website says, should be "in seven parts containing a concise overview of [the party's] position and a statement of facts, questions in issue, argument, submissions (if any) in support of the order sought concerning costs, the order or orders sought, a table of authorities and provisions of any statute, regulation, rule, ordinance or by-law relied on."[19] Each judge assigned to hear the case by the chief justice receives two sets of the appeal documents, one for that judge and one for the law clerk assigned to help.

The law clerk then prepares a "bench memo" for the judge he or she is assisting; this is a full account of the case, often with a reasoned recommendation for its disposition. Some judges take a law clerk's recommendation more seriously than others. Some are said to have no interest at all in what their clerks think. One judge told me, "I don't take my clerk's recommendations all that seriously, but I like to get them involved. A particular recommendation might make me consider some issues more closely. At least I know the academic side has been looked at." A retired justice admitted to having been very interested in what clerks had to say: "Law clerks were the only people I could discuss the issues with thoroughly." On occasion, all the law clerks may get together and try collectively to promote a particular point of view on a case.

Generally, at this early stage, the judges don't formally discuss the case amongst themselves, though they may exchange casual remarks in the corridor or over coffee. It's much like the United States Supreme Court, as described by Jan Greenburg: "The justices operate independently, almost as if they were each running their own law firms, with their own clerks and staff and law books."[20] U.S. Justice Anthony Kennedy has said that it is an "unwritten rule" in his court that judges don't talk about a case before it is heard.[21] Chief Justice McLachlin has said, "Often we're spending so much time reading and preparing that there isn't extensive discussion at all. But we certainly don't have any rules against it, and if two judges or five are having lunch, they might talk about a case they're preparing and toss it around."[22]

———————

If leave to appeal is granted, the pivotal moment in the case will be oral argument before the judges. Or, so most uninformed observers may believe; this idea perhaps is encouraged by litigation lawyers who pride themselves on their expensive skill in persuasive public speaking.

Argument takes place in a formal and intimidating courtroom. The judges are gowned and look grave. They file in solemnly, from a door at the back, in order of seniority. Beverley McLachlin has said, "Hearings are lots of fun."[23] This is a minority view. Normally the court hears one case a day while sitting. It sits two weeks a month except in the summer. Justice Ian Binnie has said that the reason leading litigators often don't want to become judges is because "it's better to spend half-a-day in court spouting drivel than a whole day listening to it."[24]

The justices sit on high-backed chairs, upholstered in red leather, on a dais. Each side has an hour or so to make their case (some exceptional cases are given more time, perhaps even days). Judges interrupt with questions, some interrupting more than others. Some questions seem penetrating; others, pointless. Questions may be motivated by a desire to make a point to other judges, to conduct a sort of indirect judicial dialogue, with the appearing lawyers in the role of extras. A retired judge told me that the main reason why questioning from the bench is disorganized, even chaotic, is because of the informal rule that judges do not talk to each other about a case before the oral argument: "No one knows what the others are thinking." Jeffrey Toobin has written about U.S. Supreme Court justices that they "are remembered for their opinions, but they are revealed by their questions."[25] It is the questions asked from the bench, writes Toobin, that reveal which way the justices are thinking on a case. U.S. Supreme Court Justice Anthony Kennedy has said, "The first time we know what our colleagues are thinking is in oral arguments, from the questions."[26]

There may be interveners in a case, persons not directly affected by the outcome but who have views on the underlying issues. Someone interested in a case can request permission to appear (a single judge, or sometimes the registrar, decides whether or not to permit the intervention). Since the Charter, interventions have become more numerous and more important. In the past decade, about half the cases heard have had one or more interveners.[27] About 90 percent of the requests to intervene are granted. Justice Iacobucci has written, "The most robust democracy is that in which considerations of public policy are sensitive to the interests and needs of all groups or individuals whose interests are at stake.... This need to ensure that courts address the interests of non-parties has led to increased involvement of interveners in constitutional adjudication."[28] With interveners, a case can look more like a general debate on a policy issue than an attempt to resolve a specific dispute between particular parties. Interveners are inclined to introduce into argument, for example, social science data and general considerations of social context.

Does oral argument really matter? This question is often asked. Most judges, lawyers, and court watchers, if pressed, agree that oral argument counts for little (but not nothing). Before they solemnly file into the courtroom, the justices have made up their minds (or come close to it), based on written submissions. This is true at all levels of the judiciary. A judge of the Ontario Superior

Court of Justice, where trials take place, wrote to me, "The factum ... is the single most important weapon in an advocate's arsenal, which, in my view, drives the result." A retired Supreme Court judge said, "We all know what we think before the hearing, and we don't change our minds very often. I've done a study of it, and a judge only changes his mind based on oral argument about 15 percent of the time." Another Supreme Court judge said, "Before you go in to hear the arguments, you've a pretty good idea of what you think about a case. You seldom change your mind, although it does happen occasionally." A third judge agreed, but added that oral arguments are still important. "They can help confirm feelings you already had. It's a way of testing your thoughts. It's an opportunity to clear up any doubts you have." Justice Rothstein pointed out in an interview that the cases are hard and a lot of preparation is required. "When you've done all that work on a case, you're likely to have formed some kind of view of what it is all about."

Justice Michel Bastarache, when still on the court, said about oral argument, "I've changed my mind very few times. It does happen, but it's very seldom."[29] By contrast, Beverley McLachlin said, "I have actually changed my mind on a number of occasions as a result of counsel."[30] She told me in an interview that she was "a big fan of oral argument. Justice is a conversation."[31] Justice Louis LeBel told an interviewer, "I have seen what I would call the feeling, the sentiment of the court, shift, during an argument, and I think there have been [perhaps a dozen] cases where oral argument made the difference as to the outcome, brought up a new aspect, or focused us on some aspects of the facts that we might have missed or underestimated."[32] Justice LeBel commented to me, "Look, we'd be pretty dumb if, having read all the papers, we didn't have some idea what we thought about the case."[33] Some say that a lawyer can lose a case in oral argument by doing a poor job or being excessively irritating but can very seldom win a case in the courtroom. Gérard La Forest, Supreme Court justice from 1985 to 1997, seriously proposed doing away with oral arguments altogether.

A senior lawyer complained to me that sometimes Supreme Court judges don't engage with counsel appearing before them. "They have their own agendas," he said. "That's what they're really interested in. They don't much care what you say." Another lawyer, Earl Cherniak, a seasoned and respected advocate, gave an example of this in a 2009 speech.[34]

> On occasion, the court is waiting for a case to come to it that gives it the opportunity to speak on an issue that it thinks is important, and grants leave even if it thinks the Court of Appeal decision is right and largely agrees with the reasons.
>
> A good example of this kind of case is the *Canadian Red Cross v. Krever,* in which the issue was the limits (or lack of limits) on the power of a commissioner to issue notices of potential findings of misconduct to targets of a public inquiry.
>
> ... It became apparent within about 30 seconds of my argument in the Supreme Court of Canada that the Red Cross position had no hope whatever of success, as I was immediately faced with a barrage of hostile questions from all nine members of the bench, delivered with machine-gun like rapidity, often simultaneously. My prepared argument was stillborn. It was perhaps the most excruciating 60 minutes of my legal career ...
>
> Quite clearly, the court wanted to make a statement about the powers of commissioners in public inquiries, given the prominence and importance of the several public inquiries going on in Canada during the 90s, and this case gave it the opportunity. But they had no interest at all in my take on the issue.[35]

In this case, the Supreme Court affirmed the wide powers of a commission of inquiry, including the power to send out broadly gauged notices warning of potential findings of misconduct.

Earl Cherniak agrees that, generally speaking, oral argument may not matter much. Along with many other practitioners, he believes the factum is what counts. Each judge will have studied it and will come to the hearing with a definite leaning to one side or another, or in some cases, with his or her mind mostly made up. "I put the very question to Justice Charron at a Cambridge Lectures bull session two years ago in this way: 'Given the amount of our time and our client's money that counsel spend preparing themselves for oral argument, does it make a difference?' Her answer was phrased very diplomatically, but the import was clear. 'Not very much'."[36]

Justice Ian Binnie gave his own account of pleading before the court in a 1998 speech to the Criminal Lawyers' Association.[37] Binnie attributes somewhat more importance to oral argument than Cherniak. He talked about the "sundown rule," which gives advocacy a real impact by giving the lawyer a voice in the decision-making process at a moment when it really matters. "When you start your submission at 9:45 in the morning, remember that the judges are probably going to want to reach a tentative decision on the appeal before the sun goes down…. Once oral argument is heard, the court wants to capitalize on some of the adrenalin pumping around the courtroom to, as Justice Estey used to say, 'get this baby airborne'. The only difference between the lawyers and judges on the day of the hearing is that you don't get to vote, and you have to leave the discussion when it's only half over."

Despite the view that oral arguments don't count for much, many lawyers place a lot of stock in appearing before the Supreme Court. One said wistfully to me, of his first appearance there after a long career in the courts below, "It was a real honour, a real honour, to appear in the Supreme Court of Canada. It's like a baseball player who plays in the World Series after thirty years in the minor leagues."[38]

Binnie's remark in his 1998 speech that lawyers "have to leave our discussion when it's only half over" was a reference to the judges' conference that immediately follows the hearing of a case. That's when "the other half" of the discussion takes place. Binnie described how a conference works (he was speaking when Lamer was still chief justice):

> The court conference is a little bit like a family dinner where the arguments continue after the guests have left and the gloves come off.
>
> From the judges' perspective, the appeal has gone through a process of ever-increasing distillation and concentration. At the time of the initial preparation there is an enormous amount of paper flowing around. Bench memos are written, the facts are gone through, the leading cases are looked at and the judges come to terms with what the appeal is all about. The oral hearing is still more focussed. When the argument moves back into the conference room it is distilled down to its most critical essentials. Thus, oral submissions should narrow, not broaden, the area of controversy. Judges at the oral hearing do not really need to be harangued in generalities as if they were bystanders at a public meeting....
>
> At court conferences the judges speak in reverse order of appointment. The junior judge goes first.... there is no insurmountable inhibition on any of the judges picking up a pen, or at what length. The Chief Justice allocates the writing of

the principal opinions, but apart from seniority where insisted upon, the exercise is generally open and largely consensual.

Some other judges tell a different and less reassuring story about post-hearing conferences. It is said that when Lamer was chief justice, the conference sometimes took only a few minutes. "Lamer would seem impatient," I was told. "He would look at his watch. He gave the impression he had something more important to do." On one occasion, to bring discussions to an end, Lamer said, "Look, we can do whatever we want. That's the end of the matter."[39] Then he left.

In the Lamer days, a full post-hearing conference (if he allowed one) had two parts. First, each judge, starting with the most junior, would speak for about five minutes and give his view of the case. This would be followed by a break. Then there was an informal discussion. Today, the conference begins with the chief justice giving her view of the issues, and then anyone can have his say. Some judges don't like the newer system. "It allows three or four judges to dominate the discussion, and just talk to each other," one said. Chief Justice McLachlin has described the post-case judges' conference in a television interview.[40] The judges sit at a round table and first have a general chat, she said, and then there is the more formal process of asking for an opinion, at least a tentative one, beginning with the most junior judge. Voices are never raised, she said, although there may be "healthy tensions" in the room.

Conferences are usually conducted in English, tacit admission that several of the anglophone judges are not fully bilingual. A practice of "reconferencing" has grown up, as part of the chief justice's drive for consensus. Justice LeBel has described reconferencing: "Instead of just discussing and voting on a case right after it is argued, the judges meet a second time to try to iron out differences and devise a common approach. Voting is sometimes deferred until the second conference."[41] There is a reconference in about one of every ten cases.[42]

The chief justice has the job of assigning justices to write judgments. Chief Justice McLachlin has said that she has this power because the other judges have given it to her.[43] (Before McLachlin, the most senior judge in a majority was entitled to write if he or she wished to do so.) Often, not much choosing is necessary. If a majority clearly emerges at the post-hearing conference, the senior judge in that majority will likely write the opinion, unless he or she doesn't want to or somebody else puts forward a strong claim, perhaps based on particular expertise. If it's not clear at the conference who should write for the majority, the chief justice may wait a week or two before suggesting to someone that they might like to do it. Sometimes, there may be a competition to write. "There are some cases where everyone wants to write," a retired judge told me. "There is a battle to write." Then, the chief justice has to choose. McLachlin has said that she chooses based on a variety of considerations—expertise, for example, and workload, and giving everyone a chance at high-profile cases.[44]

Those who plan to dissent have to figure it out for themselves. It is generally believed that McLachlin pushes for unanimity (since she became chief justice, about 70 percent of the court's decisions have been unanimous[45]) and discourages dissenting opinions and even concurring opinions. When this was put to her by Kirk Makin, justice reporter for *The Globe and Mail,* she ignored the question of dissenting opinions and commented, "I would never—and have never—gone to a judge and even suggested that they should not write a concurring opinion. I wouldn't do it. It's not right."[46] Nonetheless, a former judge told me that McLachlin would come round to see you if she suspected a concurring opinion was a possibility, and work hard to talk you out of it. She believes concurring opinions muddle the court's message. She has said as much.[47] Another retired judge complained to me that sometimes a judge will prepare a brief concurring opinion with some "quotable quotes," just to attract attention. Ironically, Beverley McLachlin is said to have done this early in her Supreme Court career. "It made me furious," a colleague of hers said. "It was insulting." One judge told me, "Concurring opinions, not dissenting opinions, are where the mischief is." Adam Liptak of *The New York Times* has described unanimous rulings with concurring opinions as "faux unanimity." He has written, "One measure of whether unanimity is authentic is the number of separate opinions in nominally unanimous decisions."[48]

There is, of course, only so much that the chief justice can do to persuade her colleagues. Liptak has written of the United States court that "Supreme Court justices are among the last people susceptible to schmoozing, flattery and arm-twisting.... Chief Justice John G. Roberts Jr. possessed a light, quick wit and can be extremely charming. But there have been few signs lately that those qualities have translated into the unified court he talked about in his early days there."[49]

⎯⎯◆⎯⎯

And then, judgments have to be written. Serious research is done, much of it by law clerks; focus becomes clear; and differences of opinion emerge. There may be reconferencing. After a time (sometimes a long time), a draft majority opinion is circulated. Comments may be offered to the author, often quite informally, sometimes quite succinctly. When I was a law clerk, I was once sitting in the office of Justice Roland Ritchie, who had just circulated a draft judgment on a case from Quebec, when Justice Louis-Philippe Pigeon appeared in the doorway, waving the offending draft. "You are wrong!" he said loudly to Justice Ritchie, in his high-pitched voice, and then disappeared. Comments on draft judgments will more typically be given in memos sent to all justices. The earlier a memo is circulated, the more influential it is likely to be. If there are going to be dissenting judgments, they will start circulating in draft form a few weeks after the draft majority judgment appeared. Views may change during the process. Professor Peter McCormick, a political scientist, has reviewed cases from the beginning of the 1984–85 term to the end of the 2006–07 term and has identified 150 "where the person initially assigned to write the majority judgment has lost enough votes that theirs became minority reasons; while conversely a colleague who started with a minority of the votes moved enough votes to write the judgment of the Court."[50]

In the 2003 *Wewaykum Indian Band* case,[51] the Supreme Court formally commented on its decision-making process. In *Wewaykum,* allegations of a reasonable apprehension of bias (actual bias was not claimed, just that someone might reasonably think there had been bias) were made against Justice Binnie because of memoranda related to the issue in the case that he had written fifteen years earlier when he was an assistant deputy minister of justice. The court found no reasonable apprehension of bias. It addressed the argument that, had there been the reasonable apprehension of bias in one judge, the judgment of the entire court would have been undermined:

Each member of the Supreme Court prepares independently for the hearing of appeals. All judges are fully prepared, and no member of the Court is assigned the task to go through the case so as to "brief" the rest of the panel before the hearing. After the case is heard, each judge on the panel expresses his or her opinion independently. Discussions take place on who will prepare draft reasons, and whether for the majority or the minority. Draft reasons are then prepared and circulated by one or more judges. These reasons are the fruit of a truly collegial process of revision of successive drafts. In that sense, it can be said that reasons express the individual views of each and every judge who signs them, and the collective effort and opinion of them all.[52]

Eventually, the case is decided. It may have taken a few weeks, a few months, or more than a year. But now, the reasons—majority, concurring, dissenting—are final and ready to be released. Unlike in the United States, judgments are not read aloud from the bench. The parties are given notice and the formal judgment is deposited with the court registrar, together with the written opinions. A news release alerts the media and anybody else who has subscribed to releases. A media briefing is held to help journalists understand the reasons for the decision. Copies of the reasons are available at the Court Records Office. They are available electronically on the day they are released. A website run collaboratively by the court and the faculty of law of the Université de Montréal[53] contains all Supreme Court decisions since 1948. Eventually, reasons for judgment will be published in the Supreme Court Reports. All that remains is for journalists, and later, law professors, to pick at the entrails and scribble their criticisms.

Nine people doing their best. Like any other group of equals working together to make a difficult decision, there will be crosswinds of competing ambitions, differences of opinion, and clashes of personality. The chief justice uneasily presides, as first among equals, over this headstrong bunch. The product of their labours and deliberations is generally good, but not always.

FOURTEEN

Ideological Soup

William O. Douglas, who sat on the U.S. Supreme Court for almost thirty-seven years (1939–75), once said that his law clerks were "the lowest form of human life."[1] Justice Byron "Whizzer" White of the same court (1962–93) said, "Clerks were 'rarely in doubt and often in error' while the Justices 'were often in doubt and rarely in error.'"[2] Ken Starr, independent counsel in the Whitewater investigation and erstwhile dean of the Pepperdine University law school, has described Supreme Court law clerks as "25-year-old legal savants, whose life experience is necessarily limited."[3] The American public has a straightforward view of law clerks: "Americans love a good conspiracy theory, and the idea that unelected, unaccountable, young law school graduates are the puppet masters of infirm and elderly justices is too irresistible to ignore."[4] Eventually, the "puppet masters" may themselves become "infirm and elderly justices": three members of the current U.S. Supreme Court—Roberts, Kagan, and Breyer—were once Supreme Court law clerks.[5]

Canadian Supreme Court law clerks have generally been described in terms more positive than those used by Justice Douglas, but not everyone is a fan. A *National Post* editorial called them "recently graduated, twentysomething law students weaned on an ideological soup of radical feminism, multiculturalism and moral relativism—who see the law as the means to translate these doctrines into public policy without the intervening necessity of election and legislation."[6] F.L. Morton and Rainer Knopff, in *The Charter Revolution and the Court Party*, write disapprovingly that the growth in the number and functions of clerks "has effected a devolution of power from the top (judges) to the middle (clerks) of the bureaucratic pyramid."[7]

Each of the nine judges of the Supreme Court of Canada has three law clerks. Each law clerk is hired for one year and begins work in August or September. A law clerk must have a law degree, get security clearance, sign a confidentiality and conflict-of-interest declaration, and swear the oath found in section 54 of the Public Service Administration Act.[8] The pay is about $60,000. Someone who wants to be a law clerk applies to the court and not to an individual judge. Successful applicants become part of a pool; judges choose from the pool according to their seniority, although recently some judges have objected to choosing in this way and have tried to make the process less dependent on the judicial pecking order.

According to the official description of the law clerk's role, "a law clerk, under the direction of the Judge for whom the clerk works, shall research points of law, prepare memoranda of law and generally assist the Judge in the work of the Court." What actually happens depends on the judge a clerk works for. Some judges use their clerks for routine research, keep them at a considerable distance, and have little or no interest in any opinions they may have and try to offer. Others are more friendly and will have freewheeling discussions with their clerks about a case, perhaps late at night over a pizza or at the weekend cottage or farm. Sometimes a clerk may draft part of a judgment. Some of a clerk's opinions and language may even survive into the final judgment (one clerk mentioned to me "the power of the first draft"), but this doesn't happen very often.[9] One retired judge told me, "Law clerks wrote parts of my judgments. But I always wrote the first paragraph!" Then the former judge added: "With a clerk who is curious, you can go somewhere." Justice LeBel, when I interviewed him, said that occasionally one of his law clerks would draft a judgment based on an outline he gave the clerk. When a clerk's opinion and language end up in reasons for judgment, the clerk is comforted and encouraged by it well into his legal career, perhaps into his dotage, and may mention it at cocktail parties, or in lectures if he is a professor. Of course, by adopting some ideas and language of a clerk, a judge makes them his own; in no meaningful sense can a law clerk be said, as a result, to have written all or part of a judgment.

One valuable contribution of law clerks is to bring to justices the recent teachings, and prevailing ethos, of Canadian and foreign law schools (many have done graduate work abroad, generally in the United States or the United Kingdom). Chief Justice Brian Dickson acknowledged this in a speech at the University of Manitoba in 1977. Law clerks, he said, "bring to the Court an awareness of current teachings and attitudes in Canadian law schools."[10] As early as 1959, Yale law professor Alexander Bickel, who in his youth clerked for Felix Frankfurter, made the same point about the American court: "Law clerks were a conduit through which new legal theories migrated from law school classrooms to the Supreme

Court … law clerks performed a valuable service by keeping the justices abreast of the newest legal theories."[11] The clerk might pass on this knowledge through informal discussion or, more likely, a bench memorandum. Some bench memoranda merely summarize the facts and arguments in a particular case but others range much further afield.

Not everyone regards this process as benign. Morton and Knopff have commented, "While factums come through the front door of the Court, advocacy scholarship comes in the back door in the persons of the clerks."[12] In this respect, clerks may have had a particular role in the years immediately following the 1982 Charter of Rights and Freedoms. They were fresh from studying it in law school, something the judges had not done. And, as one former clerk commented to me, almost invariably "the clerk got better marks in law school than the judge he worked for."

Robert Sharpe and Kent Roach, in their biography of Chief Justice Brian Dickson, give a balanced appraisal of the role and influence of law clerks. The clerks, they say, may not write judgments, but they do have "an important impact on the style of the Court's judgments."[13] Sharpe and Roach quote the late Brian Morgan, who clerked for Dickson in 1978–79. Morgan said, "The primary potential of the law clerk is to add depth of scholarship to the strength of the judgment."[14] This depth of scholarship became particularly important as the court became a powerful policy-making body after the 1982 Charter. No longer was it sufficient to rely on counsel, who might be narrowly focused on the interests of their clients rather than on what would be good policy for the entire country. And sometimes the judge may find the clerk exerting influence in unexpected ways. Justice Marshall Rothstein reports that early in his judgeship a clerk suggested he tone down some of the stories he told in public speeches. "There was one quite racy one. My clerk told me to can it."[15]

When the Supreme Court of Canada law clerk program began in 1968, modelling itself on the U.S. Supreme Court system (authorized by Congress in 1919), each judge had only one clerk, and some judges elected not to have even that. Starting in 1982, coincident with passage of the Charter of Rights, each judge was entitled to two clerks. In 1989, the number went to three. I was law clerk to Justice Wilfred Judson for the court year 1969–70; for two or three months, when Judson was ill and away, I worked for Justice Roland Ritchie. Back then, the nine clerks all worked together at desks in one large room, an arrangement that encouraged discussion and argument (and idle gossip). Set in a box on the wall was a bank of nine light bulbs, one for each clerk, rather like the old-style register in the servants' hall of a stately home. If your judge wanted to see you, he pushed a button on his desk, and your light bulb lit up.

During my year as a clerk, I got the distinct impression that most of the judges did not know what to do with invariably brash and opinionated young law graduates. It's different now. The clerks are still brash and opinionated, but judges have figured out how to use them. For the most part, in my day, we were underworked. Another clerk and I spent many afternoons playing billiards at a down-at-the-heel Ottawa private club, a mile or so from the court, on Elgin Street. We weren't missed. When I was working, it was usually writing legal memoranda for Justice Judson or Ritchie. Sometimes, I wrote one or more drafts of a judgment. In that year, the Supreme Court heard 131 cases. Only two of them were constitutional cases. It was a different time. When I arrived, the chief justice was John Cartwright. During the year, he retired and was replaced by Gérard Fauteux. At the end of our year, Ron and Iris Martland (Martland was one of the judges, from Alberta) gave a party for the clerks at their Rockcliffe house. We gathered around the piano, played by Justice Martland, and sang a song he had written—*Battle Hymn of the Supreme Court.* The first verse went:

> *We all owe our existence*
> *To the statute B.N.A.,*
> *To Confederation's fathers*
> *And to dear old Sir John A.*
> *Then they scrapped the Privy Council*
> *And now we have our own way*
> *As we go judging on.*

Are law clerks the keepers of secrets? A recent imbroglio suggests that the current court administration thinks they should be, and is determined to keep clerks' mouths shut and the secrets intact.

David Weiden is an assistant professor of political science at Indiana University–Purdue University. In 2006, he co-authored, with Artemus Ward, a well-received book called *Sorcerers' Apprentices,* about law clerks at the U.S. Supreme Court.[16] For that book, the authors interviewed 150 former U.S. Supreme Court law clerks. Weiden got interested in their Canadian counterparts. He was given a research grant by the Canadian government to study their "impact and influence." In 2009, he devised a survey and sent it to all former law clerks, hundreds of them, some having had the job thirty or forty years ago. The Supreme Court was not amused. On June 3, 2009, Jill Copeland, the court's executive legal officer, sent an email to all former clerks. It accused Professor Weiden of giving out "inaccurate information" about the court's position on his survey, a serious charge against anyone, let alone a professor pursuing research and hoping to get tenure. It said, "The Court takes the view that participation in the survey by former clerks would ... violate confidentiality obligations. The Court takes the view that confidentiality obligations of current and former law clerks are not limited to information about cases, but also extend to internal processes of each Justice's chambers." Chief Justice McLachlin authorized the Copeland email, and it is widely thought that its language was her own. As well, I was told that, at about the same time, the Chief Justice called all current clerks to a meeting and lectured them on their confidentiality obligations. "She's a control freak," I was told by an angry clerk.

Weiden was baffled by the whole thing; this had not been an issue in the United States. Some former Canadian law clerks were puzzled by the sweeping prohibition in the Copeland email; some resented it.[17] The press got on to the story. Kirk Makin wrote in *The Globe and Mail* that Weiden had drawn "a stiff rebuke" from the court, which had issued a "frosty warning" to former clerks.[18] Another story referred to the "chilling effect" of Copeland's June 3 message.[19] *The Globe* editorialized on the incident: "The court is afraid of losing its mystique. And why did it take an American to dream up the idea? Where are all the Canadian political scientists and legal academics? They are all—scholars and judges—caught up in a political-legal culture that is still fairly timid and deferential, and not terribly transparent.... The court shouldn't be so squeamish ..."[20]

It was often pointed out that writers of well-received popular books about the U.S. Supreme Court have the habit of interviewing former law clerks, and no one seems to mind—well, almost no one.[21] Bob Woodward and Scott Armstrong wrote a famous book, published in 1979, called *The Brethren: Inside the Supreme Court.*[22] They interviewed 170 former law clerks. Another well-known and more recent example of the genre is Jeffrey Toobin's *The Nine: Inside the Secret World of the Supreme Court.*[23] Toobin interviewed more than seventy former clerks. The judicial system of the United

States has emerged intact from these exposés, although some of the justices discussed in *The Brethren* were incensed by their portrayal; subsequently, confidentiality rules were made more formal and comprehensive, and the habits of some judges changed.[24] For example, after the Woodward and Armstrong book was published, Justice Byron White stopped having lunch with law clerks, nervous about who might later say what to whom. And Weiden himself has written about secrecy rules at the U.S. Supreme Court, including "the legendary 'ninety-second rule': any clerk caught talking to a journalist for more than ninety seconds will be fired."[25]

There may be more behind the Supreme Court of Canada's reaction to the Weiden survey than is generally known. A persistent rumour has it that a few years ago a judgment was leaked some two weeks before it was to be officially released. A law clerk is said to have disclosed the result, in a fit of hubris, to a lawyer friend who was counsel to one of the parties in the case. The leak was discovered, and the law clerk was fired. There was much gnashing of teeth. From that time on, confidentiality has been emphasized—overemphasized, some would say. Those who have clerked since the rumoured incident are afraid to say anything. Nonetheless, in the Weiden affair, those who run the Supreme Court of Canada—starting with the Chief Justice—overreacted, and looked secretive, even foolish.

There's nothing terribly new in all this. Chief Justice Bora Laskin was obsessed with law clerk confidentiality. He was horrified by *The Brethren*.[26]

—

Perhaps clerks are just not all that important—at least, not as important as conspiracy theorists and some clerks themselves believe. Law professor Todd Peppers, in his authoritative *Courtiers of the Marble Palace,* convincingly describes how the role of the American Supreme Court law clerk has evolved from that of stenographer, to legal assistant, to something like a law firm associate in the modern age.[27] Law clerks at the Supreme Court of Canada, like their American counterparts, are similar to junior associates in a big firm. Any partner in such a firm would agree that, with very few exceptions, the associate, helpful as he may be, has little power or influence over the conduct of a file. It is hard to imagine a historian, writing about some famous case, having much interest in the law firm associates who worked on the file. Yet, the law clerk mystique remains. "A Supreme Court clerkship is a glittering prize and the ultimate credential in American law," writes Adam Liptak.[28]

And the law clerks themselves love the job. I interviewed a number of former clerks, and they all said it had been a wonderful experience. I was frequently told that a year clerking was "the best year of my professional life." One said there were three reasons. First, she said, it's the content of the work: "Fellow law graduates were doing dog-bites-man cases, and I was working on big issues that affected the country." Second, you got to know the judges as human beings, and not just remote and important figures. "You discover their kids get sick too, and they worry like everybody else. You discover the humanity of the whole thing." Third, you get to meet and know "a group of exceptionally talented people with bright futures—your fellow law clerks."

The Change We Need

The Supreme Court of Canada runs our life. It does a good job of it, in many ways. Nine intelligent men and women work hard to understand and decide complex and important legal and public policy issues. They present the public with lengthy and reasoned accounts of the decisions they make. They are sensitive about the court's relationship to the legislative and executive branches. They remember that no one elected them to anything. They want Canadians to know more about what they do (up to a point). To those members of the public who are paying attention, the judges seem to get it right more often than they get it wrong. If sometimes they make mistakes, well, who doesn't? If some of their decisions are controversial, what else could one expect?

Despite this generally pleasing picture, big changes are needed. Most of them are beyond the court's ability to implement by itself. Action is required elsewhere. Parliament's intervention is necessary, because legislation that defines and empowers the court must be amended. Conventions and practices of the executive branch should be abandoned, particularly those that affect the selection of judges; here, in particular, the prime minister must be strapped securely into a back seat. The media must pay serious attention to what happens at the court; perhaps some of the space and resources now given over to thinly disguised legal gossip could be devoted to sophisticated coverage of one of our most powerful governmental institutions. Finally, the public must get involved and concerned; all else depends on this. And then, there is one essential thing that can only be accomplished by the judges themselves. It is the judges who must get the balance right between respecting democratic institutions and forestalling the tyranny of the majority.

———

The way judges are appointed must change. Given the essential role of the Supreme Court in the governance of Canada, and particularly its role in keeping the executive branch in check, it is not acceptable that a seat on the highest court is the gift of the prime minister acting alone. Changing this selection procedure is the single most needed reform and one that requires amendment of the Supreme Court Act.

As it now stands, a Supreme Court judge is chosen by the prime minister in private, using whatever criteria he happens to find appealing at the time. Any consultation with others is at the prime minister's discretion. If there is consultation, it is largely perfunctory and secret. The one time a public event was held—Marshall Rothstein appeared before an ad hoc parliamentary committee in 2006—it was widely acknowledged to be meaningless: the choice had already been made, the deed done. Such a selection method is inappropriate and dangerous in a political system where the judiciary is required to rein in the executive and legislative branches.[1] The person to be judged should not, untrammelled, choose his judge. And the private nature of the current practice leads to public suspicion and skepticism.

What might replace the selection process we now have? There are two broad alternatives. The first is a U.S.-style system, political and top-down. The prime minister would nominate a candidate, and his choice would require formal confirmation by Parliament following public hearings by a parliamentary committee. This process would roughly mirror what happens in the United States, where the president nominates a candidate who then must be confirmed by the Senate following public hearings and a recommendation by the Senate Judiciary Committee.

The most cogent objection to adopting a U.S.-style system in Canada is that executive control of the legislative branch makes the requirement of parliamentary approval of an executive choice a mere formality. After all, Parliament does what the government tells it to do; if the prime minister nominates someone to be a judge of the Supreme Court, it is unlikely that Parliament will reject the nomination, particularly if there is a majority government. There is no compelling response to this objection, except to note (and hope) that the political effects of a public parliamentary process might be surprising, introducing a new and unpredictable democratic dynamic.

A frequent objection to a U.S.-style system is that it would "politicize" the Canadian process[2] and discourage worthy candidates. The U.S. system is also regarded by some Canadians, particularly senior lawyers, as unseemly, demeaning to judicial dignity and offensive to the legal profession's sensibility. Another criticism sometimes made is that public hearings can be staged and misleading. But recent studies of the American system suggest that the questioning of nominees has great value. One study, based on an analysis of every question asked and every answer given at Supreme Court confirmation hearings in the last seventy years, shows that the hearings "often address real substance, illuminate the spirit of their times and change with shifts in partisan alignments and the demographic characteristics of nominees."[3] *The New York Times* has editorialized, "We have worried, especially in recent years, that nominees are far too carefully packaged and coached on how to duck all of the hard questions. A new study supports our fears: Supreme Court nominees present themselves one way at confirmation hearings but act differently on the court."[4] Yet, the same newspaper's Supreme Court correspondent, Adam Liptak, has subsequently written, "The six justices appointed in the two decades since [1990] have performed largely as expected, probably thanks to increased scrutiny of more robust paper trails and less ideological drift."[5] Liptak has also noted that a recent study by two political scientists has found that the overall level of candour by nominees answering Senate questions is fairly high.[6]

The second alternative is a bottom-up, politics-free system of the kind recently introduced into the United Kingdom. Under the Constitutional Reform Act 2005, vacancies in the new U.K. Supreme Court are, in effect, filled by an ad hoc selection committee. The prime minister is given the name of the person selected by the committee. Ad hoc committees are composed of Supreme Court judges and members of the Judicial Appointments Commission for England and Wales (which has a lay majority) and the Judicial Appointments Board for Scotland and the Northern Ireland Judicial Appointments Commission (both of which have substantial lay representation).[7] A similar system, although more political, is used in South Africa to fill vacancies of the Constitutional Court, the final court of appeal on constitutional matters. When there is a vacancy, the Judicial Service Commission (JSC), a broad-based body established by the 1996 South African Constitution, calls for nominations and holds public interviews of those nominated. Then the JSC draws up a list of approved candidates that must have at least three names more than the number of appointments to be made. South Africa's president chooses from the list, after consultation with the chief justice and the leaders of political parties represented in the National Assembly.

Either the U.S. or the U.K. model, or a hybrid, would be a substantial improvement on the current Canadian method of appointing Supreme Court judges. The dignified and less political United Kingdom model would, no doubt, be more palatable in Canada, particularly to the legal profession. But the U.S. system, with its intensely democratic aspect, is attractive, particularly considering that, once chosen, a new judge is no longer democratically accountable. The objection that good candidates will not be willing to be questioned in public by political partisans is not persuasive; it may not be true (Justice Ian Binnie said he was willing to be questioned in this way), and, in any event, why should someone seeking high office be sheltered from the democratic rough and tumble? Why should we be scared of a little public pushing and shoving when it comes to picking judges?

Someone asked me, in the course of a lively dinner table discussion, if there was an instance, just one, of a bad Canadian Supreme Court judge who would not have been appointed if a U.S.-style confirmation process had been used. No obvious example came to mind. So, said my interlocutor, if the results of the existing system are acceptable, why change it? There is force to this point of view. My reply was that process—and not just outcome—is important. After all, the point of democracy is not that it necessarily provides a more efficient government than dictatorship. The point of democracy is democracy.

In Canada, a federally appointed judge can stay in office until age seventy-five. The most recent appointment to the Supreme Court, Tom Cromwell, was born in 1952; in effect, he was appointed to serve nineteen years. A term that long is too long. Routine appointments for such lengthy periods inhibit a dynamic process of renewal. They deny an opportunity to many who would be excellent judges. They prevent the bench being properly representative of rapidly changing Canadian demographics. And they mean we will have some judges who are exhausted (a number of recent Supreme Court judges have quit long before age seventy-five, having had enough). I asked Justice Louis LeBel[8] why many judges leave before the age of seventy-five. "They just get tired," he said. "They lose the fire." When Chief Justice Lamer retired (in January 2000) at the age of sixty-six, he said he wanted to go before he lost the "sacred fire" of his passion for the law.

South Africa has a better approach. Section 176 of the South African Constitution provides that a judge of the Constitutional Court "holds office for a non-renewable term of 12 years, or until he or she attains the age of 70, whichever occurs first." A term limit like this is a good idea. Many countries in addition to South Africa have one.[9] Pulitzer Prize–winning U.S. historian James MacGregor Burns has written of the U.S. Supreme Court, which has no mandatory retirement age, "Justices throughout the court's history have clung to their seats long after their political patrons have retired and long after their parties have yielded to their opponents or even disappeared. They have often perpetuated ideologies and attitudes that are outdated or that Americans have repudiated at the ballot box. Inevitably, life tenure has produced a critical time lag, with the Supreme Court institutionally almost always behind the times. As a result, too often the Supreme Court has seemed to be fighting the progress of history."[10] Canada should be anxious to avoid the behind-the-times trap.

In 2010, Prime Minister Harper revived proposals to reform the Senate. On March 30, 2010, his government introduced legislation that would limit senators to a single term of eight years rather than allow them to serve until age seventy-five (there have been several recent attempts at this and other changes to the Senate). Steven Fletcher, the minister of state for democratic reform, said, "Canadians are rightly questioning how senators with no democratic mandate can serve terms for up to 45 years."[11] There is no good argument that appointments to the Supreme Court are different. Supreme Court judges, like senators, do not have a democratic mandate. They have more power than senators, considerably more. Their terms of office should be limited as well.

And they should be fully bilingual, when appointed. Such a requirement should be added to the Supreme Court Act. Full bilingualism has important symbolic value, which is not to be underestimated. It is also required to assure French-speaking litigants and counsel that they are at no disadvantage, and for the court to operate in an efficient manner (for one thing, reducing the extensive translation of internal documents). The bilingualism bar should be set high. Formal testing may be necessary. A modest facility in the other language is not adequate. A judge should be able to understand complex and technical written and oral argument in either official language from his or her first day on the bench. This is not so now. Justice Louis LeBel has observed that judges' conferences are usually conducted in English because many judges are not fully fluent in French.[12]

There has been a recent attempt to amend the Supreme Court Act to require genuine proficiency in both official languages. There was considerable discussion about bilingualism when Michel Bastarache's seat on the court became vacant in 2008. In May 2009, shortly after the seat was filled by the bilingual Tom Cromwell, New Democratic Party MP Yvon Godin introduced a private member's bill, Bill C-232, requiring future Supreme Court appointees to be bilingual. The bill passed in the House of Commons in March 2010, with Conservatives opposed but all the opposition parties voting in favour, and, at the time of writing, is before the Senate.

Bill C-232 reignited the bilingualism controversy with a vengeance. Once more, retired Supreme Court judge John Major, who is unilingual, argued forcefully and candidly that "Canada is a country governed by the rule of law, and the most essential fact necessary to preserve that is to have the most competent people, regardless of language skills, sit on the Supreme Court."[13] He said that, contrary to what is claimed, most Supreme Court judges are not fully bilingual—perhaps three at most (LeBel, Fish, and Charron). He told a reporter that Justice Marie Deschamps sometimes needs help with English cases, and that other franco-phone justices have relied on translation when dealing with English cases.[14]

Others bloviated in the popular press on both sides of the issue. A *National Post* editorial was entitled "How to Ruin the Supreme Court"[15] and referred to bilingualism as a "parlour trick." Most lawyers were vehemently opposed to the Godin bill. Some were not. Michel Doucet, dean of the University of Moncton's law school, and someone who has pleaded in French before the Supreme Court (three judges were listening through interpreters), wondered if some of his arguments were lost in translation.[16] The dean of civil law at the University of Ottawa has described his experience of pleading a case in French before the Supreme Court: "Overall, the interpretation was good, but inconsistencies, incomplete state-ments and, indeed, errors ... necessarily affect the force and the logic of the oral arguments presented. A legal argument is like a chain: if one piece breaks, the whole thing falls apart."[17] Retired judge Claire L'Heureux-Dubé was adamantly in favour of C-232.

The Canadian Bar Association, at its 2010 annual meeting, called for abandonment of the bill (the Quebec branch was opposed to the CBA resolution). Commissioner of Official Languages Graham Fraser and Quebec premier Jean Charest have supported the proposed legislation.

In the bilingualism debate, the hounds may be chasing the wrong fox. What about judges trained in the common law deciding civil law cases that depend on the Quebec Civil Code (and vice versa— what about judges from Quebec adjudicating cases that depend on the common law of the other provinces)? There is the statutory requirement that three judges be from Quebec, but since panels often are nine judges, and are never less than five, in every civil law case there are common law judges sitting and deciding, often in a majority. This seems like a much more substantive problem than bilingualism, yet, peculiarly, it is seldom discussed. Perhaps that is because of the illusion that a unilingual Canadian can always go to night school and learn the other language in a few months, while no senior common lawyer could ever similarly master the intricacies of another system of law (and vice versa).

Those who argue against a bilingualism requirement on the grounds that only judicial ability matters presumably should also be opposed, for the same reason, to the constitutional convention of broad geographic representation from outside Quebec (one judge from the Maritimes, three from Ontario, one from the Prairie provinces, and one from British Columbia). If all the best candidates are from Ontario, why, then, let's fill up the court with Ontario lawyers! Strangely, unperturbed by illogicality, opponents of a bilingualism requirement don't take this view.

Regional representation on the United States Supreme Court has never been an issue, and it needs reconsideration in Canada. It is also time to reconsider an unstated preference for appointing appellate court judges to the Supreme Court (on today's court, only Ian Binnie did not sit first on a court of appeal). Tracey E. George of Vanderbilt University law school has written, "The more homogenous the group, the worse the quality of the decisions they make."[18] Timothy O'Neill, in a law review article entitled "The Stepford Justices," has argued that a mix of justices with wide legal and governmental experience on the U.S. Supreme Court is "vital for the effective functioning of the nation's highest Collegial court."[19] In this respect, U.S. practice is not to be followed. Elena Kagan is the only U.S. Supreme Court judge who was not previously a judge on an appeal court. All the judges went to Harvard or Yale law school. The U.S. Supreme Court bench has a social and cultural uniformity that Canada should not emulate.[20]

How much money do judges have? How is it invested? There is no financial disclosure requirement in Canada for judges or candidates for judicial appointment. It is the same in England and Australia, but not in the United States; in the U.S., the Ethics in Government Act of 1978 requires that federal judges disclose personal and financial information each year. We know that, in 2008, Chief Justice John Roberts Jr. and Mrs. Roberts had investments in fifty-seven public companies and mutual funds, including, for example, Microsoft stock worth between $100,001 and $250,000. That same year, Clarence Thomas earned $333,334 in book royalties for *My Grandfather's Son,* his autobiography.[21] Candidates for U.S. judicial office must also disclose their assets and liabilities. When Sonia Sotomayor was nominated for the U.S. Supreme Court, we quickly learned that on November 23, 2008, she won $8,283 gambling with her mother at a Florida casino. We further discovered that she had $1.16 million in assets and $418,350 in debts, and spent a lot of money getting her teeth fixed (she owed her dentist $15,000). We found out that she drives a white Saab convertible. In India, Supreme Court judges are required to post the details of their assets on the court's website.[22] Thus, we know that Chief Justice Shri K.G. Balakrishnan drives a 2000 Santro car, and that the wife of Mr. Justice Tarun Chatterjee has seven pairs of gold earrings.

Supreme Court of Canada judges (all judges, for that matter) should be required to make full, annual, public disclosure of their assets and liabilities. We don't care what kind of car they drive, or what sort of jewellery they wear. But we do care very much, or should, about how much money they've got, where it came from, and how it's invested. The Canadian public is entitled to have this information about very senior public servants as part of a broad concept of good and transparent governance. With it, we would have a better understanding of who our judges are. Our confidence in what they do would be increased. Rumours would be easily dispelled. (I have frequently encountered speculation by lawyers about a judge's financial affairs, and conjecture about why a particular judge didn't sit on this or that case.) Judges themselves would benefit from transparency, and their public stature would increase.

One Supreme Court justice told me that there is a "soft" financial disclosure protocol in effect at the court, but, surprisingly, he wasn't certain of the details or if all the judges followed it. Some judges, he thought, might have placed their investments in a blind trust; others may have disclosed the nature of their investments to court officials. In his case, Supreme Court lawyers were aware of his portfolio and would occasionally suggest that he might have a conflict. If there were doubt, he would discuss the matter with the chief justice. There were three or four cases a year that he stepped away from because of conflict possibilities.

And so, the Supreme Court Act should be amended: to change the method of appointing judges, adopting either the U.S. or the U.K. model, preferably that of the United States; to limit the tenure of a judge to a fixed term, of twelve or possibly fifteen years; to require all appointees to possess a high level of bilingualism; and to require financial disclosure upon appointment and thereafter. The convention of regional representation should be reconsidered, and the practice of favouring appellate court judges in appointments should be abandoned. Implementing these reforms will take considerable political will and wisdom. Will the prime minister agree to give up his stranglehold over the appointment process? Will the government be bold enough to reform the court, in the name of rationality and responsibility?

The court prides itself on transparency. The pride is unjustified. Posting online documents filed with the court and putting videos of oral argument up on the official website are good practices, but they fall far short of effectively communicating the role and work of the court to the Canadian public. Not too many people in Estevan, Saskatchewan, will read factums of an evening. Not too many folk in Bridgewater, Nova Scotia, will stop watching *Dancing With the Stars* and tune in to the oral argument of counsel in a complicated case.

Effective communication with the public requires the court to embrace popular media, and to be embraced back. And if the court wants to reach out and speak to ordinary Canadians, better it use Facebook than CPAC (the Cable Public Affairs Channel). Giving dull speeches to friendly, Establishment audiences and tightly scripted interviews to deferential questioners who know little if anything about the court doesn't do the job. Ten months after Steve Paikin's December 2, 2009, TVO interview of Beverley McLachlin, the YouTube posting of the interview had 698 views and one comment ("She's no fool!"). (In contrast, less than twenty-four hours after Stephen Harper's March 16, 2010, YouTube interview, there were 29,572 views and 1,903 comments.) The YouTube posting of McLachlin's February 4, 2010, speech at the University of British Columbia law school, posted in six parts, was a flop. Eight months after the speech, only 399 people had watched the first part, and just 78 had persevered to the last part. A law student at Osgoode Hall blogged pensively, "We Canadians have to contend with Youtube [*sic*] clips of the Chief Justice's occasional speeches to law students or TVO interviews to glean any sort of information about the Court's inner workings ... Why such a strict code of *omertà*?"[23] (*Omertà* is the code of silence often favoured by criminal organizations.)

Moxy is needed. Judges, beginning with the chief justice, should give substantive, wide-ranging speeches and interviews about the court and its work, with few holds barred. There may be slip-ups, there may be controversy, there may even be occasional embarrassment, but that's a small price to pay. Will the administration of justice be threatened? Will the judiciary's dignity diminish? Will the public have less regard for judges? I don't think so. Quite the contrary. As Canadians come to know the work of the court and learn about the judges and the issues they decide, they will replace their knee-jerk deference with genuine regard. As judges establish distinct public personalities, Canadians' interest in what they do will increase.

Popular media must reciprocate. In the Introduction, I described the poor state of contemporary reporting on the Supreme Court. Canadian media devote insufficient resources to the task. For sure, there is a group of talented and knowledgeable reporters who do their best to keep us informed, but the group is too small, and their work receives little attention. Perhaps the court's code of silence (*omertà*, as the Osgoode Hall student described it) partly accounts for this lack of interest; it's hard to report well and get front-page exposure if no one will tell you anything. But, there's still much to say, and to write about. Canadian deference to authority and excessive respect for judicial mystique must be overcome. Dahlia Lithwick has written of the U.S. Supreme Court, "Perhaps for the rule of law to mean anything, Americans need to see the high court as both human and oracular, and the folks who cover it inevitably have to walk some invisible, unknowable line between two myths that are each partly true."[24]

Has the Supreme Court lost its constitutional way? This is the big debate. The divide between the two sides of the argument is clear enough. Some think that the court, using the power given it by the 1982 constitutionally entrenched Charter of Rights and Freedoms, has usurped the power of elected politicians and undermined democracy. These critics say nine unelected and unaccountable elite lawyers have become the most powerful law and policy makers in the land, and this is a bad thing. Others consider the court's role, made possible by the Charter, to be to keep in check a tyrannical executive that has emasculated the legislature and to protect minorities from oppression by the majority, and this is a good thing.

This book has given several examples of each point of view. Writers on both sides of the question (mostly professors writing for professors) continue to scribble away. In early 2010, for example, Dennis Baker (a political scientist) published a book called *Not Quite Supreme*,[25] railing against Canadian constitutional orthodoxy. Baker argues that the legislative branch should feel free to reject what the courts say. He writes, "It is often perfectly reasonable for a legislature to test the Supreme Court's resolve and conviction in its own judgment by persisting for a time longer with its contrary legislative interpretation."[26] Indeed, to Baker this testing of the judiciary by the legislature is highly desirable, since "the Canadian Supreme Court, relying on the claim of constitutional interpretive supremacy, has indeed usurped the executive and legislative powers."[27]

Another writer on the subject is Andrew Petter, one-time law professor and a former British Columbia cabinet minister. In his *Politics of the Charter*,[28] published about the same time as Baker's book, Petter argues that the Charter is a regressive political instrument used by judges to promote the interests of the economically privileged. He rejects placing democracy in servitude to "academic scribblers or imperial judges" who encroach on the prerogative of the legislature by telling elected officials how to deal with public policy.

Then we have Frederick DeCoste, of the University of Alberta faculty of law. In a 2010 paper, DeCoste says that the Supreme Court violates a core constitutional principle of federalism by promoting "Canada's fundamental values," values which the court says underlie the Charter and are superior to the law itself.[29] Citizens should be free "to choose their own values and morality, and with that, their own lives, beyond the touch and taint of law and politics."[30] After all that breast beating, it turns out that what upsets DeCoste most is the way enforcing Canadian fundamental values subverts federalism. The fix for DeCoste, something of a letdown after all the rhetoric, is to give the provinces a role in the appointment of Supreme Court judges.

So much for the academy. What does the public think? Poll results suggest that Canadians like the Charter and what the judges do with it. In Chapter 1, I quoted a pollster who reported in 2007: "It's what I'd call a big patriotic symbol for the country."[31] As respect for the executive and legislative branches diminishes (and it has),[32] regard for the judiciary tends to increase. Critics of the court, of course, say that an approving public doesn't really understand the issues, and its approval, born of ignorance, counts for little.

It's no surprise that the judges themselves are the most commanding constituency supporting their new and powerful role. Not all of them, though: there are some who are nervous about the whole thing. One judge who is not nervous is Rosalie Abella, whom I have described as a leader of the court. Abella's views have been consistent over many years. I earlier quoted a comment she made in 1989: "The legislature which relies on majority support cannot be expected to risk political self-destruction by promulgating minority causes. The courts risk nothing."[33] In an April 2000 speech,[34] she reiterated that the courts are the best place to protect minority rights and that the work of the courts in doing so supports democracy rather than impairs it. She has vigorously attacked critics of Supreme Court Charter decisions. "While their articulated target was the Supreme Court of Canada, their real target was the way the Charter was transforming their traditional expectations and entitlements." Abella is not just a leader of the court; she is a leader of those who believe in a highly interventionist judiciary.

This debate will go on forever, and there is nothing wrong with that. Those who think the court goes too far will remain in the minority—that is, as long as the court does not go much further. There remains danger that an overly active and ambitious court will upset the constitutional apple cart, to the country's detriment as a liberal democracy. The reforms I suggest earlier would help guard against this danger. Adopting a better system of appointing judges and appointing them for a limited term would enhance the court as a democratic institution and make it more responsive to the Canadian people. A court that is more open, and media that are more diligent, would promote democracy and responsiveness. An informed and vigilant citizenry is the best protection of all against an overbearing judiciary.

I wrote in the Introduction that when I began this book I thought the Supreme Court undemocratic and in need of reform. I called it intolerable that nine unknown and unelected officials should make decisions fundamental to Canadian social and political life. Two years later, I haven't changed my mind entirely (although the work of the Supreme Court is impressive in many ways). My criticisms are not so much of the judges and what they do as they are of the mismatch between the job the constitution gives them and some of the ways in which the court is structured and operates. It is as if a person of good physique was forced to wear an ill-fitting suit. I've come to favour an interventionist court, persuaded in the end of their role in guarding against the tyranny of the majority, and particularly in guarding against the executive branch. The Supreme Court of Canada is the real opposition to the government. But an interventionist court, doing this essential job, must be staffed and structured differently, to make what it does tolerable in a true democracy.

_____

As we look at the Supreme Court's history since the Charter was enacted in 1982, one thing is for certain. Every Canadian is directly affected in essential ways by what the court does. In these pages, we have heard the stories of people whose problems have reached the court of last resort: a woman seeking an abortion, a terminally ill person wanting to die, a gay man fighting discrimination, orthodox Jews and Hutterites whose religious practices were threatened, Aboriginal chiefs pursuing historical land claims, a Quebec separatist, a suspected terrorist, a black man stopped by the police, a dominatrix from the suburbs, a man with a gun, a businessman who wants to sell his company, a pensioner of a failed corporation. Though some of the situations you've read about may seem singular, or curious, the judgments handed down have implications that stretch into the corners of every Canadian's life. Whether you are one of the people directly affected by a decision of the court, or simply someone who cares about the political, social, and economic makeup of the country, have no doubt: cloistered in their strange art deco building on the banks of the Ottawa River, judges of the Supreme Court of Canada have something to say to you.

———————◆———————

Judges of the Charter

Notes on the twenty-nine judges who have sat on the Supreme Court of Canada since the Charter of Rights and Freedoms came into force (April 17, 1982), ordered by date of appointment

ROLAND RITCHIE (1959–1984) Nova Scotia. Ritchie came from a prominent family (his brother, Charles, was an eminent diplomat and diarist). Appointed by Prime Minister John Diefenbaker directly from legal practice. Perhaps best known for his majority judgment in the 1969 *Drybones* case, the only case in which the Supreme Court struck down a law for breach of the old Diefenbaker Bill of Rights (see Chapter 2). Retired shortly after the Charter came into force. Old-school, conservative.

BORA LASKIN (1970–1984; CHIEF JUSTICE, 1973–1984) Ontario. Most of Laskin's legal career before his appointment to the court by Pierre Trudeau was spent as a law professor and labour arbitrator. First Jew on the court. Described by his biographer as a "philosopher-jurist." Died in office shortly after the Charter became law. Some say that Laskin "reinvented" the Supreme Court, making it focus on issues of national importance and pushing judges to consider social realities. Independent, anti-Establishment, a bit of a maverick.

BRIAN DICKSON (1973–1990; CHIEF JUSTICE, 1984–1990) Manitoba. Old-fashioned and privileged in many respects but seen as a progressive and subtle thinker. Considered by many to be the greatest chief justice of modern times, a judge who elaborated fundamental constitutional values and laid down basic guidelines of Charter interpretation. In the *Morgentaler* case, Dickson found that the abortion provisions of the Criminal Code were unconstitutional (see Chapter 3).

JEAN BEETZ (1974–1988) Quebec. Rhodes Scholar. Beetz was a law professor for most of his career. An expert in constitutional law and a friend of Pierre Trudeau. In *Morgentaler,* Beetz agreed that abortion laws were unconstitutional.

WILLARD "BUD" ESTEY (1977–1988) Ontario. Estey was the son of a Supreme Court justice (James Estey). Agreed with the majority in *Morgentaler.* Blunt and tough, he is remembered in Justice Binnie's description of court process: "Once oral argument is heard, the court wants to capitalize on some of the adrenalin pumping around the courtroom to, as Justice Estey used to say, 'get this baby airborne'."

WILLIAM MCINTYRE (1979–1989) British Columbia. McIntyre dissented in *Morgentaler,* which he saw as an unwise attempt by the court to take power that rightly belonged to Parliament. Seen by many as an arch-conservative, not in tune with the times. But, when he died in 2009, an obituary quoted lawyers who described him as a civil libertarian, a tremendous supporter of the Charter, an important tempering voice, and twenty years ahead of his time.

JULIEN CHOUINARD (1979–1987) Quebec. Rhodes Scholar. High-ranking Quebec civil servant. Appointed to the court by Joe Clark. Died at age fifty-eight.

ANTONIO LAMER (1980–2000; CHIEF JUSTICE, 1990–2000) Quebec. Lamer was a dominant figure, likeable but flawed. Primarily a criminal defence lawyer. As chief justice, he failed to promote harmony on the court or foster good working relationships among the judges. Considered the *Secession Reference* his greatest achievement (but see Chapter 5). Some lesser-heralded Lamer judgments showed considerable wisdom, such as the 1997 *Delgamuukw* case on Aboriginal title, when he wrote, "Let's face it, we are all here to stay."

BERTHA WILSON (1982–1991) Ontario. Wilson, appointed by Pierre Trudeau, was the first woman justice on the court. Considered a feminist, and almost a cult figure in certain quarters. Found it difficult to thrive in the court's "old boys' club" atmosphere that prevailed at the time. When Beverley McLachlin was sworn in (in 1979), Justice Wilson leaned over to her and whispered, "Three down, six to go." (Claire L'Heureux-Dubé was also on the court.)

GERALD LE DAIN (1984–1988) Ontario (succeeded Bora Laskin on the court). Le Dain was probably best known for chairing the Commission of Inquiry into the Non-Medical Use of Drugs (1969–73), which recommended the decriminalization of marijuana possession. An innovative dean of Osgoode Hall Law School. Known as a man of passion and temper. Wasn't on the court long enough to leave much of a mark.

GÉRARD LA FOREST (1985–1997) New Brunswick. Rhodes Scholar. Most of La Forest's career was spent as a law professor and public servant. Conservative: he agreed with McIntyre in *Morgentaler,* believing that the abortion question should be dealt with by Parliament. Proposed doing away with oral argument before the court, on the ground that it made no difference to the outcome of a case.

CLAIRE L'HEUREUX-DUBÉ (1987–2002) Quebec. L'Heureux-Dubé was the second woman to be appointed to the court. Wore her heart on her sleeve. Admired by some for her candour and passion; thought by others to be abrasive. Dissented in the 1993 *Rodriguez* case, believing that the law against assisting a suicide was unconstitutional (see Chapter 3). Considered a crusader for women's rights. Adamant in favour of a formal requirement that Supreme Court justices be bilingual.

JOHN SOPINKA (1988–1997) Ontario. Sopinka was a hard-driving Toronto trial lawyer and expert on the law of evidence, appointed directly from practice. Once played professional football (Toronto Argonauts, Montreal Alouettes). A good amateur violinist. Gave the majority judgment in the 1993 *Rodriguez* case.

CHARLES GONTHIER (1989–2003) Quebec. Described by some as the intellectual leader of the court during his time. Said to be the brains behind the court's "most important judgment ever," the 1998 *Secession Reference* (see Chapter 5).

PETER CORY (1989–1999) Ontario. Bomber pilot during World War Two. Cory dissented in *Rodriguez,* and gave a powerful judgment (in the majority) in the 1998 *Vriend* case, which read the words "sexual orientation" into the prohibited grounds of discrimination in Alberta's human rights statute, even though the legislature had deliberately left them out (see Chapter 4).

BEVERLEY MCLACHLIN (1989–   ; CHIEF JUSTICE, 2000–   ) British Columbia. McLachlin looms large because of how long she has been on the court, and because she is chief justice. Known as a crisp and effective administrator. Seeks consensus. No clear judicial or legal point of view giving coherence to her judgments.

WILLIAM STEVENSON (1990–1992) Alberta. Resigned for health reasons after less than two years on the court. Stevenson was counsel on the last case from Canada to be appealed to the Judicial Committee of the Privy Council in London (1959).

FRANK IACOBUCCI (1991–2004) Ontario. Highly respected and a powerful intellectual presence in the court. In *Vriend,* Iacobucci said the Canadian people had chosen to replace a system of parliamentary supremacy with a system of constitutional supremacy. His judgment in the 2004 *Amselem* case, giving a very broad interpretation of Charter-protected religious freedom, has been much criticized and is perhaps an aberration (see Chapter 5). Son of an Italian steelworker, Iacobucci had hoped to be chief justice but lost out to Beverley McLachlin.

JOHN MAJOR (1992-2005) Alberta. Unilingual. Plain-speaking. Conservative. After he left the court, Major conducted an extraordinary inquiry into the 1985 Air India bombing and produced a lengthy (perhaps too lengthy) and excellent report that was largely ignored.

MICHEL BASTARACHE (1997-2008) New Brunswick. Staunch protector of French-language rights. Bastarache resigned from the court at an early age, apparently finding the atmosphere disagreeable. Gave strong (and convincing) dissents in *Amselem* and the *Labaye* case (see Chapters 3 and 4).

IAN BINNIE (1998-) Ontario. Patrician background. Fiercely independent. Binnie is perhaps the smartest judge on the current court—certainly the funniest (though he has a tendency to go for an easy laugh and sometimes gets into trouble because of it). The best writer. Dissented in the 2005 *Chaoulli* case about private health care insurance, agreeing with LeBel that it was about social policy, not constitutional law, and that the questions it raised should be decided by the Quebec National Assembly, not the courts.

LOUISE ARBOUR (1999-2004) Ontario. Before being appointed, Arbour was chief prosecutor for the International Criminal Tribunals for the former Yugoslavia and for Rwanda. Left to become United Nations High Commissioner for Human Rights. Preferred a public stage to the cloistered world of the court.

LOUIS LEBEL (2000-) Quebec. A scholar and a gentleman. Influential in his quiet and understated way. LeBel showed considerable political courage in the 2009 case of *Nguyen v. Quebec,* giving a unanimous judgment striking down Quebec's Bill 104, which amended the Charter of the French language known as Bill 101 and blocked thousands of children from attending English-language schools.

MARIE DESCHAMPS (2002–   ) Quebec. In her first eighteen months on the court, Deschamps wrote more dissenting or separate opinions than any other judge. Shows considerable independence, particularly in criminal law matters. In *Chaoulli*, Deschamps (in the majority) said a prohibition on paying for private health insurance infringed "the right to personal inviolability and … is not justified by a proper regard for democratic values, public order and the general well-being of the citizens of Quebec."

MORRIS FISH (2003–   ) Quebec. Fish was the first anglophone appointed from Quebec since Doug Abbott in 1954. A strong advocate of the rights of the criminally accused. Fish's passion for the Charter was shown in 2010 by his *Cornell* dissent, where he fulminated against aggressive police practices, and in his majority judgment in *Morelli*, where he took a similar dim view of police behaviour.

ROSALIE ABELLA (2004–   ) Ontario. A powerful presence in the court because of her strong personality and her coherent commitment to minority rights. Abella has an expansive view of the role of the judiciary. U.S. legal commentator Dahlia Lithwick has called Abella "a cross between Celine Dion and Ruth Bader Ginsburg."

LOUISE CHARRON (2004–   ) Ontario. Franco-Ontarian. Has a special interest in criminal law. Charron joined with McLachlin in giving the majority reasons in the 2009 *Grant* cases and the 2010 *Sinclair* case; both of these judgments show a strong law-and-order bias and favour the police rather than the accused, which pitted Charron against LeBel, Fish, and Abella (see Chapter 6).

MARSHALL ROTHSTEIN (2006–   ) Manitoba. Conservative. Rothstein is the only Supreme Court nominee to have appeared publicly before a House of Commons committee before formal appointment (see Chapter 8). Overtly unilingual, and something of a whipping boy because of it. Famous for his hard work. Particular expertise in intellectual property.

TOM CROMWELL (2008–   ) Nova Scotia. Not afraid to disagree. In his first judgment, the 2009 *Van* case (a criminal law matter), he gave forceful dissenting reasons for a court split five to four. A judge of strong and independent opinions, particularly interested in the traditional private law subjects of contract and tort, which may now receive more sophisticated attention than in recent times. A good pianist: has said that lawyers could learn a lot from the composer Johann Sebastian Bach.

Canadian Charter
of Rights and Freedoms

Whereas Canada is founded upon principles that recognize the supremacy of God and the rule of law:

GUARANTEE OF RIGHTS AND FREEDOMS
Rights and freedoms in Canada

1. The *Canadian Charter of Rights and Freedoms* guarantees the rights and freedoms set out in it subject only to such reasonable limits prescribed by law as can be demonstrably justified in a free and democratic society.

FUNDAMENTAL FREEDOMS
Fundamental freedoms

2. Everyone has the following fundamental freedoms:

(a) freedom of conscience and religion;

(b) freedom of thought, belief, opinion and expression, including freedom of the press and other media of communication;

(c) freedom of peaceful assembly; and

(d) freedom of association.

DEMOCRATIC RIGHTS

Democratic rights of citizens

3. Every citizen of Canada has the right to vote in an election of members of the House of Commons or of a legislative assembly and to be qualified for membership therein.

Maximum duration of legislative bodies

4. (1) No House of Commons and no legislative assembly shall continue for longer than five years from the date fixed for the return of the writs of a general election of its members.

Continuation in special circumstances

(2) In time of real or apprehended war, invasion or insurrection, a House of Commons may be continued by Parliament and a legislative assembly may be continued by the legislature beyond five years if such continuation is not opposed by the votes of more than one-third of the members of the House of Commons or the legislative assembly, as the case may be.

Annual sitting of legislative bodies

5. There shall be a sitting of Parliament and of each legislature at least once every twelve months.

MOBILITY RIGHTS

Mobility of citizens

6. (1) Every citizen of Canada has the right to enter, remain in and leave Canada.

Rights to move and gain livelihood

(2) Every citizen of Canada and every person who has the status of a permanent resident of Canada has the right

(a) to move to and take up residence in any province; and

(b) to pursue the gaining of a livelihood in any province.

Limitation

(3) The rights specified in subsection (2) are subject to

(a) any laws or practices of general application in force in a province other than those that discriminate among persons primarily on the basis of province of present or previous residence; and

(b) any laws providing for reasonable residency requirements as a qualification for the receipt of publicly provided social services.

Affirmative action programs

(4) Subsections (2) and (3) do not preclude any law, program or activity that has as its object the amelioration in a province of conditions of individuals in that province who are socially or economically disadvantaged if the rate of employment in that province is below the rate of employment in Canada.

LEGAL RIGHTS

Life, liberty and security of person

7. Everyone has the right to life, liberty and security of the person and the right not to be deprived thereof except in accordance with the principles of fundamental justice.

Search or seizure

8. Everyone has the right to be secure against unreasonable search or seizure.

Detention or imprisonment

9. Everyone has the right not to be arbitrarily detained or imprisoned.

Arrest or detention

10. Everyone has the right on arrest or detention

(a) to be informed promptly of the reasons therefor;

(b) to retain and instruct counsel without delay and to be informed of that right; and

(c) to have the validity of the detention determined by way of *habeas corpus* and to be released if the detention is not lawful.

Proceedings in criminal and penal matters

11. Any person charged with an offence has the right

(a) to be informed without unreasonable delay of the specific offence;

(b) to be tried within a reasonable time;

(c) not to be compelled to be a witness in proceedings against that person in respect of the offence;

(d) to be presumed innocent until proven guilty according to law in a fair and public hearing by an independent and impartial tribunal;

(e) not to be denied reasonable bail without just cause;

(f) except in the case of an offence under military law tried before a military tribunal, to the benefit of trial by jury where the maximum punishment for the offence is imprisonment for five years or a more severe punishment;

(g) not to be found guilty on account of any act or omission unless, at the time of the act or omission, it constituted an offence under Canadian or international law or was criminal according to the general principles of law recognized by the community of nations;

(h) if finally acquitted of the offence, not to be tried for it again and, if finally found guilty and punished for the offence, not to be tried or punished for it again; and

(i) if found guilty of the offence and if the punishment for the offence has been varied between the time of commission and the time of sentencing, to the benefit of the lesser punishment.

Treatment or punishment

12. Everyone has the right not to be subjected to any cruel and unusual treatment or punishment.

Self-crimination

13. A witness who testifies in any proceedings has the right not to have any incriminating evidence so given used to incriminate that witness in any other proceedings, except in a prosecution for perjury or for the giving of contradictory evidence.

Interpreter

14. A party or witness in any proceedings who does not understand or speak the language in which the proceedings are conducted or who is deaf has the right to the assistance of an interpreter.

EQUALITY RIGHTS

Equality before and under law and equal protection and benefit of law

15. (1) Every individual is equal before and under the law and has the right to the equal protection and equal benefit of the law without discrimination and, in particular, without discrimination based on race, national or ethnic origin, colour, religion, sex, age or mental or physical disability.

Affirmative action programs

(2) Subsection (1) does not preclude any law, program or activity that has as its object the amelioration of conditions of disadvantaged individuals or

groups including those that are disadvantaged because of race, national or ethnic origin, colour, religion, sex, age or mental or physical disability.

OFFICIAL LANGUAGES OF CANADA

Official languages of Canada

16. (1) English and French are the official languages of Canada and have equality of status and equal rights and privileges as to their use in all institutions of the Parliament and government of Canada.

Official languages of New Brunswick

(2) English and French are the official languages of New Brunswick and have equality of status and equal rights and privileges as to their use in all institutions of the legislature and government of New Brunswick.

Advancement of status and use

(3) Nothing in this Charter limits the authority of Parliament or a legislature to advance the equality of status or use of English and French.

English and French linguistic communities in New Brunswick

16.1 (1) The English linguistic community and the French linguistic community in New Brunswick have equality of status and equal rights and privileges, including the right to distinct educational institutions and such distinct cultural institutions as are necessary for the preservation and promotion of those communities.

Role of the legislature and government of New Brunswick

(2) The role of the legislature and government of New Brunswick to preserve and promote the status, rights and privileges referred to in subsection (1) is affirmed.

Proceedings of Parliament

17. (1) Everyone has the right to use English or French in any debates and other proceedings of Parliament.

Proceedings of New Brunswick legislature

(2) Everyone has the right to use English or French in any debates and other proceedings of the legislature of New Brunswick.

Parliamentary statutes and records

18. (1) The statutes, records and journals of Parliament shall be printed

and published in English and French and both language versions are equally authoritative.

New Brunswick statutes and records

(2) The statutes, records and journals of the legislature of New Brunswick shall be printed and published in English and French and both language versions are equally authoritative.

Proceedings in courts established by Parliament

19. (1) Either English or French may be used by any person in, or in any pleading in or process issuing from, any court established by Parliament

Proceedings in New Brunswick courts

(2) Either English or French may be used by any person in, or in any pleading in or process issuing from, any court of New Brunswick.

Communications by public with federal institutions

20. (1) Any member of the public in Canada has the right to communicate with, and to receive available services from, any head or central office of an institution of the Parliament or government of Canada in English or French, and has the same right with respect to any other office of any such institution where

(a) there is a significant demand for communications with and services from that office in such language; or

(b) due to the nature of the office, it is reasonable that communications with and services from that office be available in both English and French.

Communications by public with New Brunswick institutions

(2) Any member of the public in New Brunswick has the right to communicate with, and to receive available services from, any office of an institution of the legislature or government of New Brunswick in English or French.

Continuation of existing constitutional provisions

21. Nothing in sections 16 to 20 abrogates or derogates from any right, privilege or obligation with respect to the English and French languages, or either of them, that exists or is continued by virtue of any other provision of the Constitution of Canada.

Rights and privileges preserved

22. Nothing in sections 16 to 20 abrogates or derogates from any legal or customary right or privilege acquired or enjoyed either before or after the

coming into force of this Charter with respect to any language that is not English or French.

MINORITY LANGUAGE EDUCATIONAL RIGHTS

Language of instruction

23. (1) Citizens of Canada

(a) whose first language learned and still understood is that of the English or French linguistic minority population of the province in which they reside, or

(b) who have received their primary school instruction in Canada in English or French and reside in a province where the language in which they received that instruction is the language of the English or French linguistic minority population of the province,

have the right to have their children receive primary and secondary school instruction in that language in that province.

Continuity of language instruction

(2) Citizens of Canada of whom any child has received or is receiving primary or secondary school instruction in English or French in Canada, have the right to have all their children receive primary and secondary school instruction in the same language.

Application where numbers warrant

(3) The right of citizens of Canada under subsections (1) and (2) to have their children receive primary and secondary school instruction in the language of the English or French linguistic minority population of a province

(a) applies wherever in the province the number of children of citizens who have such a right is sufficient to warrant the provision to them out of public funds of minority language instruction; and

(b) includes, where the number of those children so warrants, the right to have them receive that instruction in minority language educational facilities provided out of public funds.

ENFORCEMENT

Enforcement of guaranteed rights and freedoms

24. (1) Anyone whose rights or freedoms, as guaranteed by this Charter, have been infringed or denied may apply to a court of competent jurisdiction

to obtain such remedy as the court considers appropriate and just in the circumstances.

Exclusion of evidence bringing administration of justice into disrepute

(2) Where, in proceedings under subsection (1), a court concludes that evidence was obtained in a manner that infringed or denied any rights or freedoms guaranteed by this Charter, the evidence shall be excluded if it is established that, having regard to all the circumstances, the admission of it in the proceedings would bring the administration of justice into disrepute.

GENERAL

Aboriginal rights and freedoms not affected by Charter

25. The guarantee in this Charter of certain rights and freedoms shall not be construed so as to abrogate or derogate from any aboriginal, treaty or other rights or freedoms that pertain to the aboriginal peoples of Canada including

(a) any rights or freedoms that have been recognized by the Royal Proclamation of October 7, 1763; and

(b) any rights or freedoms that now exist by way of land claims agreements or may be so acquired.

Other rights and freedoms not affected by Charter

26. The guarantee in this Charter of certain rights and freedoms shall not be construed as denying the existence of any other rights or freedoms that exist in Canada.

Multicultural heritage

27. This Charter shall be interpreted in a manner consistent with the preservation and enhancement of the multicultural heritage of Canadians.

Rights guaranteed equally to both sexes

28. Notwithstanding anything in this Charter, the rights and freedoms referred to in it are guaranteed equally to male and female persons.

Rights respecting certain schools preserved

29. Nothing in this Charter abrogates or derogates from any rights or privileges guaranteed by or under the Constitution of Canada in respect of denominational, separate or dissentient schools.

Application to territories and territorial authorities

30. A reference in this Charter to a province or to the legislative assembly or legislature of a province shall be deemed to include a reference to the Yukon Territory and the Northwest Territories, or to the appropriate legislative authority thereof, as the case may be.

Legislative powers not extended

31. Nothing in this Charter extends the legislative powers of any body or authority.

APPLICATION OF CHARTER

Application of Charter

32. (1) This Charter applies

(a) to the Parliament and government of Canada in respect of all matters within the authority of Parliament including all matters relating to the Yukon Territory and Northwest Territories; and

(b) to the legislature and government of each province in respect of all matters within the authority of the legislature of each province.

Exception

(2) Notwithstanding subsection (1), section 15 shall not have effect until three years after this section comes into force.

Exception where express declaration

33. (1) Parliament or the legislature of a province may expressly declare in an Act of Parliament or of the legislature, as the case may be, that the Act or a provision thereof shall operate notwithstanding a provision included in section 2 or sections 7 to 15 of this Charter.

Operation of exception

(2) An Act or a provision of an Act in respect of which a declaration made under this section is in effect shall have such operation as it would have but for the provision of this Charter referred to in the declaration.

Five year limitation

(3) A declaration made under subsection (1) shall cease to have effect five years after it comes into force or on such earlier date as may be specified in the declaration.

Re-enactment

(4) Parliament or the legislature of a province may re-enact a declaration made under subsection (1).

Five year limitation

(5) Subsection (3) applies in respect of a re-enactment made under subsection (4).

CITATION

Citation

34. This Part may be cited as the *Canadian Charter of Rights and Freedoms*.

NOTES

———◆———

INTRODUCTION **The Voice Passed Down from the Mountain**

1. The Canadian Press, "Prostitution is safest indoors: dominatrix," 7 June 2008, www.ctv.ca/servlet/ArticleNews/story/CTVNews/20080607/ont_dominatrix_080607/20080607 (accessed 22 January 2010).

2. The Charter is part of the Constitution Act, 1982, which is Schedule B to the Canada Act 1982 (U.K.), 1982, c. 11. For the Charter's full text, see Appendix B; the Charter is also available online at http://laws.justice.gc.ca/en/charter/1.html.

3. I wrote about this in "A trial in error? Why should a Toronto court decide Canada's prostitution laws?" *Maclean's*, 24 December 2009, www2.macleans.ca/2009/12/24/a-trial-in-error (accessed 22 January 2010).

4. *Bedford v. Canada*, 2010 ONSC 4264.

5. John Ibbitson, "Securities case a battle that will test the nation," *The Globe and Mail*, 17 October 2009, A12.

6. There may be one exception. The Constitution Act, 1982, stipulates that a change in the composition of the Supreme Court is one of several amendments to the Constitution that require a unanimous vote of all the provinces plus both Houses of Parliament. But some scholars argue that this provision is ineffective, because the Supreme Court Act is not listed in the Constitution Act as a constitutional instrument.

7. See Treasury Board of Canada Secretariat, "Supreme Court of Canada: 2008–2009 Departmental Performance Report," www.tbs-sct.gc.ca/dpr-rmr/2008-2009/inst/jsc/jsc00-eng.asp (accessed 22 January 2010).

8. Reported by Jake Cole, "Supreme Court of Canada one of the top 10 best places to work in public service," *The Hill Times*, 5 April 2010, www.hilltimes.com/page/view/-04-05-2010 (accessed 28 April 2010).

9. See "Bulletin of Proceedings: Special Edition, Statistics 1999 to 2009," www.scc-csc.gc.ca/stat/pdf/doc-eng.pdf (accessed 19 March 2010).

10. Cristin Schmitz, "Drop in caseload worries Supreme Court of Canada observers," *The Lawyers Weekly,* 1 October 2010, www.lawyersweekly.ca/index.php?section=article&articleid=1260 (accessed 14 October 2010).

11. There has even been a conference at Yale Law School to consider the mystery of the U.S. Supreme Court's shrinking docket. See Adam Liptak, "The Case of the Plummeting Supreme Court Docket," *The New York Times,* 29 September 2009, www.nytimes.com/2009/09/29/us/29bar.html (accessed 2 October 2009).

12. See, for example, Yu-Sung Soh, "The Case of the Missing Cases," *The Court,* 8 February 2007, www.thecourt.ca/2007/02/08/the-case-of-the-missing-cases (accessed 24 October 2009).

13. Dahlia Lithwick, "Supreme Court Dispatch, Eh: How the United States' never-ending legal mess at Gitmo is spilling over into Canada," *Slate,* 13 November 2009, www.slate.com/id/2235467/ (accessed 24 November 2009).

14. Philip Girard writes in his biography of former chief justice Bora Laskin, "I have not found a single layperson who has been able to identify any of Laskin's successors as chief justice of Canada." *Bora Laskin: Bringing Law to Life* (Toronto: University of Toronto Press, 2005), xvi.

15. See Robert Barnes, "Even for the Experienced Sotomayor, Many Changes Await," *The Washington Post,* 8 August 2009, www.washingtonpost.com/wp-dyn/content/article/2009/08/07/AR2009080702078_pf.html (accessed 14 September 2009).

16. The survey was by FindLaw.com. See www.prnewswire.com/news-releases/two-thirds-of-americans-cant-name-any-us-supreme-court-justices-says-new-findlawcom-survey-95298909.html (accessed 2 June 2010).

17. "Did a Supreme Court judge throw away the briefs," *The Globe and Mail,* 31 October 2006, A1.

18. *Supreme Conflict: The Inside Story of the Struggle for Control of the United States Supreme Court* (New York: Penguin Books, 2007), 161.

19. Quoted by Mark Bernstein, "Balancing Justice," *Syracuse University Magazine,* Winter 2005–06, http://sumagazine.syr.edu/archive/winter05-06/features/feature2/index.html (accessed 4 January 2010).

20. For example, see the bibliography published on the Supreme Court's official website, www.scc-csc.gc.ca/court-cour/biblio/index-eng.asp (accessed 11 December 2009).

21. *The Nine: Inside the Secret World of the Supreme Court* (Toronto: Random House of Canada, 2008).

22. See note 18.

23. Adam Liptak, "Tailgating Outside the Supreme Court, Without the Cars," *The New York Times,* 3 March 2010, A18.

24. "Courts, Transparency and Public Confidence—To the Better Administration of Justice," (2003) 8 *Deakin Law Review* 1, www.austlii.edu.au/au/journals/DeakinLRev/2003/1.html (accessed 22 January 2010).

25. Karol Kudyba, "Guarding the Chief Justice of the Supreme Court, the Queen and other important people," *The Sheaf.com* (University of Saskatchewan Student Newspaper), 3 November 2010, http://thesheaf.com/2010/11/03/guarding-

the-chief-justice-of-the-supreme-court-the-queen-and-other-important-people/ (accessed 4 November 2010).

26. See Christin Schmitz, "McLachlin Court turns ten," *The Lawyers Weekly,* 25 December 2009, http://lawyersweekly.ca/index.php?section=article&volume=29& number=32&article=3 (accessed 3 January 2010).

27. 10 June 2010 interview.

28. See Girard, note 14, 437.

29. Bob Woodward and Scott Armstrong, *The Brethren: Inside the Supreme Court* (New York: Simon & Schuster, 1979).

30. See Kevin Libin, "Chronicler of the truth," *Financial Post,* 2 May 2009, www.financialpost.com/scripts/story.html?id=658e43e3-d2c6-4ea8-96b6-a4e26b7a2a32&k=99586 (accessed 22 January 2010).

31. See www.cbsnews.com/stories/2008/04/24/60minutes/main4040290.shtml (accessed 20 March 2010).

32. *Making Our Democracy Work: A Judge's View* (New York: Knopf, 2010).

33. Quoted by Ian Binnie, "Interpreting the Constitution: The Living Tree vs. Original Meaning," *Policy Options,* October 2007, 104 at 107.

34. Tom Bingham, *The Rule of Law* (London: Allen Lane, 2010), 42–43. Adam Liptak of *The New York Times* has described an emerging critique of the United States Supreme Court "concerned with the quality of the court's judicial craftsmanship. In decisions on questions great and small, the court often provides only limited or ambiguous guidance to lower courts. And increasingly it does so at enormous length." Adam Liptak, "Justices are Long on Words but Short on Guidance," *The New York Times,* 17 November 2010, www.nytimes.com/2010/11/18/us/18rulings. html?scp=1&sq=%22long%20on%20words%22&st=cse (accessed 19 November 2010).

35. In his chambers, 25 May 2010.

36. The reference is to Weiler's book, *In the Last Resort: A Critical Study of the Supreme Court of Canada* (Toronto: Carswell Methuen, 1974).

ONE Law Out of Their Guts

1. Christie wrote about this trip in a privately printed memoir—*A Journey Into Justice* (2000).

2. Christie, 69.

3. The quixotic Christie was killed in a traffic accident on July 31, 2006. His bicycle was hit by a minivan on the Trans-Canada Highway, in the hamlet of Iron Bridge, near Sault Ste. Marie, Ontario. Christie was on his third cross-country bicycle trip, this time heading to Newfoundland, where he planned to attend the Canadian Bar Association's annual meeting.

4. James G. Snell and Frederick Vaughan, *Supreme Court of Canada: History of the Institution* (Toronto: The Osgoode Society for Canadian Legal History, 1985), 177. Snell and Vaughan are very critical of the building.

5. Chris Hume, email message to the author, 10 June 2008.

6. Dennis Baker, *Not Quite Supreme: The Courts and Coordinate Constitutional Interpretation* (Montreal: McGill-Queen's University Press, 2010), 45.

7. See Seth Stern and Stephen Wermiel, *Justice Brennan: Liberal Champion* (New York: Houghton Mifflin Harcourt, 2010). In a review of this book, Dahlia Lithwick comments: "Where this book truly soars is in its account of Brennan's skills at—as he always described it to his clerks—getting to five... He emerges as so carefully attuned to the concerns and passions of his colleagues that he was able, time after time, to draft opinions, or help them draft opinions, in ways that could achieve five votes." Dahlia Lithwick, "Getting to Five," *The New York Times Book Review,* 10 October 2010, 20.

8. Jaclyn Delligatti and Nicholas Rugoff, "The Court's Witness: An Interview with Linda Greenhouse," *The Politic,* March 2010, www.thepolitic.org/articles/39/an-interview-with-linda-greenhouse (accessed 7 March 2010).

9. From 1984 to 2005, there were a total of 2009 appeals heard by the Court: 477 were assigned to panels of five, 956 were assigned to panels of seven, and 576 were assigned to panels of nine. See Benjamin Alarie, Andrew Green, and Edward M. Iacobucci, "Is Bigger Always Better? On Optimal Panel Size, with Evidence from the Supreme Court of Canada," CLEA 2008 Meetings Paper, 16 September 2008, available at SSRN: http://ssrn.com/abstract=1152322 (accessed 3 October 2008). A thorough discussion of the considerations at play in forming a panel can be found in Donald R. Songer, *The Transformation of the Supreme Court of Canada: An Empirical Examination* (Toronto: University of Toronto Press, 2008), 111–18. Chief Justice McLachlin apparently favours panels of nine in principle. She has said at a press conference that if the court sits seven judges instead of nine, "there might be a little bit of uncertainty. It detracts somewhat, I believe, from the certainty that attends the resolution of a legal issue." Kirk Makin, "Top judge didn't vote in Morgentaler decision," *The Globe and Mail,* 16 August 2008, www.theglobeandmail.com/servlet/story/RTGAM.20080816.wmclachlin0816/BNStory/National/home (accessed 17 August 2008).

10. Peter McCormick has argued that reasons, including concurring and dissenting reasons, are more important than outcome. "It is the outcome that gets the headlines, but it is the reasons that cast their shadow over future judicial decisions." See "The Reasons Why Reasons Are (Reasonably) Important," *The Court,* 24 June 2009, www.thecourt.ca/2009/06/24/the-reasons-for-reasons/ (accessed 3 August 2009).

11. See Chapter 8 for an account of this committee hearing.

12. See "Judges should apply law, not make it: Rothstein," www.ctv.ca/servlet/ArticleNews/story/CTVNews/20060227/rothstein_grilling_060227/20060228? (accessed 11 June 2008).

13. Interview with Rothstein in his chambers, 11 June 2010.

14. Beverley McLachlin, "Appellate Review in Canada," International Summit of High Courts, Istanbul, Turkey, November 2010, 6, www.summitofhighcourts.com/docs/papers/canada.pdf (accessed 19 October 2010).

15. Hearing on the Nomination of John Roberts to Be Chief Justice of the Supreme Court before the Senate Judiciary Committee, 109th Cong., 1st Sess. 56 (12 September 2005). For an amusing and enlightening comparison of umpires and judges, see Bruce Weber, "Umpires v. Judges," *The New York Times,* 11 July 2009, www.nytimes.com/2009/07/12/weekinreview/12weber.html?_r=1&scp=5&sq=bruce%20

weber&st=cse (accessed 13 July 2009). U.S. Supreme Court judges are known to be fanatical baseball fans and frequently use baseball metaphors in their judgments. See Adam Liptak, "This Bench Belongs in a Dugout," *The New York Times,* 1 June 2010, www.nytimes.com/2010/06/01/us/01bar.html?emc=tnt&tntemail0=y (accessed 1 June 2010).

16. Charles Eisgruber, *The Next Justice: Repairing the Supreme Court Appointments Process* (Princeton: Princeton University Press, 2007), 17.

17. Ronald Dworkin, "The Supreme Court Phalanx," *The New York Review of Books,* 27 September 2007, 92.

18. Richard Posner, *How Judges Think* (Cambridge: Harvard University Press, 2008), 81.

19. Peter Baker, "Obama v. Roberts," *The New York Times,* 18 April 2010, WK1.

20. "The Court's Aggressive Term," *The New York Times,* 4 July 2010, www.nytimes.com/2010/07/05/opinion/05mon1.html?hp (accessed 5 July 2010).

21. See www.whitehouse.gov/blog/Judge-Sotomayors-Opening-Statement/ (accessed 2 August 2009).

22. Jeffrey Toobin, "Answers to Questions," *The New Yorker,* 27 July 2009, 19.

23. Ronald Dworkin, "Justice Sotomayor: The Unjust Hearings," *The New York Review,* 24 September 2009, 37.

24. Posner, note 18, 8.

25. Posner, 11. A quantitative study of Charter cases decided since 2000 suggests that "ideology" has had little effect. See Benjamin Alarie and Andrew James Green, "Charter Decisions in the McLachlin Era: Consensus and Ideology at the Supreme Court of Canada," 16 April 2009, http://ssrn.com/abstract=1387039 (accessed 18 June 2009).

26. Brian Z. Tamanaha, *Beyond the Formalist-Realist Divide: The Role of Politics in Judging* (Princeton: Princeton University Press, 2010).

27. Tamanaha, 181–82.

28. The 2001 Judge Mario G. Olmos Memorial Lecture, delivered at the University of California, Berkeley, School of Law. For the full text, see www.nytimes.com/2009/05/15/us/politics/15judge.text.html (accessed 30 May 2009).

29. Peter Baker, Jeff Zeleny, "Obama Nominates Hispanic Judge for Supreme Court," *The New York Times,* 27 May 2009, A1.

30. Posner, note 18, 82.

31. Posner, 151.

32. Posner, 125.

33. Posner has his own theory about why judges, like Roberts and Rothstein, deny they make law. "For judges to acknowledge even just to themselves the political dimension of their role would open a psychologically unsettling gap between their official job description and their actual job. Acknowledging that they were making political choices would also undermine their confidence in the soundness of their decisions, since judges' political choices cannot be justified by reference to their professional background or training." Note 18, 289.

34. Songer, note 9, 8.

35. See "The Agenda with Steve Paikin," TVO, 1 December 2009, www.tvo.org/TVO/WebObjects/TVO.woa?video?TAWSP_Int1_20091201_779664_0 (accessed 2

January 2010). The most thorough (and quantitative) study of the gender issue in Canada, although now dated, is Candace C. White, "Gender Difference in the Supreme Court of Canada," University of Calgary M.A. thesis, 1998, www.collectionscanada.gc.ca/obj/s4/f2/dsk2/ftp01/MQ38554.pdf (accessed 9 January 2010).

36. Songer, note 9, 208–9.

37. In an interview in her chambers, 10 June 2010. She said the same thing in an October 2010 web interview: Rebecca Lowe, "Interview with Beverley McLachlin," International Bar Association, www.ibanet.org/Article/Detail.aspx?ArticleUid=634cd6e1-ddba-4510-b69a-924e3c87b65e (accessed 19 October 2010).

38. Ian Bushnell, *The Captive Court: A Study of the Supreme Court of Canada* (Montreal: McGill-Queen's University Press, 1992), xii–xiii.

39. Florian Sauvageau, David Schneiderman, and David Taras, *The Last Word: Media Coverage of the Supreme Court of Canada* (Vancouver: UBC Press, 2006), 8.

40. Claire Bernstein, "How top judges came to grips with Charter," *Toronto Star*, 20 May 1990, B1.

41. Beverley McLachlin, "Human Rights Protection in Canada," Fourth Annual Human Rights Lecture, Law Society of Ireland, Dublin, Ireland, 7 May 2008, 9, www.flac.ie/download/pdf/attachment_to_piln_bulletin_24jul08.pdf (accessed 10 January 2010).

42. Every observer has his own list of the most important Charter cases. For example, see "Charter of Rights anniversary," *The Globe and Mail*, 10 April 2007, A7, which gives the "top cases" lists of three constitutional experts, or "Key cases in Charter's young history," *Toronto Star*, 7 April 2007, A20.

43. A compelling, if occasionally intemperate, account of the huge expansion of judicial power and activism since the 1982 Charter can be found in F.L. Morton and Rainer Knopff, *The Charter Revolution and the Court Party* (Peterborough, Ontario: Broadview Press, 2000). Morton and Knopff describe the "Court Party" as comprising all those elite interests, throughout Canada, which seek to politicize the judiciary in pursuit of various left-wing political agendas. They write: "Our primary objection to the Charter Revolution is that it is deeply and fundamentally undemocratic, not just in the simple and obvious sense of being anti-majoritarian, but also in the more serious sense of eroding the habits and temperament of representative democracy..." (149).

44. Some argue that labour law is central to the evolution of constitutional law. See Kelly Harris, "Labour Law Central to Constitutional Fight," *Canadian Lawyer*, February 2010, www.canadianlawyermag.com/Labour-law-central-to-constitutional-fight.html (accessed 12 February 2010).

45. For example, the decision in *MiningWatch Canada v. Canada (Fisheries and Oceans)*, 2010 SCC 2, http://scc.lexum.umontreal.ca/en/2010/2010scc2/2010scc2.html (accessed 14 February 2010). This case emphasized federal environmental assessment requirements.

46. 1999 CanLII 665.

47. Alex M. Cameron, *Power Without Law: The Supreme Court of Canada, the Marshall Decisions, and the Future of Judicial Activism* (Montreal: McGill-Queen's University Press, 2009).

48. Cameron, 148–49.
49. See Baker, note 6.
50. Baker, 136.
51. *Vancouver (City) v. Ward,* 2010 SCC 27.
52. Paragraph 25.
53. See www.g20defence.ca/pdfs/Statement_of_Claim.pdf (accessed 22 September 2010).
54. Janice Tibbetts, "Charter issues fine tuned: McLachlin," *National Post,* 7 January 2010, www.nationalpost.com/news/canada/story.html?id=2414472 (accessed 10 January 2010).
55. "The Supreme Court 2005 Term," 120 *Harvard Law Review* 4 (2006).
56. By contrast, in 2008 Professor Noah Feldman of Harvard Law School wrote a lengthy article in *The New York Times Magazine* about the importance of the U.S. Supreme Court in the making of U.S. foreign policy. "When Judges Make Foreign Policy," 28 September 2008, 50.
57. *BCE Inc. v. 1976 Debentureholders,* 2008 SCC 69 (CanLII).
58. (Montreal: McGill-Queen's University Press, 2003).
59. Nigel Hannaford, "Will the real radical please stand up?" *Calgary Herald,* 4 July 2009, www.calgaryherald.com/news/Will+real+radical+please+stand/1759640/story. html (accessed 5 July 2009).
60. Don Butler, "Charting the impact of the Charter; Canadians love their Charter of Rights and Freedoms—even if they don't know much about it," *Ottawa Citizen,* 15 April 2007, A6. According to a 2001 Gallup poll, Canadians had greater respect for the Supreme Court than for just about any other Canadian institution. See Sauvageau, Schneiderman, and Taras, *The Last Word,* 26–27.
61. Kent Roach, *The Supreme Court on Trial: Judicial Activism or Democratic Dialogue* (Toronto: Irwin Law, 2001), 7–8.
62. Roach, 207.
63. In his chambers, 25 May 2010.
64. (Oxford: Oxford University Press, 2007).
65. "Moving Houses," The *Times Literary Supplement,* 4 April 2008, http://tls. timesonline.co.uk/article/0,,25368-2651149_1,00.html (accessed 14 June 2008).
66. (London: Hart Publishing, 2009).
67. James Allan, Grant Huscroft, and Nessa Lynch, "The Citation of Overseas Authority in Rights Litigation in New Zealand: How Much Bark? How Much Bite?" *Otago Law Review,* Vol. 11, No. 3, 2007. See also Adam Liptak, "U.S. Court Is Now Guiding Fewer Nations," *The New York Times,* 18 September 2008, www.nytimes. com/2008/09/18/us/18legal.html?scp=1&sq=%22supreme%20court's%20 global%20influence%22&st=cse (accessed 7 April 2009).
68. 2010 SCC 3 (CanLII).
69. Paragraph 2.
70. Although, a few months later, the court backed away from an argument that the Charter's guarantee of free expression implies a right to disclosure of information in the government's hands. *Ontario (Public Safety and Security) v. Criminal Lawyers' Association,* 2010 SCC 23 (CanLII).

71. 000 U.S. 08-205 (2010), www.supremecourtus.gov/opinions/09pdf/08-205.pdf (accessed 18 February 2010).

72. James MacGregor Burns, *Packing the Court: The Rise of Judicial Power and the Coming Crisis of the Supreme Court* (New York: The Penguin Press, 2009), 250.

73. Quoted by Kirk Makin, "Charting a course in the age of judicial review," *The Globe and Mail,* 11 April 2007, A8.

74. During the 10 June 2010 interview.

75. "It's Complicated: David Souter finally tells Americans to grow up," *Slate,* 9 June 2010, www.slate.com/id/2256458 (accessed 14 June 2010).

76. 11 June 2010 interview.

77. *How Judges Think,* 306.

TWO A Brief History

1. Two full studies of the court's history are Ian Bushnell's *The Captive Court: A Study of the Supreme Court of Canada* (Montreal: McGill-Queens University Press, 1992) and James G. Snell and Frederick Vaughan's *Supreme Court of Canada: History of the Institution* (Toronto: The Osgoode Society for Canadian Legal History, 1985). The latter can be downloaded free from www.thecourt.ca/resources/snell-and-vaughan/. Snell and Vaughan are particularly interesting on the appointment process and give biographic details of appointees. Another good source is Peter McCormick, *Supreme at Last: The Evolution of the Supreme Court of Canada* (Toronto: James Lorimer & Company, 2000). McCormick concentrates on the post-1949 period; his book has a statistical bent.

2. "Sir William Buell Richards," *Dictionary of Canadian Biography Online* www.biographi.ca/009004-119.01-e.php?&id_nbr=5793 (accessed 25 October 2009).

3. See David E. Rempel, "First Chief Justice of the Supreme Court of Canada: Potsdam Alumnus," *The Racquette,* 19 November 2010 http://media.www.theracquette.com/media/storage/paper1301/news/2010/11/19/CollegeLife/First.Chief.Justice.Of.The.Supreme.Court.Of.Canada.Potsdam.Alumnus-3961225.shtml (accessed 20 November 2010).

4. "Sir William Johnston Ritchie," *Dictionary of Canadian Biography Online* www.biographi.ca/009004-119.01-e.php?&id_nbr=6395&interval=20&&PHPSESSID=0cc4a1mvavcalmq4mfmb9v79a0 (accessed 25 October 2009).

5. "Sir Samuel Henry Strong," *Dictionary of Canadian Biography Online,* www.biographi.ca/009004-119.01-e.php?&id_nbr=7088&interval=20&&PHPSESSID=0ig5guqe9rsvi53lns8vmntia0 (accessed 25 October 2009).

6. The newspaper *L'Électeur,* quoted in "Jean-Thomas Taschereau," *Dictionary of Canadian Biography Online* www.biographi.ca/009004-119.01-e.php?&id_nbr=6456&interval=20&&PHPSESSID=0ig5guqe9rsvi53lns8vmntia0 (accessed 25 October 2009).

7. "William Alexander Henry," *Dictionary of Canadian Biography Online* www.biographi.ca/009004-119.01-e.php?&id_nbr=5577&interval=20&&PHPSESSID=0ig5guqe9rsvi53lns8vmntia0 (accessed 25 October 2009).

8. Snell and Vaughan, note 1, 18.

9. *Brassard v. Langevin* (1877), 1 S.C.R. 145.

10. *Severn v. The Queen* (1878), 2 S.C.R. 70.

11. Bushnell, note 1, 87.
12. Quoted by Snell and Vaughan, note 1, 171.
13. Bushnell, note 1, 156.
14. Strong's personal conduct apparently deteriorated as the years went by. For a detailed account of various incidents involving Strong, see Snell and Vaughan, note 1, 59–64.
15. Bushnell, note 1, 171.
16. Bushnell, 194.
17. (1921), 62 S.C.R. 424.
18. The story is most recently told by Ian Blue, "On the Rocks; The Gold Seal Case: A Surprising Second Look," 36 *Advocates Quarterly* 363 (2010).
19. S.C. 1927, c.38, sections 1 and 2.
20. *Reference as to Meaning of the Word "Persons" in Section 24 of the British North America Act, 1867,* [1928] S.C.R. 276. There is a book about this case—Robert J. Sharpe and Patricia I. McMahon, *The Persons Case: The Origins and Legacy of the Fight for Legal Personhood* (Toronto: The University of Toronto Press, 2007). The judgments of both the Supreme Court and the Privy Council can be found at www2.law.columbia.edu/faculty_franke/CLT2009/Persons%20Case.pdf (accessed 28 January 2010).
21. Snell and Vaughan, note 1, 141.
22. *Edwards v. Attorney General for Canada,* [1930] A.C. 124.
23. Speech to the law faculty of the University of British Columbia, 4 February 2010, www.youtube.com/watch?v=hsvYwnpjCQc (accessed 28 February 2010).
24. William Kaplan, *Canadian Maverick: The Life and Times of Ivan C. Rand* (Toronto: University of Toronto Press, 2009), xiv.
25. *Attorney General for Ontario v. Attorney General for Canada,* [1947] A.C. 127.
26. S.C. 1949, c.37.
27. *Ponoka-Calmar Oils v. Wakefield,* [1960] A.C. 18.
28. Kaplan, note 24, xii.
29. [1951] S.C.R. 265.
30. [1953] 2 S.C.R. 299.
31. [1959] S.C.R. 122.
32. Kaplan, note 24, 151.
33. Beverley McLachlin, "Human Rights Protection in Canada," Fourth Annual Human Rights Lecture, Law Society of Ireland, Dublin, Ireland, 7 May 2008, 5, www.flac.ie/download/pdf/attachment_to_piln_bulletin_24jul08.pdf (accessed 10 January 2010).
34. Bushnell, note 1, 322.
35. Bushnell, 331.
36. There are two biographies of Hall: Frederick Vaughan, *Aggressive in Pursuit: The Life of Justice Emmett Hall* (Toronto: University of Toronto Press, 2004), and Dennis Gruending, *Emmett Hall: Establishment Radical* (Markham, Ontario: Fitzhenry and Whiteside, 2005).
37. *The Queen v. Drybones,* 1969 CanLII 1 (S.C.C.).
38. S.C. 1960, c.44.
39. Philip Girard, *Bora Laskin: Bringing Law to Life* (Toronto: University of Toronto Press, 2005), 366.

40. Girard, 369.

41. Supreme Court Act, R.S.C. 1970, c. S-19, s. 41(1), as amended by S.C. 1974-75-76, c.18, s.5.

THREE **Life and Death**

1. *R. v. Morgentaler,* 1988 CanLII 90. The paragraph references in the end notes below are to this citation.

2. Kent Roach, *The Supreme Court on Trial: Judicial Activism or Democratic Dialogue* (Toronto: Irwin Book, 2001), 193.

3. Robert Sharpe and Kent Roach, in their biography of Brian Dickson, have written about the Supreme Court's internal deliberations in *Morgentaler,* drawing upon Dickson's papers. See *Brian Dickson: A Judge's Journey* (Toronto: The Osgoode Society, 2003).

4. Quoted by Sharpe and Roach, 22.

5. Paragraph 22.

6. Paragraph 47 of Dickson's judgment:

   Consider then the case of a pregnant married woman who wishes to apply for a therapeutic abortion certificate because she fears that her psychological health would be impaired seriously if she carried the foetus to term. The uncontroverted evidence reveals that there are many areas in Canada where such a woman would simply not have access to a therapeutic abortion. She may live in an area where no hospital has four doctors; no therapeutic abortion committee can be created. Equally, she may live in a place where the treatment functions of the nearby hospitals do not satisfy the definition of "accredited hospital" in s. 251(6). Or she may live in a province where the provincial government has imposed such stringent requirements on hospitals seeking to create therapeutic abortion committees that no hospital can qualify. Alternatively, our hypothetical woman may confront a therapeutic abortion committee in her local hospital which defines "health" in purely physical terms or which refuses to countenance abortions for married women. In each of these cases, it is the administrative structures and procedures established by s. 251 itself that would in practice prevent the woman from gaining the benefit of the defence held out to her in s. 251(4).

7. Paragraph 217.

8. Paragraphs 238–239.

9. Paragraphs 190–191.

10. Paragraph 215.

11. W.H. McConnell, *William R. McIntyre: Paladin of the Common Law* (Montreal: Carleton University Press, 2000), 65.

12. McIntyre's death in 2009 prompted a re-evaluation of his judicial career that some observers might find ironic. In an obituary, Kirk Makin of *The Globe and Mail* quoted lawyers who now described McIntyre as a "civil libertarian," "a tremendous supporter of the Charter," "an important tempering voice," and "20 years ahead of his time." Kirk Makin, "William McIntyre was wrongly labelled an arch-conservative," *The Globe and Mail,* 17 June 2009, R5.

13. "Morgentaler's victory transcends abortion issue," *Toronto Star,* 30 January 2008, AA6.

14. "It's time to talk about abortion," *Maclean's,* 21 July 2008, 16.
15. See Stanley Tromp, "Mulroney gov't wrestled with abortion debate," *The Gazette* (Montreal), 29 June 2009, www.montrealgazette.com/news/Mulroney+wrestled+with+abortion+debate+Documents/1744477/story.html (accessed 1 July 2009).
16. For minutes of all the meetings, see www.canada.com/pdf/1988cabinetminutes.pdf (accessed 1 July 2009).
17. Richard A. Posner, *How Judges Think* (Cambridge: Harvard University Press, 2008), 286.
18. These quotations are from Sarah Barmak and Richard Brennan, "'I deserve' Order of Canada, Morgentaler says," *Toronto Star,* 2 July 2008, www.thestar.com/prntArticle/452487 (accessed 3 July 2008).
19. See www.nanosresearch.com/news/in_the_news/Globe%20and%20Mail%20August%2014%202009.pdf (accessed 22 August 2010).
20. *Shape the Future of Health Care,* Commission on the Future of Health Care in Canada, Interim Report, February 2002, 3.
21. *Chaoulli v. Quebec (Attorney General),* 2005 SCC 35 (CanLII). The paragraph references in the endnotes below are to this citation.
22. Quoted by Graeme Hamilton, "Crusading doctor seen as rebel," *National Post,* 10 June 2005, A5.
23. Section 15 of the Health Insurance Act, R.S.Q., c. A-29, and section 11 of the Hospital Insurance Act, R.S.Q., c. A-28.
24. R.S.Q., c. C-12.
25. Paragraph 4.
26. Paragraphs 87–90.
27. Paragraph 107.
28. Paragraph 124.
29. Paragraph 161.
30. "The Supreme Court decision that will change Canada," *Ottawa Citizen,* 10 June 2005, A1.
31. "Our top court comes under scrutiny," *Toronto Star,* 17 June 2005, A23.
32. Graeme Hamilton, "Crusading doctor seen as a rebel," *National Post,* 10 June 2005, A5.
33. For example, in 2008 the British Columbia Automobile Association offered its members insurance that would cover the cost of a private medical clinic in B.C. or in the United States if they are on a Canadian waiting list for longer than forty-five days.
34. See D. Cohn, "*Chaoulli* Five Years On: All Bark and No Bite?" a paper presented at the 2010 annual meeting of the Canadian Political Science Association, www.cpsa-acsp.ca/papers-2010/Cohn.pdf (accessed 23 August 2010).
35. See André Picard, "Private health care slips under radar," *The Globe and Mail,* 17 July 2009, www.theglobeandmail.com/life/health/private-health-care-slips-under-radar/article1220145/ (accessed 22 July 2009).
36. Peggy Curran, "Your money, your health," *The Gazette* (Montreal), 3 October 2010 www.montrealgazette.com/health/Your+Money+Your+Health/3614174/story.html (accessed 14 October 2010).

37. Arnold Relman, "Health Care: The Disquieting Truth," *The New York Review*, 30 September 2010, 45.
38. Janice Tibbetts, "Judges must consider medical wishes of 'mature minors,' Supreme Court rules," *The Vancouver Sun*, 27 June 2009, B3.
39. C.C.S.M. c. C80. The relevant provisions state:
    25(8) Subject to subsection (9), upon completion of a hearing, the court may authorize a medical examination or any medical or dental treatment that the court considers to be in the best interests of the child.
    25(9) The court shall not make an order under subsection (8) with respect to a child who is 16 years of age or older without the child's consent unless the court is satisfied that the child is unable
    (a) to understand the information that is relevant to making a decision to consent or not consent to the medical examination or the medical or dental treatment; or
    (b) to appreciate the reasonably foreseeable consequences of making a decision to consent or not consent to the medical examination or the medical or dental treatment.
40. This appeared in an affidavit filed with the Supreme Court, and is quoted by Tibbetts, note 38.
41. *A.C. v. Manitoba (Director of Child and Family Services)*, 2009 SCC 30 (CanLII). The paragraph references in the endnotes below are to this citation.
42. Paragraph 21.
43. Paragraph 46.
44. Paragraph 87.
45. Paragraph 98.
46. Paragraph 143.
47. Paragraph 162.
48. "Immaturity is no mere stereotype," *The Globe and Mail*, 1 July 2009, www.theglobeandmail.com/news/opinions/editorials/immaturity-is-no-mere-stereotype/article1203067/ (accessed 10 July 2009).
49. *Rodriguez v. British Columbia (Attorney General)*, 1993 CanLII 75 (S.C.C.). The page references in the endnotes below are to this citation.
50. Page 79.
51. Pages 84–85.
52. Page 86.
53. Page 105.
54. Page 33.
55. Pages 59–60.
56. Pages 115–16.
57. Page 130.
58. For example, in 2006 Marielle Houle pleaded guilty to assisting the suicide of her son, and was sentenced to three years' probation. *R. c. Houle*, [2006] R.J.Q. 787.
59. Kirk Makin, "Ten years as top judge and she's still losing sleep," *The Globe and Mail*, 7 January 2010, www.theglobeandmail.com/news/national/ten-years-as-top-judge-and-shes-still-losing-sleep/article1421731/ (accessed 10 January 2010).

FOUR **The Bedrooms of the Nation**

1. *Vriend v. Alberta,* 1998 CanLII 816 (S.C.C.). Paragraph references in the endnotes below are to this citation.
2. Reported by Marina Jimenez, "College flock divided over firing of gay instructor: Individual's rights versus institution's dogma," *Edmonton Journal,* 1 February 1991, B1.
3. R.S.A. 1980, c. I-2. The Act was amended after Vriend made his 1992 claim (by the Individual's Rights Protection Amendment Act, 1996, S.A. 1996, c. 25). At the time of the Supreme Court hearing, the statute was known as the Human Rights, Citizenship and Multiculturalism Act.
4. Paragraph 53.
5. Paragraph 56.
6. Paragraph 80.
7. See paragraphs 131-142.
8. See Donald R, Songer, *The Transformation of the Supreme Court of Canada: An Empirical Examination* (Toronto: University of Toronto Press, 2008), 6.
9. For a full analysis of media reaction to *Vriend,* see Florian Sauvegeau, David Schneiderman, and David Taras, *The Last Word: Media Coverage of the Supreme Court of Canada* (Vancouver: UBC Press, 2006), chapter 2.
10. Reported by Joe Woodward, "Landmark case only one battle in an ongoing fight," *Calgary Herald,* 9 April 2000, A13.
11. Joe Woodward, "A ruling for the ruling class," *Ottawa Citizen,* 7 April 1998, A15.
12. Quoted by Paula Simons, "Long, rocky road to a rights ruling," *Edmonton Journal,* 11 April 1998, F1.
13. C.L. Ostberg and Matthew E. Weinstein, *Attitudinal Decision Making in the Supreme Court of Canada,* (Vancouver, UBC Press, 2007), 135.
14. Quoted by Ian Hunter, "Equality in slavery," *National Post,* 27 May 1999, A19.
15. Sheila Pratt, "Reluctant gay rights hero seeks serenity abroad," *Edmonton Journal,* 30 March 2008, A1.
16. The judge was referring to the cases of *EGALE Canada Inc. v. Canada (Attorney General)* 2002 BBCA 396 (CanLII) (B.C. Court of Appeal); *Halpern v. Canada (Attorney General)* 2003 CanLII 26403 (Ontario Court of Appeal); and *Hendricks v. Quebec (Procureur général),* 2002 CanLII 23808 (Quebec Superior Court).
17. *Reference re Same-Sex Marriage* 2004 SCC 79 (CanLII), paragraph 11. The paragraph references in the endnotes below are to this citation.
18. Paragraph 22.
19. Paragraph 46.
20. Paragraph 60.
21. "Stop! In the name of love (for Canada)," *The Globe and Mail,* 2 February 2005, A15.
22. S.C. 2005, c.33.
23. "Bill C-38: The Civil Marriage Act," *Legislative Summaries,* Library of Parliament, www.parl.gc.ca/common/bills_ls.asp?Parl=38&Ses=1&ls=c38 (accessed 20 July 2008).

24. Clifford Kraus, "Gay Marriage Is Extended Nationwide in Canada," *The New York Times,* 29 June 2005, www.nytimes.com/2005/06/29/international/americas/29canada.html?pagewanted=print (accessed 20 July 2008).

25. See Cristin Schmitz, "A view from the top: Justice LeBel speaks," *The Lawyers Weekly,* 30 April 2010 www.lawyersweekly.ca/index.php?section=article&article id=1152 (accessed 15 May 2010).

26. In his chambers, 25 May 2010.

27. Don Butler, "Charting the impact of the Charter; Canadians love their Charter of Rights and Freedoms—even if they don't know much about it," *Ottawa Citizen,* 15 April 2007, A6.

28. *R. v. Labaye,* 2005 SCC 80 (CanLII). Paragraph references in the endnotes below are to this citation. *R. v. Kouri,* [2005] 3 S.C.R. 789, a so-called "companion case," was decided at the same time. In *Kouri,* the accused operated a Montreal bar in which, every half-hour, a translucent curtain closed around the dance floor and people engaged in group sex. The accused's acquittal on a charge of keeping a bawdy house was affirmed by the Supreme Court, Bastarache and LeBel dissenting.

29. Paragraph 30. Paragraph 62 of McLachlin's judgment has a full summary of the test: Indecent criminal conduct will be established where the Crown proves beyond a reasonable doubt the following two requirements: 1. That, by its *nature,* the conduct at issue causes harm or presents a significant risk of harm to individuals or society in a way that undermines or threatens to undermine a value reflected in and thus formally endorsed through the Constitution or similar fundamental laws by, for example: (a) confronting members of the public with conduct that significantly interferes with their autonomy and liberty; or (b) predisposing others to anti-social behaviour; or (c) physically or psychologically harming persons involved in the conduct, and 2. That the harm or risk of harm is of a *degree* that is incompatible with the proper functioning of society.

30. "Supreme Court swings in favour of group-sex clubs," Canwest News Service, 21 December 2005, www.canada.com/topics/news/story.html?id=df5ac2e9-351c-4973-bbf2-756403fb1184 (accessed 29 September 2009).

31. Paragraph 81.

32. Paragraph 137.

33. 23 December 2005, A30.

34. "Redefining perversion," *National Post,* 28 December 2005, A18.

35. Quoted by Joe Woodward, "Canada's 'culture of modesty' under attack," *Calgary Herald,* 15 January 2006, B5.

36. Andrea Houston, "Bringing sexy back to the Church St Village," *Xtra!,* 12 November 2010, www.xtra.ca/public/National/Bringing_sexy_back_to_the_Church_St_Village-9422.aspx (accessed 15 November 2010).

FIVE **True Believers**

1. *Syndicat Northcrest v. Amselem,* 2004 SCC 47 (CanLII). Paragraph references in the endnotes below are to this citation.

2. Paragraph 52.

3. Section 6 of the Quebec Charter reads: "Every person has a right to the peaceful enjoyment and free disposition of his property, except to the extent provided by

law." Section 1 reads: "Every human being has a right to life, and to personal security, inviolability and freedom."

4. Paragraph 84.
5. Paragraph 87.
6. Paragraph 135.
7. Paragraphs 184–185.
8. Julius Grey, "A peculiar Canadian paradox," *The Globe and Mail*, 13 September 2007, A19.
9. "Supreme Court never fails to astonish," *The Gazette*, 8 July 2004, A25.
10. "Supreme Court was way out of line with kirpan ruling," *The Gazette*, 8 March 2006, A27.
11. *Alberta v. Hutterian Brethren of Wilson Colony*, 2009 SCC 37 (CanLII). Paragraph references in the endnotes below are to this citation.
12. Paragraph 4.
13. Paragraphs 36–37.
14. Sue Bailey, "Hutterites lose Old World–New World court clash over photos," Canadian Press, 25 July 2009, www.canadaeast.com/search/article/739441 (accessed 23 September 2009).
15. Paragraph 115.
16. Quoted by Bailey, note 14.
17. "No real risk of identity theft," *The Globe and Mail*, 28 July 2009, http:// v1.theglobeandmail.com/servlet/story/LAC.20090801.ASELF01ART1155/ TPStory/TPEntertainment/?pageRequested=2 (accessed 28 July 2009).
18. Ian Mulgrew, "Canada's guarantees of religious freedom face multiple threats," *The Vancouver Sun*, 26 April 2010, www.vancouversun.com/news/Canada+guarantees +religious+freedom+face+multiple+threats/2951495/story.html (accessed 30 April 2010).
19. Colby Cosh, "Say cheese!" *National Post*, 28 July 2009, www.nationalpost.com/ scripts/story.html?id=1834729 (accessed 26 September 2009).
20. "A fine balance," *Ottawa Citizen*, 29 July 2009, www.ottawacitizen.com/news/ fine+balance/1839392/story.html (accessed 26 September 2009).
21. The trial judge noted in his judgment (*Delgamuukw v. British Columbia*, 1991 CanLII 2372):

> A total of 61 witnesses gave evidence at trial, many using translators from their native Gitksan or Wet'suwet'en language; "word spellers" to assist the official reporters were required for many witnesses; a further 15 witnesses gave their evidence on commission; 53 territorial affidavits were filed; 30 deponents were cross-examined out of court; there are 23,503 pages of transcript evidence at trial; 5,898 pages of transcript of argument; 3,039 pages of commission evidence and 2,553 pages of cross-examination on affidavits (all evidence and oral arguments are conveniently preserved in hard copy and on diskettes); about 9,200 exhibits were filed at trial comprising, I estimate, well over 50,000 pages; the plaintiffs' draft outline of argument comprises 3,250 pages, the province's 1,975 pages, and Canada's over 1,000 pages; there are 5,977 pages of transcript of argument in hard copy and on diskettes. All parties filed some excerpts from the exhibits they referred to in argument. The province alone submitted 28 huge

binders of such documents. At least 15 binders of reply argument were left with me during that stage of the trial.

22. *Delgamuukw v. British Columbia,* 1997 CanLII 302. Paragraph references in the endnotes below are to this citation.

23. Paragraph 111.

24. Paragraphs 128–129.

25. "A distant court, an imprudent decision," *The Vancouver Sun,* 20 December 1997, A21.

26. "Who owns this land? Aboriginal rights cast pall over B.C. economy," *The Globe and Mail,* 6 June 1998, A1.

27. "Natives ponder future of difficult victory," *The Globe and Mail,* 8 June 1998, A4.

28. "Delgamuukw ruling makes a bad situation worse," *The Windsor Star,* 20 June 1998, H2.

29. Troy Donovan Hunter, "Aboriginal court judgment must be honoured," *Times Colonist* (Victoria), 12 October 2010, www.timescolonist.com/story_print. html?id=3656363&sponsor= (accessed 15 October 2010).

30. Shawn McCarthy, "At what price 'white man's money'?" *The Globe and Mail,* 20 July 2009, www.theglobeandmail.com/news/politics/at-what-price-white-mans-money/article1223426/ (accessed 13 September 2009).

31. The government asked the court to answer three questions:
    1. Under the Constitution of Canada, can the National Assembly, legislature or government of Quebec effect the secession of Quebec from Canada unilaterally?
    2. Does international law give the National Assembly, legislature or government of Quebec the right to effect the secession of Quebec from Canada unilaterally? In this regard, is there a right to self-determination under international law that would give the National Assembly, legislature or government of Quebec the right to effect the secession of Quebec from Canada unilaterally?
    3. In the event of a conflict between domestic and international law on the right of the National Assembly, legislature or government of Quebec to effect the secession of Quebec from Canada unilaterally, which would take precedence in Canada?

32. See William Johnston, "Still speaking with forked tongues: The Supreme Court's historic Quebec secession ruling has been misinterpreted for a decade," *The Globe and Mail,* 20 August 2008, A17.

33. Hauser Global Law School Program, NYU School of Law, Distinguished Fellow Lecture Series, "To Be a Chief Justice: A Conversation with Chief Justice Beverley McLachlin," 29 March 2004, www.nyulawglobal.org/events/dfls/documents/McLachlin_script.rtf (accessed 3 October 2008).

34. See Gretta Chambers, "Covering the Case of the Century," *The Gazette* (Montreal), 20 February 1998, B3.

35. Norma Greenaway, "Passions mount as Supreme Court hears case against Quebec secession," *The Record* (Kitchener–Waterloo), 17 February 1998, A1.

36. Lorne Sossin of the University of Toronto wrote in *The Globe and Mail* that "deciding not to decide is the only just decision" because of "the harm that deciding cases in the abstract can produce, not least by diminishing public confidence

in the Supreme Court itself." Patrick Monahan of Osgoode Hall Law School, writing in the same newspaper, described it as "baffling" that "otherwise sensible commentators from outside Quebec, including the editorial board of *The Globe and Mail*, have questioned the wisdom of the Supreme Court reference." Lorne Sossin, "The Supreme Court should decide not to decide Quebec Secession," *The Globe and Mail*, 24 February 1998, A17; Patrick Monahan, "Why the court reference made sense," *The Globe and Mail*, 5 March 1998, A19.

37. *Reference re Secession of Quebec*, 1998, CanLII 793. Paragraph references in the endnotes below are to this citation.

38. Paragraph 32.

39. Paragraph 77.

40. Paragraph 104.

41. Sujit Choudhry and Robert Howse, "Constitutional Theory and *The Quebec Secession Reference*," *Canadian Journal of Law and Jurisprudence*, Vol. XIII, No.2 (July 2000), 143.

42. NYU interview, note 33.

43. *Charkaoui v. Canada (Citizenship and Immigration)*, 2008 SCC 38 (CanLII). Paragraph references in the endnotes below are to this citation. For an interesting account of how the judges behaved during the hearing, see Kirk Makin, "Case illuminates court's inner workings," *The Globe and Mail*, 16 June 2006, A8. Two other appellants in the case, Mohamed Harkat and Hassan Almrei, were refugees living in Canada. They were also suspected of having links to al-Qaeda. In December 2009, the Federal Court quashed the Almrei security certificate on the grounds that the information provided in support of the certificate was inadequate.

44. S.C. 2001, c. 27.

45. Section 77(2) of IRPA says: "The Minister shall file with the Court the information and other evidence on which the certificate is based, and a summary of information and other evidence that enables the person who is named in the certificate to be reasonably informed of the case made by the Minister but that does not include anything that, in the Minister's opinion, would be injurious to national security or endanger the safety of any person if disclosed."

46. In his 2010 commencement speech at Harvard. See http://news.harvard.edu/gazette/story/2010/05/text-of-justice-david-souters-speech (accessed 6 June 2010).

47. Quoted by Janice Tibbetts, "Judge questions right of security above all," *National Post*, 15 June 2006, A4.

48. Paragraph 28.

49. Paragraph 65. Section 7 of the Charter says, "Everyone has the right to life, liberty and security of the person and the right not to be deprived thereof except in accordance with the principles of fundamental justice." The full text of the Charter is reprinted in Appendix B of this book.

50. Paragraph 87.

51. *Charkaoui v. Canada (Citizenship and Immigration)*, 2008 SCC 38 (CanLII).

52. Colin Freeze, "R. v. Charkaoui: A David and Goliath story," *The Globe and Mail*, 24 September 2009, www.theglobeandmail.com/news/national/r-v-charkaoui/article1300159 (accessed 28 September 2009).

53. *Re Charkaoui*, 2009 CF 1030 (CanLII).
54. "Frustrating standoff," *The Globe and Mail*, 26 September 2009, www. theglobeandmail.com/news/opinions/editorials/frustrating-standoff/article 1302738 (accessed 28 September 2009).
55. "Justice prevails in security cases," *Toronto Star*, 30 September 2009, www.thestar.com/article/702820 (accessed 5 October 2009).
56. The full text of the speech can be found on the Supreme Court website; seewww.scc-csc.gc.ca/court-cour/ju/spe-dis/bm2009-09-22-eng.asp (accessed 13 January 2010). McLachlin also discussed the *Charkaoui* case at some length in a speech she gave in Charlottetown on October 21, 2008: Sixth Annual Symons Lecture on the State of Canadian Confederation www.cpac.ca/forms/index.asp?dsp=template&act =view3&pagetype=vod&hl=e&clipID=2074 (accessed 19 October 2010).
57. "McLachlin's fine line," *National Post*, 24 September 2009, www.nationalpost.com/opinion/story.html?id=2026176 (accessed 28 September 2009).

SIX   True Crime

1. Cristin Schmitz, "Supreme Court of Canada appointments must be non-partisan: McLachlin," *The Lawyers Weekly*, 15 January 2010, www.lawyersweekly.ca/index.php p?section=article&volume=29&number=33&article=1 (accessed 13 January 2010).
2. 2009 SCC 32 (CanLII). Paragraph references in the endnotes below are to this citation.
3. "'And the winner is ...'": The First Annual OZZY Awards," www.thecourt.ca/2010/02/24/introducing-the-first-annual-ozzy-awards.
4. "Tainted evidence can be used to convict: court," *The Globe and Mail*, 18 July 2009, A4.
5. See Adam Liptak, "The Roberts Court Comes of Age," *The New York Times*, 30 June 2010, http://query.nytimes.com/gst/fullpage.html?res=9406E7DF163CF9 33A05755C0A9669D8B63&scp=2&sq=liptak%20%22roberts%20court%20 comes%20of%20age%22&st=cse (accessed 17 September 2010).
6. See Supreme Court of Canada, "Bulletin of Proceedings: Special Edition, Statistics 1999–2009," www.scc-csc.gc.ca/stat/pdf/doc-eng.pdf (accessed 22 March 2010).
7. Paragraph 153.
8. Stuart's academic writings were quoted several times in *R. v. Grant*. He appeared in the case as counsel to the Canadian Civil Liberties Association, an intervener, and has expressed pleasure at the decision. See Robert Todd, "New test for tainted evidence," *Law Times*, 27 July 2009,   www.lawtimesnews.com/200907275133/ Headline-News/New-test-for-tainted-evidence (accessed 18 January 2010).
9. Reported by Kirk Makin, "Court report card," *The Globe and Mail*, 25 June 2009, www.theglobeandmail.com/news/national/court-report-card/article1190488/ (accessed 29 June 2009).
10. Quoted in the judgment of Chief Justice McLachlin and Justice Charron, paragraph 7.
11. Paragraph 12.
12. Paragraph 44.
13. Paragraph 50.
14. Paragraph 85.

15. Paragraph 140.
16. There was a surprise at the end of the judgment. Grant had been convicted of possessing a firearm for the purposes of transferring it, under s.100(1) of the Criminal Code. McLachlin and Charron thought that both the trial judge and the Ontario Court of Appeal took too broad a view of the meaning of "transfer." Just moving the gun from one place to another was not a transfer. Donnohue Grant was acquitted on the arms trafficking charge. He became an outreach worker, counselling youth to avoid drugs. See Kelly Grant, "Where public housing meets the market," *The Globe and Mail,* 24 April 2010, M1.
17. Paragraph 151.
18. Paragraph 195.
19. Paragraph 209.
20. *R. v. Wray,* 1970 CanLII 2 (S.C.C.).
21. 2009 SCC 33 (CanLII). Paragraph references in the endnotes below are to this citation.
22. Paragraph 50.
23. 2009 SCC 35 (CanLII).
24. 2009 SCC 34 (CanLII). Paragraph references in the endnotes below are to this citation.
25. Paragraph 3.
26. Paragraph 44.
27. "Fair suspicion, not caprice," *The Globe and Mail,* 7 December 2009, A14. *The Globe*'s editorial was peculiar. It seemed to think that *Grant,* where the gun was allowed into evidence, and which is generally regarded as somewhat pro-police, was not that at all ("The police have an important job to do. It is becoming harder all the time, as the Supreme Court loads more on to the expectation of privacy than it can reasonably bear").
28. 2009 SCC 57 (CanLII). Paragraph references in the endnotes below are to this citation.
29. Paragraph 3.
30. Quoted in paragraph 6.
31. *R. v. Patrick,* 2009 SCC 17. Paragraph references in the endnotes below are to this citation.
32. Paragraph 13.
33. Paragraph 30.
34. Paragraph 32.
35. Paragraph 55.
36. Paragraph 73.
37. Paragraph 77.
38. 2010 SCC 31. Paragraph references in the endnotes below are to this citation.
39. Paragraph 46.
40. Paragraph 80.
41. Paragraphs 115–116.
42. Paragraph 120.
43. *R. v. Sinclair,* 2010 SCC 35; *R. v. McCrimmon,* 2010 SCC 36; *R. v. Willier,* 2010 SCC 37.

44. "The right to counsel, diminished," *The Globe and Mail,* 8 October 2010, www.theglobeandmail.com/news/opinions/editorials/the-right-to-counsel-diminished/article1750413 (accessed 16 October 2010).

45. Quoted by Tim Naumetz, "Defence lawyers reeling at SCC rulings on right to counsel," *Law Times,* 18 October 2010, 4.

46. Kirk Makin, "No right to counsel during interrogation: top court," *The Globe and Mail,* 8 October 2010, www.theglobeandmail.com/news/national/no-right-to-a-lawyer-during-interrogation-supreme-court-rules/article1749557/ (accessed 16 October 2010).

47. *Sinclair,* Paragraph 86.

48. Paragraph 131.

49. Paragraph 125.

50. Paragraph 172.

SEVEN **Money Talks**

1. Donald Songer points out that since 1975 the court "has been transformed from a Court primarily concerned with resolving private disputes between individuals and businesses into a court of public law." (In 1975, appeals as of right were abolished in almost all cases.) Donald R. Songer, *The Transformation of the Supreme Court of Canada: An Empirical Examination* (Toronto: University of Toronto Press, 2008), 58. But that doesn't mean the court has been doing nothing in private law. For example, Anthony Duggan, of the University of Toronto faculty of law, has written, "During the period 1989–2009, the Supreme Court substantially reshaped the law of fiduciary obligations …" "Fiduciary Obligations in the Supreme Court of Canada: A Retrospective" (May 5, 2010), available at the Social Science Research Network: http://papers.ssrn.com/sol3/papers.cfm?abstract_id=1600928.

2. See Supreme Court of Canada, "Bulletin of Proceedings: Special Edition, Statistics 1999 to 2009," www.scc-csc.gc.ca/stat/pdf/doc-eng.pdf (accessed 22 March 2010).

3. An earlier version of my discussion of the *BCE* case appeared in *Canadian Lawyer,* August 2008, 24.

4. *BCE Inc. v. 1976 Debentureholders,* 2008 SCC 69 (CanLII). Page references in the endnotes below are to this citation.

5. *BCE inc. (Arrangement relatif à),* 2008 QCCA 935 (CanLII).

6. "BCE ruling misreads equity vs. debt," *The Globe and Mail,* 22 May 2008, www.farris.com/images/pdf_archive/ALH-BCERuling.pdf (accessed 1 September 2008).

7. "Court 'functioning at its best' on BCE," *The Globe and Mail,* 20 August 2008, B1.

8. In an interview in her chambers, 10 June 2010.

9. In an email to the author, 14 June 2010.

10. See Jacquie McNish, Derek Decloet, and Sinclair Stewart, "How a tiny clause spelled the end of the biggest deal," *The Globe and Mail,* 26 November 2008, http://v1.theglobeandmail.com/servlet/story/RTGAM.20081126.wbcetictock27/GSStory/Business (accessed 12 February 2010).

11. R.S., 1985, c. C-44. Section 241(2) reads:
    If, on an application under subsection (1), the court is satisfied that in respect of a corporation or any of its affiliates

(*a*) any act or omission of the corporation or any of its affiliates effects a result,

(*b*) the business or affairs of the corporation or any of its affiliates are or have been carried on or conducted in a manner, or

(*c*) the powers of the directors of the corporation or any of its affiliates are or have been exercised in a manner that is oppressive or unfairly prejudicial to or that unfairly disregards the interests of any security holder, creditor, director or officer, the court may make an order to rectify the matters complained of.

12. Paragraph 113.

13. *Metcalfe & Mansfield Alternative Investments II Corp., (Re)*, 2008 ONCA 587 (CanLII). Page 4 of the judgment gives a description of asset-backed commercial paper:

Asset Backed Commercial Paper is a sophisticated and hitherto well-accepted financial instrument. It is primarily a form of short-term investment—usually 30 to 90 days—typically with a low interest yield only slightly better than that available through other short-term paper from a government or bank. It is said to be "asset backed" because the cash that is used to purchase an ABCP Note is converted into a portfolio of financial assets or other asset interests that in turn provide security for the repayment of the notes.

14. R.S.C. 1985, c. C-36 as amended.

15. All quoted by Julius Melnitzer, "Lawyers surprised top court denies leave in ABCP," *Law Times*, 29 September 2008, 1.

16. *Confédération des syndicats nationaux v. Canada (Attorney General)*, 2008 SCC 68 (CanLII).

17. Paragraph 1.

18. "53. Bills for appropriating any Part of the Public Revenue, or for imposing any Tax or Impost, shall originate in the House of Commons."

19. "Making good use of EI to repay old mistake," *The Chronicle-Herald* (Halifax), 3 January 2009.

20. *Lipson v. Canada*, 2009 SCC 1 (CanLII). Paragraph references in the endnotes below are to this citation.

21. Quoted by Cristin Schmitz, "Top court boosts tax avoidance rule," *The Lawyers Weekly*, 23 January 2009, www.lawyersweekly.ca/index.php?section=article&articleid=840 (accessed 3 May 2009).

22. R.S.C. 1985, c. 1 (5th Supp.).

23. Paragraph 119.

24. Section 245(1) reads:

Subsection (2) [i.e. the denial of a tax benefit] applies to a transaction only if it may reasonably be considered that the transaction

(*a*) would, if this Act were read without reference to this section, result directly or indirectly in a misuse of the provisions of any one or more of

(i) this Act,

(ii) the *Income Tax Regulations*,

(iii) the *Income Tax Application Rules*,

(iv) a tax treaty, or

(v) any other enactment that is relevant in computing tax or any other amount payable by or refundable to a person under this Act or in determining any amount that is relevant for the purposes of that computation; or

(*b*) would result directly or indirectly in an abuse having regard to those provisions, other than this section, read as a whole.

25. Paragraph 61.
26. *Nolan v. Kerry (Canada) Inc.,* 2009 SCC 39 (CanLII). Paragraph references in the endnotes below are to this citation.
27. Paragraph 70.
28. Paragraph 134.
29. Paragraph 147.
30. "*Nolan v. Kerry* and Its Place in Pension Deliberation," www.thecourt.ca/2009/08/22/nolan-v-kerry-and-its-place-in-pension-deliberation (accessed 5 October 2009).

EIGHT **Pretty Sweet Work**

1. Some of this chapter appeared in an earlier form in my article "Ottawa's Best-Kept Secret?" *Maclean's,* 2 February 2009, 20.
2. R.S., 1985, c. S-26.
3. "Minister Calls for Newfoundland and Labrador Representation on Supreme Court of Canada," news release of the Government of Newfoundland and Labrador, 16 April 2008, www.releases.gov.nl.ca/releases/2008/just/0416n06.htm (accessed 29 June 2008).
4. Quoted by Kirk Makin, "Newfoundland seeks judge on Supreme Court," *The Globe and Mail,* 28 May 2008, A9.
5. "Kennedy's comments curioser and curioser," *The Telegram,* 31 May 2008, www.thetelegram.com/index.cfm?sid=139585&sc=86 (accessed 30 June 2008).
6. See Janice Tibbetts, "Lawyers want in on Supreme Court justice hearings," *The Vancouver Sun,* 20 April 2008, www.canada.com/vancouversun/story.html?id=f74045f8-1d05-4124-89bf-42a318e63769&k=97910 (accessed 29 June 2008).
7. Bernard Amyot, "A judge's personal beliefs should be off limits," *Toronto Star,* 4 May 2008, www.thestar.com/columnists/article/420907 (accessed 29 June 2008).
8. Senate Committee on the Judiciary: S. Hrg. 109-158, Confirmation Hearing on the Nomination of John G. Roberts, Jr. to be Chief Justice of the United States, 2, www.gpoaccess.gov/congress/senate/judiciary/sh109-158/2-4.pdf (accessed 29 June 2008).
9. This process goes on even when there are no vacancies and no retirements imminent. See Cristin Schmitz, "Lawyers debate what makes top court candidates supreme," *The Lawyers Weekly,* 12 March 2010, www.lawyersweekly.ca/index.php?section=article&volume=29&number=41&article=5 (accessed 10 March 2010).
10. Janice Tibbetts, "Bilingualism not a priority for top court, ex-judge says," *The Gazette* (Montreal), 8 May 2008, www.canada.com/montrealgazette/news/story.html?id=2b92b955-c2a4-48a1-a334-55391f29d784 (accessed 30 June 2008).
11. "High-court bilingualism is supremely desirable," *The Gazette* (Montreal), 13 May 2008, www.canada.com/montrealgazette/news/editorial/story.html?id=e2e6b2e0-9d63-43df-acab-885f869534ce (accessed 30 June 2008).
12. "Denis Coderre's bad idea," *National Post,* 16 May 2008, A14.

13. Rhéal Séguin, "Quebec issues demand for bilingual judges," *The Globe and Mail,* 22 May 2008, A4.

14. 28 May 2008, A16.

15. "To mandatory bilingualism, just say 'non'," The *Globe and Mail,* 27 May 2008, A17.

16. "Bilingual judges is the perfect accommodation," *The Globe and Mail,* 29 May 2008, A17.

17. "Canada's top court needs the most competent jurists—and they're bilingual," *The Globe and Mail,* 3 June 2008, http://listserv.linguistlist.org/cgi-bin/wa?A2=ind0806&L=lgpolicy-list&P=4783 (accessed 7 April 2009).

18. Kirk Makin, "Newfoundland wants judge on the Supreme Court," *The Globe and Mail,* 28 May 2008, http://license.icopyright.net/user/viewContent.act?tag=3.7441%3Ficx_id%3D%2FLAC.20080528.APPOINT28%2FTPStory%2FTPNational%2FAtlantic (accessed 29 June 2008).

19. See Kirk Makin, "Newfoundland lawyer accused of misconduct," *The Globe and Mail,* 15 January 2005, A12.

20. In May 2009, New Democratic Party member of Parliament Yvon Godin introduced a private member's bill, Bill C-232, requiring future Supreme Court appointees to be bilingual. The bill was passed in the House of Commons, with Conservatives opposed but all the opposition parties voting in favour. It is currently before the Senate. See the discussion in the Conclusion.

21. Kirk Makin, "Court 'functioning at its best' on BCE," *The Globe and Mail,* 20 August 2008, B1.

22. Quoted by Cristin Schmitz, "Seven Supreme Court of Canada judges could retire in 2010," *The Lawyers Weekly,* 26 February 2010, www.lawyersweekly.ca/index.php?section=article&articleid=1108 (accessed 23 March 2010).

23. Janice Tibbetts, "High court lacks allure for Quebec judges," *National Post,* 18 June 2002, A8.

24. R.S.C. 1985, c. J-1.

25. *Reference re Remuneration of Judges of the Provincial Court (P.E.I.),* 1997 CanLII 317 (S.C.R.).

26. Adam Dodek, "Chief Justice Lamer and Policy Design at the Supreme Court of Canada," 2009 46 *Supreme Court Law Review (2d)* 93, 97.

27. See www.quadcom.gc.ca/Media/Pdf/2007/RapportFinalEn.pdf (accessed 5 April 2009).

28. See www.quadcom.gc.ca/Media/Pdf/2009/NewsReleaseGovResponse.pdf (accessed 23 March 2010).

29. See www.supremecourtus.gov/publicinfo/year-end/2006year-endreport.pdf (accessed 5 April 2009).

30. "How much should judges make?" 20 January 2009, www.nytimes.com/2009/01/20/washington/20bar.html?_r=1&scp=5&sq=liptak%20pay&st=cse (accessed 5 April 2009).

31. "Should we pay federal circuit judges more?" 88 B.U. L. Rev. 63 (2008).

32. Stephen J. Choi, G. Mitu Gulati, and Eric A. Posner, "Are Judges Overpaid? A Skeptical Response to the Judicial Salary Debate," The Law School, The University of Chicago, John M. Olin Law and Economics Working Paper No. 376 (2d series),

December 2007, https://www.law.uchicago.edu/files/376.pdf (accessed 7 April 2009).

33. William O. Douglas, *Go East, Young Man: The Early Years* (New York: Random House, 1974), 463, quoted by James MacGregor Burns, *Packing the Court: The Rise of Judicial Power and the Coming Crisis of the Supreme Court* (New York: The Penguin Press, 2009), 160.

34. Supreme Court Act, R.S.C. 1985, c. S-26. S. 4(2) reads: "The judges shall be appointed by the Governor in Council by letters patent under the Great Seal."

35. "Welcome to the court, but fix the entrance," *The Globe and Mail,* 2 August 2003, A14.

36. Chris Purdy, "Appointments OK," *Edmonton Journal,* 8 May 200 4, A1.

37. Kirk Makin, "Osgoode Professors on Chief Justice Beverley McLachlin," *The Globe and Mail,* 8 January 2005, http://osgoode.yorku.ca/media2.nsf/releases/27767BD5 6D67B0E685256F8500700AE7 (accessed 14 November 2008).

38. Kirk Makin, "'Lawyer's lawyer' Binnie named to Supreme Court," *The Globe and Mail,* 9 January 1998, A1.

39. See Irwin Cotler, "The Supreme Court appointment process: chronology, context and reform," *University of New Brunswick Law Journal,* 2008, http://findarticles.com/p/articles/mi_7000/is_58/ai_n28556216/?tag=content;col1 (accessed 7 April 2008).

40. See University of Toronto Faculty of Law, "Chronology of Supreme Court Appointments Reform," www.law-lib.utoronto.ca/conferences/judiciary/chronology .htm (accessed 25 November 2009).

41. Cotler effectively summarizes the reasons for changing the appointments process in his *University of New Brunswick Law Journal* article. See note 39.

42. John Geddes, "Critics Lambaste Review Process for Supreme Court Nominations," *Maclean's,* 6 September 2004, www.thecanadianencyclopedia.com/index.cfm?PgN m=TCE&Params=M1ARTM0012649 (accessed 29 June 2008).

43. See Department of Justice press release, "New Supreme Court of Canada appointments process launched," 8 August 2005, www.justice.gc.ca/eng/news-nouv/nr-cp/2005/doc_31586.html (accessed 29 June 2008).

44. Jacob Ziegel, "Supreme Court selection process needs more thought," *The Globe and Mail,* 13 April 2005, www.theglobeandmail.com/servlet/story/RTGAM.20050413. wwebcomment12/BNStory/National (accessed 29 June 2008).

45. Story told by Rothstein, author interview, 11 June 2010.

46. P.W. Hogg, "Appointment of Justice Marshall Rothstein to the Supreme Court of Canada" (2006) 44 *Osgoode Hall L.J.* 527.

47. Alan Kellogg, "Judge TV just plain optics, not that there's anything wrong with that: Justice Marshall Rothstein deftly handled questions without tipping his hand; let's hope his performance will be repeated on the bench," *Edmonton Journal,* 28 February 2006, A3.

48. "Lightly grilled: Polite, but pointless, the Supreme Court nomination hearing could have used a lot more American style," *Maclean's,* 8 March 2006, www.macleans. ca/article.jsp?content=20060313_122895_122895&source=srch (accessed 29 June 2008).

49. "A show trial in reverse," *andrewcoyne.com,* 1 March 2006, http://andrewcoyne. com/columns/2006/03/show-trial-in-reverse.php (accessed 29 June 2008).

50. Quoted by Cristin Schmitz, "Supreme Court of Canada appointments must be non-partisan: McLachlin," *The Lawyers Weekly,* 15 January 2010 www.lawyersweekly.ca/index.php?section=article&volume=29&number=33&article=1 (accessed 13 January 2010).

51. See Department of Justice press release, "Minister of Justice announces selection process for Supreme Court of Canada," 28 May 2008, www.justice.gc.ca/eng/news-nouv/nr-cp/2008/doc_32258.html (accessed 14 June 2008).

52. Janice Tibbetts, "New judge for top court is not likely by fall," *Ottawa Citizen,* 13 August 2008, A3.

53. Rob Linke, "MP says Harper's comment untrue," *Telegraph-Journal* (Saint John), 10 September 2008, A1.

54. 347 U.S. 483.

55. Further testimony of Hon. Clarence Thomas, of Georgia, to be Associate Justice of the U.S. Supreme Court, *Hearings Before the Committee on the Judiciary, United States Senate, One Hundred Second Congress, First Session, on the Nomination of Clarence Thomas to be Associate Justice of the Supreme Court of the United States.* October 11, 12, and 13, 1991, Part 4 of 4. Washington, DC: Government Printing Office, 1993.

56. Linda Greenhouse, "2,691 Decisions," *The New York Times,* 13 July 2008, www.nytimes.com/2008/07/13/weekinreview/13linda.html?scp=5&sq=greenhouse&st=cse (accessed 13 July 2008).

57. Jeffrey Toobin, "Answer to Questions," *The New Yorker,* 27 July 2009, 19.

58. Christopher Eisgruber, *The Next Justice: Repairing the Supreme Court Appointments Process* (Princeton: Princeton University Press, 2007).

59. Eisgruber, 4.

60. Eisgruber, 99.

61. "How to judge a would-be justice," *The New York Times,* 14 April 2008, www.nytimes.com/2008/04/14/opinion/14mon3.html?scp=6&sq=senate+confirmation&st=nyt (accessed 30 June 2008).

62. Schmitz, note 22.

NINE **The Chief**

1. For example, see Yves Faguy, "A conversation with the Chief Justice," *National* magazine, June 2010, 20. McLachlin often says this: "As I was told when I was first appointed, they hand you the reins of power and it takes you about three days to discover that they aren't connected to anything."

2. An earlier and shorter version of this discussion appeared in *Maclean's*—"Judging Beverley," *Maclean's,* 6 July 2009, 48.

3. Nahlah Ayed, "Chief justice reveals importance of religion in candid TV Interview," *National Post,* 25 May 2000, A11.

4. Quoted by Sean Fine, "The most important woman in Canada," *Saturday Night,* December 1995, 46.

5. Susan Harada, "The McLachlin Group," *The Walrus,* April 2009, www.walrusmagazine.com/articles/2009.05-law-the-mclachlin-group/2/ (accessed 10 April 2009).

6. Hauser Global Law School Program, NYU School of Law, Distinguished Fellow Lecture Series, "To Be a Chief Justice: A Conversation with Chief Justice Beverley

McLachlin," 29 March 2004, www1.law.nyu.edu/nyulawglobal/events/dfls/DFLSMcLauchlin.htm (accessed 19 February 2010).

7. See Statistics Canada, Pincher Creek community profile, http://www12.statcan.ca/english/census06/data/profiles/community/Details/Page.cfm?Lang=E&Geo1=CSD&Code1=4803014&Geo2=PR&Code2=48&Data=Count&SearchText=Pincher%20Creek&SearchType=Begins&SearchPR=01&B1=All&GeoLevel=&GeoCode=4803014 (accessed 17 September 2008).

8. www.cbc.ca/news/canadavotes/riding/261/ridingtalk.html (accessed 25 September 2008).

9. Tracey Tyler, "Small Alberta town, big footprint," *Toronto Star*, 14 October 2007, A7.

10. Gwendolyn Richards, "Menzies takes Macleod handily," *Calgary Herald*, 29 June 2004, AA02.

11. Tamara Gignac, "Farm vote bountiful in Macleod," *Calgary Herald*, 8 January 2006, A4.

12. "Beverley McLachlin: Small-town Justice," Canadian Council on Learning (CCL) interview, 3 April 2008, www.ccl-cca.ca/CCL/Newsroom/Profiles/PILBMcLachlin.html (accessed 3 October 2008).

13. Margaret Wente, "The making of Beverley McLachlin," *The Globe and Mail*, 9 November 1999, A19.

14. See CCL interview, note 12.

15. See Fine, note 4.

16. "New justice 'displayed great promise'," *Edmonton Journal*, 1 April 1989, B1.

17. Neal Hall, "Top chief justice candidates both have B.C. roots," *The Vancouver Sun*, 30 August 1999, A7.

18. See Emily Bazelon, "The place of women on the Court," *The New York Times*, 12 July 2009, www.nytimes.com/2009/07/12/magazine/12ginsburg-t.html (accessed 14 September 2009).

19. See Wente, note 13.

20. See NYU conversation, note 6.

21. This anecdote was told by McLachlin in a speech to the law faculty of the University of British Columbia, 4 February 2010, www.youtube.com/watch?v=GXL8GG0GTv4&NR=1 (accessed 28 February 2010).

22. See "New justice," note 16.

23. "Mulroney appoints 3rd woman to court," *The Globe and Mail*, 31 March 1989, A1.

24. Dan Gardner, "It's an English-speaking world out there," *Ottawa Citizen*, 16 April 2010,www2.canada.com/ottawacitizen/news/archives/story.html?id=aa8e75dd-0c7d-4d25-aafd-4a005a3de021 (accessed 30 November 2010).

25. See Bruce Wallace, "Beverley McLachlin," *Maclean's*, 15 November 1999, reprinted in *The Canadian Encyclopedia*, www.thecanadianencyclopedia.com/index.cfm?PgNm=TCE&Params=M1ARTM0012039 (accessed 6 October 2008).

26. Janice Tibbetts, "A new order in the court," *The Vancouver Sun*, 22 November 2003, C3. President Ronald Reagan was similarly motivated when in 1981 he nominated Sandra Day O'Connor to be the first woman to sit on the Supreme Court of the United States. O'Connor has said of her nomination, "It had nothing to do with

me ... He was hoping to get votes from women ... there were not that many women judges ... Face it. Where are you going to find them?" See Jan Crawford Greenburg, *Supreme Conflict: The Inside Story of the Struggle for Control of the United States Supreme Court* (New York: Penguin Books, 2007), 12.

27. See, for example, Janice Tibbetts, "McLachlin has spent life on legal fast track," *The Gazette* (Montreal), 4 November 1999, A12.

28. *RJR-MacDonald Inc. v. Canada (Attorney-General),* [1995] 3 S.C.R 199.

29. *Vriend v. Alberta,* 1998 CanLII 816. See the discussion of this case in Chapter 4.

30. 1991 CanLII 84. In this case, the Supreme Court held that a Vancouver police "buy-and-bust" program did not constitute entrapment. McLachlin considered that the individual interest in being left alone and free to pursue one's daily business without being confronted by undercover police operatives vastly outweighs the state interest in the repression of crime. L'Heureux-Dubé also dissented, but only in part.

31. *R. v. Keegstra,* [1990] 3 S.C.R. 697.

32. 1999 CanLII 711.

33. "Charter Decisions in the McLachlin Era: Collegiality and Ideology at the Supreme Court of Canada" (2009) 47 *Supreme Court Law Review* 475.

34. Janice Tibbetts, "Chief Justice is chief dissenter," *National Post,* 20 June 2009, A12.

35. Kirk Makin, "Key rulings tend to favour state, expert finds," *The Globe and Mail,* 20 June 2009, A9.

36. 2009 SCC 32 (CanLII).

37. *R. v. Hess; R. v. Nguyen,* 1990 CanLII 89.

38. Fine, note 4.

39. *Hess,* page 30.

40. *R. v. Seaboyer; R. v. Gayme,* 1991 CanLII 76 (S.C.C.). Page references in the endnotes below are to this citation.

41. See page 44.

42. Page 92.

43. Fine, note 4.

44. Fine.

45. The 2005 Lord Cooke lecture, 1 December 2005, www.scc-csc.gc.ca/court-cour/ju/spe-dis/bm05-12-01-eng.asp (accessed 11 March 2009). She repeated many of the same arguments, in an abbreviated form, in an interview with Christopher Guly, "Question period: Beverley McLachlin," *Western Standard* magazine, 24 April 2006, www.westernstandard.ca/website/article.php?id=1622 (accessed 11 March 2009).

46. See Wente, note 13.

47. NYU conversation, note 6.

48. Richard Posner, *How Judges Think* (Cambridge: Harvard University Press, 2008), 8.

49. Kirk Makin, "Osgoode professors on Chief Justice Beverley McLachlin," *The Globe and Mail,* 8 January 2005, http://osgoode.yorku.ca/media2.nsf/releases/27767BD5 6D67B0E685256F8500700AE7 (accessed 14 November 2008).

50. Ronald Dworkin, *The Supreme Court Phalanx: The Court's New Right Wing Bloc* (New York: New York Review Books, 2008), xi.

51. Andrew Cohen, "The Governor General sweepstakes," *Ottawa Citizen,* 4 May 2010, www2.canada.com/ottawacitizen/columnists/story.html?id=1c0732bf-f66a-492b-9222-af1c856df9c3&p=2 (accessed 12 May 2010).

52. See Makin, note 49.

53. Interview with author, 10 June 2010.

54. Quoted by Christin Schmitz, "McLachlin Court turns ten," *The Lawyers Weekly,* 25 December 2009, http://lawyersweekly.ca/index.php?section=article&volume=29&number=32&article=3 (accessed 3 January 2010).

55. See Cristin Schmitz, "A view from the top: Justice LeBel speaks," *The Lawyers Weekly,* 30 April 2010 www.lawyersweekly.ca/index.php?section=article&articleid=1152 (accessed 15 May 2010).

56. David Brooks, "What it takes," *The New York Times,* 10 May 2010, www.nytimes.com/2010/05/11/opinion/11brooks.html?scp=1&sq="what%20it%20takes"&st=cse (accessed 12 May 2010).

57. Interview with author, 10 June 2010.

58. Makin, note 49.

59. *The Agenda with Steve Paikin,* TVO, 1 December 2009, www.tvo.org/TVO/WebObjects/TVO.woa?video?TAWSP_Int1_20091201_779664_0 (accessed 2 January 2010).

TEN   Leaders of the Court

1. Robert Lewis, "The Right Hon. Mr. Malaprop," *Maclean's,* 23 March 1998, 4.

2. Rae Corelli, "Binnie Appointed to Supreme Court, *Maclean's,* 19 January 1998, www.thecanadianencyclopedia.com/index.cfm?PgNm=TCE&Params=M1ARTM0011477 (accessed 29 November 2008).

3. Jan Wong, "Lunch with Ian Binnie," *The Globe and Mail,* 22 January 1998, C1.

4. Interview with Ahmed Farahat, "Law is Cool," 4 April 2009, http://lawiscool.com/2009/04/04/amicus-curiae-sits-down-with-justice-binnie-of-the-supreme-court-of-canada/ (accessed 12 April 2009).

5. "A better way to court Mr. Binnie," *The Globe and Mail,* 12 January 1998, A10.

6. See Farahat, note 4.

7. Farahat.

8. Professor Allan Hutchinson of Osgoode Hall Law School wrote, "The practice of appointing a legal practitioner directly to the country's highest court ... is a bad idea.... There is little evidence to say what kind of job he will do." "Let's stop gambling on Supreme Court judges," *The Toronto Star,* 19 January 1998, www.efc.ca/pages/media/toronto.star.19jan98.html (accessed 1 March 2010).

9. See Lewis, note 1.

10. Quoted by Stephen Bindman, "New judge has 'em in stitches," *Ottawa Citizen,* 3 February 1998, A3.

11. Quoted by Kirk Makin, "'Lawyer's lawyer' Binnie named to Supreme Court," *The Globe and Mail,* 9 January 1998, A1.

12. See Bindman, note 10.

13. Bindman. The "raucous laughter" at Binnie's reference to shouting may have been because the justices were aware of the probable origins of the comment. President Lyndon Johnson said of FBI director J. Edgar Hoover, "I would rather have him inside the tent pissing out than outside the tent pissing in."

14. Kirk Makin, "Supreme Court's Binnie apologizes for gay slur," *The Globe and Mail,* 13 March 1998, A1.

15. See Makin.

16. "Supreme Court wastes no time, Binnie says," *The Globe and Mail*, 28 November 1998, A5.

17. "Advance reading," *The Globe and Mail*, 5 December 1998, D7.

18. Janice Tibbetts, "Top court judges tear into media," *Edmonton Journal*, 15 August 2001, A3.

19. *R. v. Marshall*, 1999 CanLII 665 (S.C.C.).

20. Florian Sauvageau, David Schneiderman, David Taras, *The Last Word: Media Coverage of the Supreme Court of Canada* (Vancouver: UBC Press, 2006), 137. This book devotes an entire chapter to the Marshall cases and press coverage of them.

21. "The burden of language in the Mi'kmaq case," *The Globe and Mail*, 6 October 1999, A14.

22. Robert Fife, "High Court accused of 'distorting' history," *National Post*, 28 October 1999, A1. See also Lorne Gunter, "Supreme Court admits error," *Edmonton Journal*, 9 December 1999, A12. Professor Peter Russell does not agree that Binnie distorted Patterson's testimony at trial: see "Great hedge," *National Post*, 2 November 1999, A19.

23. *R. v. Marshall*, 1999 CanLII 666 (S.C.C.). The Marshall decisions are still of much interest in the Maritimes. See, e.g., Tom Sheppard, "Eel fishing and the Supreme Court of Canada," *The Queens County Advance*, 2 December 2008, 6.

24. "Supremes retreat," *National Post*, 19 November 1999, A15.

25. "Mi'kmaq patty whack," *The Globe and Mail*, 19 November 1999, A19.

26. "Court ruling the country," *The Windsor Star*, 2 December 1999, A6.

27. See Sauvageau, note 20, 139.

28. Alex M. Cameron, *Power Without Law: The Supreme Court of Canada, the Marshall Decisions, and the Failure of Judicial Activism*, (Montreal: McGill-Queen's University Press, 2009).

29. Cameron, 5.

30. Cameron, 87.

31. "Five years on, Binnie settles into the bench," *The Globe and Mail*, 10 February 2003, A3.

32. *Wewaykum Indian Band v. Canada*, 2002 SCC 79 (CanLII).

33. *Wewaykum Indian Band v. Canada*, 2003 SCC 45 (CanLII).

34. Adam Dodek has argued that *Wewaykum* is an important constitutional law case. See "Constitutional Legitimacy and Responsibility: Confronting Allegations of Bias After *Wewaykum Indian Band v. Canada*,"(2004) *Supreme Court Law Review (2d)* 165.

35. *R. v. Neil*, 2002 SCC 70 (CanLII).

36. 2 April 2004. See McGill News Archives, www.mcgill.ca/scarlettkey/news/archives (accessed 7 December 2008).

37. Kirk Makin, "Senior U.S., Canadian judges spar over judicial activism," *The Globe and Mail*, 17 February 2007, A2.

38. "Interpreting the Constitution: The Living Tree vs. Original Meaning," *Policy Options*, October 2007, 104.

39. Ian Binnie, "Legal Redress for Corporate Participation in International Human

Rights Abuses: A Progress Report," *The Brief*, Summer 2009, www.icj.org/IMG/20091022093202185.pdf (accessed 4 January 2010).

40. Dahlia Lithwick, "Supreme Court Dispatch, Eh: How the United States' never-ending legal mess at Gitmo is spilling over into Canada," *Slate*, 13 November 2009, www.slate.com/id/2235467 (accessed 24 November 2009).

41. Reported by Cristin Schmitz, "Justice needs more than words: Abella," *The Lawyers Weekly*, 12 June 2009, www.lawyersweekly.ca/index.php?section=article&articleid=939 (accessed 18 June 2009). Abella also criticized the United Nations in a speech at the University of Alberta in November 2009. See Geoff McMaster, "Supreme Court Justice decries failure of international human rights law," *Express News*, www.expressnews.ualberta.ca/article.cfm?id=10574 (accessed 22 November 2009).

42. Lead gifts came from, among others, Charles and Andrea Bronfman, Hal Jackman, Jonas Prince, Joseph Rotman, Lionel and Carol Schipper, Gerald Schwartz, Edward Sonshine, Avie Bennett, Martin Goldfarb, Leo Kolber, Larry Tannenbaum, and Gluskin Sheff & Associates. See Kathleen O'Brien, "A Room of Her Own," *University of Toronto Magazine*, Summer 2009, www.magazine.utoronto.ca/great-gifts/rosalie-abella-u-of-t-law-alumni (accessed 3 August 2009).

43. James Yap, "'And the Winner is …': The First Annual Ozzy Awards," *The Court*, www.thecourt.ca/2010/02/24/introducing-the-first-annual-ozzy-awards (accessed 9 July 2010).

44. Gail J. Cohen, "The Top 25 Most Influential: Canadian Lawyer's picks of this country's most powerful lawyers," *Canadian Lawyer*, August 2010, www.canadianlawyermag.com/Canadian-Lawyer (accessed 6 August 2010).

45. Kirk Makin, "Justice tempered with a soft heart," *The Globe and Mail*, 12 June 2009, www.theglobeandmail.com/news/national/justice-tempered-with-a-soft-heart/article1179006 (accessed 16 June 2009).

46. Wilfred List, "Family Court judge appointed new chairman of labour board," *The Globe and Mail*, 10 April 1984, M3.

47. "People always feel better after they talk to Rosie Abella," *The Globe and Mail*, 20 November 1986, A2.

48. Quoted by Martin Knelman, "Court of Appeal judge gavels for Giller," *Toronto Star*, 1 November 2003, A10.

49. See Michael Posner, "Surviving the Nazis helped make her unstoppable," *The Globe and Mail*, 5 March 2010, S6.

50. Reported by Allison Dawe, "Public policy comes out of the judicial closet," *The Kingston Whig-Standard*, 19 April 1989, 1.

51. Tom Bingham, *The Rule of Law* (London: Allen Lane, 2010), 82.

52. Mia Stainsby, "A prominent architect of public policy, Rosalie Abella assesses other players," *The Vancouver Sun*, 25 November 1991, C2.

53. "The Media and the Courts," in Julie Hannaford and Edward Badovinac (eds.), *The Empire Club of Canada Speeches 1996–1997* (Toronto: The Empire Club Foundation, 1997), 546.

54. "Judge blames lawyers' behaviour for low confidence in legal system," *Toronto Star*, 30 October 1991, 1.

55. In her 1997 Canadian Club speech (see note 53), Abella said, "I think the media's tendency to use labels or epithets instead of analysis is not particularly enlightening.... Not every pro-female decision is feminist and not every pro-male one reflects a chauvinist bias."

56. For example, at a March 1993 human rights forum at McGill University's faculty of law. See John Kalbfleisch, "Judge Abella says feminism enables women to catch up," *The Gazette* (Montreal), 11 March 1993, A6.

57. (1995), 22 OR (3d) 481.

58. Paragraph 41.

59. Although an editorial on the case welcomed the "rebalancing" of rights that it created. "Revisiting child custody," *The Globe and Mail*, 10 April 1995, A12.

60. Sean Fine, "Abella sees judges as partners in family lawmaking," *The Globe and Mail*, 7 April 1995, A5.

61. Sean Fine, "Ruling leaves dads out in cold," *The Globe and Mail*, 24 June 1995, A1.

62. "Right-wing attack sets sights on female judges," *Toronto Star*, 1 July 1995, K1.

63. Barry Lillie, "Abella on Supreme Court spells trouble for broken families," *The Record* (Kitchener-Waterloo), 2 September 2004, A9.

64. "No one knows the rules in the Supreme Court's bareknuckle fight," *The Globe and Mail*, 16 December 1997, A20.

65. "A second swing on who is being pitched as a Supreme Court judge," *The Globe and Mail*, 8 January 1998, A16.

66. Janice Tibbetts, "Ontario judge takes shot at Supreme Court critics," *Ottawa Citizen*, 8 April 2000, A5.

67. "Abella the perfect choice for governor-general," *The Globe and Mail*, 24 August 1999, A9.

68. "The Judicial Role in a Democratic State," www.ontariocourts.on.ca/coa/en/ps/speeches/judicialrole.htm (accessed 21 February 2009).

69. "Judges and the public interest," *The Globe and Mail*, 14 April 2000, A14.

70. "Abella expected to be a superb communicator," *The Globe and Mail*, 25 August 2004, A6.

71. "A purely political choice," *National Post*, 25 August 2004, A1.

72. "Robed revolutionary? Not quite," *National Post*, 27 August 2004, A16.

73. *Rosenberg v. Canada (Attorney General)*, 1998 CanLII 3243.

74. *M. v. H.*, 1996 CanLII 2218. The Supreme Court of Canada upheld the decision—*M. v. H.*, 1999 CanLII 686.

75. Tonda MacCharles, "'So proud to be a Canadian,'" *Toronto Star*, 5 October 2004, A8.

76. As reported by MacCharles.

77. 2009 SCC 54.

78. Paragraph 69.

79. 2010 SCC 16.

80. Paragraph 100.

81. *Toronto Star Newspapers Ltd. v. Canada*, 2010 SCC 21.

82. Paragraph 65.

83. Donna Bailey Nurse, "Just 'Rosie'," *University of Toronto Magazine*, Winter 2006, http://magazine.utoronto.ca/06winter/rosie.asp (accessed 5 March 2009).

ELEVEN **Middle of the Pack**

1. Kirk Makin, "A dark horse," *The Globe and Mail,* 23 December 1999, A16.
2. Janice Tibbetts and Luiza Chwialkowska, "Louis LeBel appointed to Supreme Court," *National Post,* 23 December 1999, A1.
3. See Makin, note 1, and Tibbetts and Chwialkowska.
4. Makin.
5. Janice Tibbetts, "PM's choice of new top court judge a question of language," *Ottawa Citizen,* 13 December 1999, A4.
6. 1989 CanLII 894.
7. Alexander Norris, "Was ruling legal compromise or religious view of judges?" *The Windsor Star,* 31 July 1989, A7.
8. Norris.
9. *Tremblay v. Daigle,* 1989 CanLII 33.
10. Edison Stewart, "Top court's new judge is abortion foe," *Toronto Star,* 23 December 1999, 1.
11. Stewart.
12. Makin, note 1.
13. Janice Tibbetts, "New top court judge wants to improve PR," *Ottawa Citizen,* 29 December 1999, A7.
14. Cristin Schmitz, "New top judge changes abortion view," *The Vancouver Sun,* 15 February 2000, A13.
15. Lysiane Gagnon, "A dissenting view on Judge LeBel," *The Globe and Mail,* 22 January 2000, A21.
16. Tibbetts, note 13.
17. Chantal Hébert, "Consultative process on judges is cloaked in secrecy," *The Hamilton Spectator,* 25 August 2004, A10.
18. See Cristin Schmitz, "A view from the top: Justice LeBel speaks," *The Lawyers Weekly,* 30 April 2010, www.lawyersweekly.ca/index.php?section=article&article id=1152 (accessed 15 May 2010).
19. 2009 SCC 47.
20. "Against absolutism," *The Globe and Mail,* 23 October 2009, http://proquest.umi. com.ezproxy.torontopubliclibrary.ca/pqdweb?index=0&did=1884691501&SrchM ode= 1&sid=1&Fmt=3&VInst=PROD&VType=PQD&RQT=309&VName=PQ D&TS=1284906657&clientId=1525 (accessed 19 September 2010).
21. Quoted by Rhéal Seguin, "Ruling puts nationalist sentiments on bubble," *The Globe and Mail,* 22 October 2009, A6.
22. Graeme Hamilton, "Judges' ruling rekindles Quebec language wars," *National Post,* 22 October 2009, www.nationalpost.com/language+reignited/2134111/story.html (accessed 10 July 2010).
23. Note 21.
24. Quoted by Rhéal Séguin, "PQ fumes as Jean Charest shuts down debate on language bill," *The Globe and Mail,* 18 October 2010, www.theglobeandmail.com/ news/politics/pq-fumes-and-jean-charest-shuts-down-debate-on-language-bill/ article1762175 (accessed 20 October 2010).
25. Schmitz, note 18.
26. Author interview, in LeBel's chambers, 25 May 2010.

27. Reported by Tonda MacCharles, "New judge 'dumbfounded' at appointment," *Ottawa Citizen,* 1 October 1988, A1.
28. See MacCharles.
29. See, for example, Michael Valpy, "Charron seen as progressive on social rulings," *The Globe and Mail,* 25 August 2004, A6; Norma Greenaway, "Charron a top-notch legal mind, hard-working, ex-colleagues say," *The Vancouver Sun,* 25 August 2004, A2.
30. Tim Naumetz, "'Priority of profit' a barrier for women lawyers: Charron," *Law Times,* 15 February 2010, www.lawtimesnews.com/201002156388/Headline-News/Priority-of-profit-a-barrier-for-women-lawyers-Charron (accessed 2 March 2010).
31. See "The Rothstein family Christmas vacation: All the makings of a feature-length comedy," *Maclean's,* 27 February 2006, www.macleans.ca/article.jsp?content=20060225_160936_4968 (accessed 12 September 2009).
32. Don Martin, "How to make a judge blush," *National Post,* 28 February 2006, A4.
33. "A 'show' about nothing," *National Post,* 3 March 2006, A16.
34. Reported by Terry O'Neill, "The right to make new rights," *The Gazette* (Montreal), 14 May 2006, A17.
35. "A delicate balancing act with the scales of justice," *The Gazette* (Montreal), 10 June 2009, www.lianmacdonald.ca/columns/gazette/20090610.html.
36. *President and Fellows of Harvard College v. Canada (Commissioner of Patents),* 2000 CanLII 16058; overruled by the Supreme Court of Canada, *Harvard College v. Canada (Commissioner of Patents),* 2002 SCC 76 (CanLII).
37. "IP Shakeup," *Ottawa Citizen,* 2 March 2006, F4.
38. See Richard Blackwell, "Rothstein like 'homing missile' on legal issues," *The Globe and Mail,* 24 February 2006, A4.
39. Author interview, in Rothstein's chambers, 11 June 2010.
40. Julie Smyth, "Meet the wife," *National Post,* 1 July 2006, A8.
41. Rosemary Sexton, "Chef Justice of the court," *Maclean's,* 1 March 2006, www.macleans.ca/canada/national/article.jsp?content=20060306_122385_122385 (accessed 30 June 2009).
42. "Fight over bilingual Supreme Court," *Law Times,* 15 June 2009, 7.
43. Marshall Rothstein, "Some Appellate Advocacy Advice," *The Advocates Journal,* September 2008, 6.

TWELVE **Bringing Up the Rear**

1. Janice Tibbetts, "The new 'great dissenter'," *Ottawa Citizen,* 8 March 2004, A5.
2. Cristin Schmitz, "Top court's 2009 track record: Fish 'The Great Dissenter'," *The Lawyers Weekly,* 29 January 2010, www.lawyersweekly.ca/index.php?section=article&articleid=1087 (accessed 24 March 2010).
3. Some of this account first appeared in my *Canadian Lawyer* column, "Top Court Tales." See "The surprising Justice Deschamps," *Canadian Lawyer,* March 2009, 26.
4. Janice Tibbetts, "Deschamps appointed to high court position," *Calgary Herald,* 9 August 2002, A11.
5. Sean Gordon and Irwin Block, "PM's pick 'out of the blue'," *The Gazette* (Montreal), 9 August 2002, A1.

6. Sue Bailey, "Quebec judge named to top court," *The Kingston Whig-Standard,* 9 August 2002, 9.

7. Gordon and Block, note 5.

8. Tibbetts, note 4.

9. Norman Spector, "Chretien's court legacy will long outlive him," *The Vancouver Sun,* 9 September 2002, A10.

10. Janice Tibbetts, "Deschamps: 'Tough, inquisitive'," *Ottawa Citizen,* 9 August 2002, A4.

11. Gordon and Block, note 5.

12. See, for example, Gordon and Block.

13. Janice Tibbetts, "New Justice the fifth chosen by Chretien," *National Post,* 9 August 2002, A6.

14. "Supreme questions," *The Globe and Mail,* 10 August 2002, A16.

15. Tibbetts, note 1.

16. *Canadian Foundation for Children, Youth and the Law v. Canada (Attorney General),* 2004 SCC 4 (CanLII).

17. *R. v. Caine,* 2003 SCC 74 (CanLII).

18. 2003 SCC 24 (CanLII).

19. Tom Blackwell, "Deschamps not afraid to stand alone," *National Post,* 10 June 2005, A3.

20. James Yap, "'And the Winner is ...': the First Annual OZZY Awards," *The Court,* 24 February 2010, www.thecourt.ca/2010/02/24/introducing-the-first-annual-ozzy-awards/ (accessed 24 March 2010).

21. *R. v. Morelli,* 2010 SCC 8.

22. Paragraph 89.

23. (London: Andre Deutsch, 1959).

24. Mordecai Richler, *On Snooker* (Toronto: Vintage Canada, 2002).

25. "Next up: a Quebec anglophone on the top court," *The Globe and Mail,* 13 November 1999, A25.

26. "McLachlin was an obvious choice," *The Gazette* (Montreal), 8 November 1999, B3.

27. Andrew McIntosh, "Mulroney urges PM to promote judge," *National Post,* 11 September 2000, A4.

28. "Welcome to the court, but fix the entrance," *The Globe and Mail,* 2 August 2003, A14.

29. "Quebeckers lead pack in judicial derby," *The Globe and Mail,* 29 May 2002, A7.

30. Janice Tibbetts, "Judicial friend of the underdog finally named to the Supreme Court," *Ottawa Citizen,* 1 August 2003, A1.

31. L. Ian MacDonald, "Morris Fish is a supremely wise and popular choice," *The Gazette* (Montreal), 4 August 2003, A19.

32. See Tibbetts, note 30.

33. Quoted by Mary Gordon, "Morris Fish joins Supreme Court," *The Hamilton Spectator,* 1 August 2003, C3.

34. Quoted by Lynn Moore, "New Supreme Court justice fights to overcome 'mediocrity'," *Ottawa Citizen,* 1 August 2003, A3.

35. See Lisa Fitterman, "Hospital staff will miss Fish motif: Moving to Ottawa after husband is named to top court," *The Gazette* (Montreal), 26 August 2003.

36. Peter Desbarats, "Red fish, blue fish, Justice, too, Fish," *Ottawa Citizen,* 12 August 2003, A15.

37. Desbarats.

38. Contrast Fish's technology sophistication with the ignorance on these matters of judges on the U.S. Supreme Court. During argument in the 2010 case of *City of Ontario v. Quom* (www.supremecourt.gov/opinions/09pdf/08-1332.pdf), Chief Justice Roberts wondered about how text messaging worked. "I thought, you know, you push a button; it goes right to the other thing," he said. Justice Scalia said: "You mean it doesn't go right to the other thing?" Roberts also wondered what the difference was between email and a pager.

39. 2009 SCC 22 (CanLII).

40. Paragraph 53.

41. *Tercon Contractors Ltd. v. British Columbia (Transportation and Highways),* 2010 SCC 4 (CanLII).

42. 2010 SCC 5.

43. See Lauren Collins, "Number Nine: Sonia Sotomayor's high-profile début," *The New Yorker,* 11 January 2010, 42, www.newyorker.com/reporting/2010/01/11/100111fa_ fact_collins (accessed 8 January 2010).

44. Collins, 43.

45. Peter Hendra, "Passion, devotion music to his ears," *The Kingston Whig-Standard,* 12 June 2010, www.thewhig.com/ArticleDisplay.aspx?e=2620270 (accessed 10 July 2010).

THIRTEEN   **Working Together in the Tower of Song**

1. Section 8 of The Supreme Court Act says, "The judges shall reside in the National Capital Region described in the schedule to the *National Capital Act* or within forty kilometres thereof." A one-bedroom apartment will satisfy this requirement.

2. Susan Harada, "The McLachlin Group," *The Walrus,* April 2009, www.walrus magazine.com/articles/2009.05-law-the-mclachlin-group/3/ (accessed 11 April 2009).

3. In a television interview. See *The Agenda with Steve Paikin,* TVO, 1 December 2009, www.tvo.org/TVO/WebObjects/TVO.woa?video?TAWSP_Int1_20091201_ 779664_0 (accessed 2 January 2010).

4. See Adam Liptak, "In a Polarized Court, Getting the Last Word," *The New York Times,* 8 March 2010, www.nytimes.com/2010/03/09/us/09bar.html (accessed 24 March 2010). "A few times a year, Supreme Court justices go out of their way to emphasize their unhappiness by reading a dissent from the bench out loud, supplementing the dry reason on the page with vivid tones of sarcasm, regret, anger and disdain."

5. See William Blake and Hans Hacker, "The Brooding Spirit of the Law: Supreme Court Justices Reading Dissents from the Bench," 31 *Justice System Journal* 1 (2010), www.ncsc.org/Web%20Documents/Blake_%20Hacker_030710.pdf (accessed 30 April 2010). Some courts prohibit dissenting or other separate opinions—for example, the constitutional courts of France, Italy, and Austria, and the European Court of Justice. See Linda Greenhouse, "American (Judicial) Idol," *The New*

York Times, 23 April 2010, http://opinionator.blogs.nytimes.com/2010/04/23/american-judicial-idol (accessed 30 April 2010). For many years, it was the practice of the Judicial Committee of the Privy Council to have a single judgment, "although members who disagreed could record their dissent in a register which was never seen by anyone." See Tom Bingham, *The Rule of Law* (London: Allen Lane, 2010), 44.

6. Janice Crawford Greenburg, *Supreme Conflict: The Inside Story of the Struggle for Control of the United States Supreme Court* (New York: Penguin Books, 2007), 115.

7. For an interesting and balanced account of tensions within the court when Bora Laskin was chief justice, see Philip Girard, *Bora Laskin: Bringing Law to Life* (Toronto: University of Toronto Press, 2005), chapter 19.

8. Donald R. Songer, *The Transformation of the Supreme Court of Canada: An Empirical Examination* (Toronto: University of Toronto Press, 2008).

9. For example, in a speech to the law faculty of the University of British Columbia, 4 February 2010, www.youtube.com/watch?v=GXL8GG0GTv4&NR=1 (accessed 28 February 2010).

10. "The Place of Women on the Court," *The New York Times,* 7 July 2009, www.nytimes.com/2009/07/12/magazine/12ginsburg-t.html?scp=1&sq=bazelon%20ginsburg&st=cse (accessed 11 December 2009).

11. Janice Tibbetts, "From leader to law: PM's former chef heads to the Supreme Court," *The Vancouver Sun,* 29 September 2010, www.vancouversun.com/life/From+leader+former+chef+heads+Supreme+Court/3600141/story.html (accessed 20 October 2010).

12. Greenburg, note 6, 161–62.

13. Girard, note 7, 368.

14. Supreme Court Act (R.S., 1985, c. S-26), s. 40(1).

15. Artemus Ward and David L. Weiden, *Sorcerers' Apprentices: 100 Years of Law Clerks at the United States Supreme Court* (New York: New York University Press, 2006), 109.

16. For details, see "Bulletin of Proceedings: Special Edition, Statistics 1999–2009," www.scc-csc.gc.ca/stat/index-eng.asp (accessed 24 March 2010).

17. See Cristin Schmitz, "Drop in caseload worries Supreme Court of Canada observers," *The Lawyers Weekly,* 1 October 2010, www.lawyersweekly.ca/index.php?section=article&articleid=1260 (accessed 20 October 2010).

18. Author interview, in her chambers, 10 June 2010.

19. www.scc-csc.gc.ca/faq/faq/index-eng.asp#f22 (accessed 9 December 2009).

20. Greenburg, note 6, 67.

21. Interview with Susan Swain of C-SPAN, 25 June 2009, transcript at http://supremecourt.c-span.org/assets/pdf/AKennedy.pdf (accessed 17 May 2010).

22. Yves Faguy, "A conversation with the Chief Justice," *The National,* June 2010, 21.

23. UBC speech, note 9, www.youtube.com/watch?v=74hkS56m0MY&feature=related (accessed 28 February 2010).

24. Ian Binnie, "Is There Nobody Smarter than a Toronto Lawyer?" Speech to the Empire Club of Canada, 31 March 2010.

25. Jeffrey Toobin, "After Stevens: What will the Supreme Court be like without its liberal leader?" *The New Yorker,* 22 March 2010, 39.

26. C-SPAN interview, note 21.
27. See Benjamin Alarie and Andrew Green, "Interventions at the Supreme Court of Canada: Accuracy, Affiliation, and Acceptance" (June 21, 2010). Available at SSRN: http://ssrn.com/abstract=1498747.
28. Frank Iacobucci, "The *Charter*: Twenty Years Later," (2002) 21 *Windsor Y.B. Access Just.* 3, at 6.
29. Quoted in "Three judges talk about their first time," *National Post*, 6 April 2000, B4.
30. Quoted in "Three judges."
31. Interview with author, 10 June 2010.
32. See Cristin Schmitz, "A view from the top: Justice LeBel speaks," *The Lawyers Weekly*, 30 April 2010, www.lawyersweekly.ca/index.php?section=article&article id=1152 (accessed 15 May 2010).
33. Author interview, in his chambers, 25 May 2010.
34. At the Canadian Defence Lawyers Conference, Vancouver, 4–5 June 2009. For the full text, see www.lerners.ca/content/Canadian%20Defencer%20Lawyers%20 Conference.pdf.
35. The correct citation for the case referred to by Cherniak is *Canada (Attorney General) v. Canada (Commission of Inquiry on the Blood System)*, [1997] 3 S.C.R. 440.
36. Cherniak, note 34.
37. "A Survivor's Guide to Advocacy in the Supreme Court of Canada," 27 November 1998, www.scai-ipcs.ca/pdf/Binnie-SurvivorsGuidetoAdvocacy.pdf (accessed 2 December 2008).
38. Justice Louis LeBel has written an interesting paper on the role of an advocate before the Supreme Court. "La Cour suprême du Canada: Le dialogue de l'avocat et de la Cour," *Actes de la XVIIe Conférence des juristes de l'Etat*, Editions Yvon Blais, 2006, 345–59.
39. I was told this anecdote by another judge, now retired, who was present.
40. Paikin interview, note 3.
41. See Schmitz, note 32.
42. Author interview with Chief Justice McLachlin, 10 June 2010.
43. Paikin interview, note 3.
44. Interview with Rebecca Lowe, International Bar Association, October 2010, www.ibanet.org/Article/Detail.aspx?ArticleUid=634cd6e1-ddba-4510-b69a-924e3c87b65e (accessed 19 October 2010).
45. James Gotowiec, "The Decade That Was: Fewer Judgments, but Does it Matter?" *The Court*, 4 January 2010, www.thecourt.ca/2010/01/04/the-decade-that-was-fewer-judgments-but-does-it-matter (accessed 10 January 2010).
46. Kirk Makin, "Ten years as top judge and she's still losing sleep," *The Globe and Mail*, 7 January 2010 www.theglobeandmail.com/news/national/ten-years-as-top-judge-and-shes-still-losing-sleep/article1421731 (accessed 10 January 2010).
47. Radio interview with Alison Crawford, "The House," 7 May 2010, www.cbc.ca/politics/insidepolitics/2010/05/one-on-one-with-canadas-chief-justice.html (accessed 12 May 2010).
48. Adam Liptak, "Justices Long on Words but Short on Guidance," *The New York Times*, 18 November 2010, A1.

49. Adam Liptak, "No Vote-Trading Here," *The New York Times,* 14 May 2010, www. nytimes.com/2010/05/16/weekinreview/16liptak.html (accessed 17 May 2010).

50. Peter McCormick, "'Was it Something I Said?': Losing the Majority on the Supreme Court of Canada, 1984–2007." Paper prepared for presentation at Midwest Political Science Association Annual Meeting, Chicago, Illinois, April 2008, 2.

51. *Wewaykum Indian Band v. Canada,* 2003 SCC 45 (CanLII).

52. Paragraphs 92–93.

53. http://scc.lexum.umontreal.ca/en/index.html.

FOURTEEN **Ideological Soup**

1. See Noah Feldman, "When Arrogance Takes the Bench," *The New York Times,* 11 June 2009, www.nytimes.com/2009/06/11/opinion/11feldman. html?scp=1&sq=feldman&st=cse (accessed 16 June 2009).

2. Todd C. Peppers, *Courtiers of the Marble Palace: The Rise and Influence of the Supreme Court Law Clerk* (Stanford: Stanford University Press, 2006), 165.

3. Kenneth W. Starr, "The Supreme Court and Its Shrinking Docket: The Ghost of William Howard Taft," 2006 *Minnesota Law Review* 1363, http://local.law.umn. edu/uploads/images/3274/Starr_Final.pdf (accessed 2 October 2009).

4. Peppers, note 2, 2.

5. See Adam Liptak, "A Sign of the Court's Polarization: Choice of Clerks," *The New York Times,* 6 September 2010, www.nytimes.com/2010/09/07/us/politics/07clerks. html?scp=1&sq=%22clerks%20highlight%22&st=cse (accessed 25 September 2010). Liptak's article discusses how justices tend to pick clerks who share their political views.

6. "Supremes retreat," *National Post,* 19 November 1999, A15.

7. (Peterborough, Ontario: Broadview Press, 2000), 110.

8. The section 54 oath reads:

> I, ..., swear (*or* solemnly affirm) that I will faithfully and honestly fulfil the duties that devolve on me by reason of my employment in the public service of Canada and that I will not, without due authority, disclose or make known any matter that comes to my knowledge by reason of such employment. (*Add, in the case where an oath is taken,* "So help me God" *(or name of deity).*)

9. Two University of Toronto professors have recently conducted a statistical study designed to quantify the influence of U.S. Supreme Court law clerks. "It is believed that certain USSC justices (e.g. Scalia ...) primarily write their own legal decisions, while others (e.g. Kennedy ...) rely heavily on their law clerks to do much of the writing, though there are few hard facts about this and it is mostly a matter of speculation. We attempt to verify this hypothesis by measuring the variability of writing style of the majority opinions written by the various justices. We conclude that, indeed, majority opinions written by Kennedy have significantly greater variability than do those by Scalia ..." See Jeffrey S. Rosenthal and Albert H. Yoon, "Detecting Multiple Authorship of United States Supreme Court Legal Decisions Using Function Words," 3 December 2009, http://probability.ca/jeff/ftpdir/ textvarart.pdf (accessed 11 December 2009).

10. Quoted in Robert J. Sharpe and Kent Roach, *Brian Dickson: A Judge's Journey* (Toronto: University of Toronto Press, 2003), 207.
11. As described by Todd Peppers. See note 2. Bickel wrote about this in "The Court: An Indictment Analyzed," *The New York Times,* 27 April 1958.
12. Morton/Knopff, note 7, 146.
13. Sharpe/Roach, note 10, 208.
14. Sharpe/Roach, 208. The quotation is from Brian Morgan, "A View of Clerking at the Supreme Court of Canada," (1978), 3(2) *Hearsay,* 6.
15. Author interview with Justice Rothstein, 11 June 2010.
16. Artemus Ward and David L. Weiden, *Sorcerers' Apprentices: 100 Years of Law Clerks at the United States Supreme Court* (New York: New York University Press, 2006).
17. See Cristin Schmitz, "Supremely secret: top court wants law clerks muzzled," *The Lawyers Weekly,* 26 June 2009, www.lawyersweekly.ca/index.php?section=article&articleid=947 (accessed 30 June 2009). Schmitz sought reaction from seven former law clerks and reported, "Most indicated that they thought the judges were overreaching in their apparent insistence on very broad law clerk secrecy in perpetuity."
18. Kirk Makin, "Top court orders clerks to keep quiet," *The Globe and Mail,* 19 June 2009, www.theglobeandmail.com/news/national/top-court-orders-clerks-to-keep-quiet/article1188221 (accessed 30 June 2009). As of noon on 30 June 2009, there were 27 online comments on Kirk Makin's article. Comments ranged from "If the legal system were to open itself up it might regain some of the credibility and respect it once had," to "The Supreme Court is a political organization like any other, and deserves scrutiny accordingly," to "These judges are being handled with kid gloves compared to politicians ... Why the double standard? I should think the operations of unelected powers in society should be subject to more inquiry, if anything!"
19. Tim Naumetz, "Gag on SCC law clerks has 'chilling effect'," *Law Times,* 29 June 2009, www.lawtimesnews.com/200906294937/Headline-News/Gag-on-SCC-law-clerks-has-chilling-effect (accessed 22 July 2009).
20. "The juridical mystique," *The Globe and Mail,* 20 June 2009, A20.
21. See David Lane, "Bush v. Gore, Vanity Fair, and a Supreme Court Law Clerk's Duty of Confidentiality," *The Georgetown Journal of Legal Ethics,* Summer 2005, http://findarticles.com/p/articles/mi_qa3975/is_200507/ai_n14684194/ (accessed 30 June 2009).
22. (New York: Simon and Schuster, 1979).
23. (New York: Doubleday, 2007).
24. Todd Peppers describes how many former law clerks, particularly those who served justices still sitting on the Supreme Court, refused his requests for an interview. See note 2. I had a similar experience.
25. Ward and Weiden, note 16, 11.
26. See Philip Girard, *Bora Laskin: Bringing Law to Life* (Toronto: University of Toronto Press, 2005), 449.
27. Peppers, note 2.
28. "A Justice Slows His Hiring, and Some Wonder About His Future," *The New York Times,* 3 September 2009, www.nytimes.com/2009/09/03/us/03stevens.html?_r=1&scp=2&sq=liptak%20stevens&st=cse (accessed 12 September 2009).

CONCLUSION   **The Change We Need**

1. Almost all constitutional lawyers consider that, since the Charter, the judiciary has the last word on constitutional interpretation. An exception is Dennis Baker, who sets out a different view in *Not Quite Supreme: The Courts and Coordinate Constitutional Interpretation* (Montreal: McGill-Queen's University Press, 2010).

2. Beverley McLachlin has said this in a television interview. *The Agenda with Steve Paikin,* TVO, 1 December 2009, www.tvo.org/TVO/WebObjects/TVO. woa?video?TAWSP_Int1_20091201_779664_0 (accessed 2 January 2010).

3. Adam Liptak, "Study Finds Questioning of Nominees to Be Useful," *The New York Times,* 27 June 2010, www.nytimes.com/2010/06/28/us/politics/28questions. html?_r=1&scp=1&sq=liptak%20questioning&st=cse (accessed 11 July 2010). The study referred to by Liptak is Lori A. Ringhand and Paul M. Collins, "May it Please the Senate: An Empirical Analysis of the Senate Judiciary Committee Hearings of Supreme Court Nominees, 1939–2009," UGA Legal Studies Research Paper No. 10-12, 25 June 2010, available at SSRN: http://ssrn.com/abstract=1630403.

4. "How to Judge a Would-be Justice," *The New York Times,* 14 April 2008, www. nytimes.com/2008/04/14/opinion/14mon3.html?_r=1&scp=1&sq=%22how%20 to%20judge%20a%20would-be%20justice%22&st=cse (accessed 7 April 2009). The study referred to is Jason J. Czarnezki, William K. Ford, and Lori A. Ringhand, "An Empirical Analysis of the Confirmation Hearings of the Justices of the Rehnquist Natural Court," Constitutional Commentary, Vol. 24, p. 127, 2007. A related Canadian study is Andrew James Green, Andrew James, and Benjamin Alarie, "Policy Preference Change and Appointments to the Supreme Court of Canada," 2nd Annual Conference on Empirical Legal Studies, available at Social Science Research Network: http://ssrn.com/abstract=1013560 (accessed 13 June 2008).

5. Adam Liptak, "Why Newer Appointees Offer Fewer Surprises," *The New York Times,* 17 April 2010, www.nytimes.com/2010/04/18/us/18memo.html?scp= 1&sq=liptak%20"fewer%20surprises"&st=cse (accessed 28 April 2010).

6. Liptak, note 3. This study is Dion Farganis and Justin Wedeking, "No Hints, No Forecasts, No Previews: Analyzing Supreme Court Nominee Evasiveness, 1955– 2009" (June 22, 2010). Available at SSRN: http://ssrn.com/abstract=1628813.

7. See Vernon Bogdanor, *The New British Constitution* (Portland: Hart Publishing, 2009), 65–68. A similar system has been suggested for Canada: see B. Thomas Hall and W.T. Stanbury, "An independent judicial appointments commission for Canada," *The Hill Times,* 8 February 2010, www.thehilltimes.ca/page/view/ stanburyhall-02-08-2010 (accessed 10 March 2010).

8. Author interview, in his chambers, 25 May 2010.

9. See Linda Greenhouse, "American (Judicial) Idol," *The New York Times,* 23 April 2010, http://opinionator.blogs.nytimes.com/2010/04/23/american-judicial-idol (accessed 30 April 2010).

10. James MacGregor Burns, *Packing the Court: The Rise of Judicial Power and the Coming Crisis of the Supreme Court* (New York: The Penguin Press, 2009), 4.

11. Steven Chase, "Harper proposes eight-year Senate term," *The Globe and Mail,* 30 March 2010, A6.

12. See Cristin Schmitz, "A view from the top: Justice LeBel speaks," *The Lawyers Weekly,* 30 April 2010, www.lawyersweekly.ca/index.php?section=article&article id=1152 (accessed 15 May 2010). In this interview with Schmitz, LeBel had much to say about the importance of French:

> Justice LeBel says most of the time he writes in the language in which appeals are argued. He points out it is useful to be able to think in both English and French "because simply you get a better sense of the language of the expression, of the way the idea should be translated or transferred into the language. It's a clarity, a better understanding of the culture behind each language, and I would say it's also more efficient," he explains.
>
> He notes that comparative law—resolving issues around the interrelationship of Canada's civil and common law systems—is a growing preoccupation for the court, which in turn demands a facility with both official languages.
>
> "We are often dealing with the relationship, for example, between federal law ... like bankruptcy law ... and provincial laws, and then you have to compare what's being done in the common law system [and] in the civil law system. We have to apply a set of laws and make sure that they will work in both legal systems," he says. "We have to work both in French and in English and it has made me far more aware of the difficulty, and the need, to express oneself clearly, to express legal concepts as clearly as possible, [to] reconcile the concepts in French and in English."

13. CBC, "Bilingualism for top court judges essential: MP," 6 April 2010, www.cbc.ca/canada/new-brunswick/story/2010/04/06/nb-godin-supreme-court-judges-bilingual-442.html (accessed 4 May 2010).

14. Brian Lilley, "Bilingualism law could divide the nation over the court," AM1150, 25 May 2010, www.newstalk1010.com/blog/1140112 (accessed 7 June 2010).

15. 20 April 2010, www.network.nationalpost.com/NP/blogs/fullcomment/archive/2010/04/20/national-post-editorial-board-how-to-ruin-the-supreme-court.aspx (accessed 24 December 2010).

16. Quoted by Janice Tibbetts, "Legal community divided over bilingualism on Supreme Court," *National Post,* 2 May 2010, www.nationalpost.com/related/topics/Legal+community+divided+over+bilingualism+Supreme+Court/2977850/story.html (accessed 24 December 2010).

17. Sébastien Grammond, "Unilingual Supreme Court of Canada judges just don't get it," *The Lawyers Weekly,* 21 May 2010, www.lawyersweekly.ca/index.php?section=article&articleid=1171 (accessed 11 July 2010). Grammond gives specific examples: "When I said, in French, 'The Gosset case affirmed the principle of full compensation of the injury', the interpreter translated 'Gosset says that there has to be comprehensive damage'. When I wanted to contrast the civil law and the common law, which adopt different positions on the compensation of grief, I said, in French, that 'at common law grief is not compensable'. The interpreter omitted to translate 'at common law', making it sound as if the statement related to the civil law, thus inserting a contradiction in the English version of my argument. Other examples of errors are the translation of 'droit commun' (which means general law) by 'common law' (a totally different concept), saying that one's rights were not breached without specifying that I was talking about 'Charter rights', which makes

my argument incomprehensible, or saying that the second paragraph of article 1610 of the Civil Code was not applicable when I said that it was."

18. Quoted in Adam Liptak, "Judging a Court with Ex-Judges Only," *The New York Times*, 17 February 2009, A14.

19. Timothy P. O'Neill, "'The Stepford Justices': The Need For Experiential Diversity on the Roberts Court," *Oklahoma Law Review*, Vol. 60, No. 4, 2007, www.ssrn. com/abstract=1021598.

20. The U.S. Supreme Court has not always been this way. In President Franklin Roosevelt's day, there was a justice who'd been a member of the Ku Klux Klan (Hugo Black), one who'd only gone to law school for one year (Robert Jackson), one who'd fed sheep to buy a train ticket to law school (William O. Douglas), and one who at age twelve had emigrated with his family from Austria (Felix Frankfurter). See Noah Feldman, *Scorpions: The Battles and Triumphs of FDR's Great Supreme Court Justices* (New York: Twelve Books, 2010).

21. Go to www.oyez.org/courts/roberts/robt4. There you can study the financial disclosure forms for several years of each sitting U.S. Supreme Court justice. (Click on the name of a justice on the right, then click on the listing for Financial Disclosure Reports on the left.)

22. http://supremecourtofindia.nic.in/assets.htm (accessed 11 March 2010).

23. www.thecourt.ca/2010/03/15/why-cant-someone-reveal-the-inner-workings-of-our-supreme-court (accessed 17 March 2010).

24. "Court Orders: *Slate* readers weigh in on how to fix Supreme Court reporting," *Slate*, 15 April 2008, www.slate.com/id/2189185 (accessed 18 March 2010).

25. See Baker, note 1.

26. Baker, 103.

27. Baker, 124.

28. Andrew Petter, *The Politics of the Charter: The Illusive Promise of Constitutional Rights* (Toronto: University of Toronto Press, 2010).

29. F.C. DeCoste, "The Jurisprudence of 'Canada's Fundamental Values' and Appointment to the Supreme Court of Canada," Special Series on the Federal Dimensions of Reforming the Supreme Court of Canada, Institute of Intergovernmental Relations, School of Policy Studies, Queen's University, SC Working Paper 2010-2, 1.

30. DeCoste, 4.

31. Don Butler, "Charting the impact of the Charter; Canadians love their Charter of Rights and Freedoms—even if they don't know much about it," *Ottawa Citizen*, 15 April 2007, A6. According to a 2001 Gallup poll, Canadians had greater respect for the Supreme Court than just about any other Canadian institution.

32. See, for example, John Ibbitson, "Few countries can claim such a pathetic Parliament," *The Globe and Mail*, 8 January 2010, www.theglobeandmail.com/news/politics/few-countries-can-claim-such-a-pathetic-parliament/article1424937 (accessed 18 March 2010); Campbell Clark, "PMO has too much power, poll finds," *The Globe and Mail*, 23 February 2010, www.theglobeandmail.com/news/politics/pmo-has-too-much-power-poll-finds/article1478681 (accessed 18 March 2010). To set on the other side is the 27 April 2010 ruling by the Speaker of the House of Commons, Peter Milliken, on the Afghan detainee documents issue.

Milliken held that Parliament had the right to see uncensored documents, saying, "Accepting an unconditional authority of the executive to censor the information provided to Parliament would in fact jeopardize the very separation of powers that is purported to lie at the heart of our parliamentary system and the independence of its constituent parts." See http://www2.parl.gc.ca/HousePublications/Publication. aspx?Language=E&Mode=1&Parl=40&Ses=3&DocId=4470112#SOB-3122448. John Ibbitson more recently seems to take a positive view of Parliament's role. See "The detainee deal, how sweet it is for Ottawa," *The Globe and Mail,* 15 May 2010, http://v1.theglobeandmail.com/servlet/story/LAC.20100515. AFGHANDOCANALYSIS15GTA/TPStory/TPNational (accessed 6 June 2010).

33. Reported by Allison Dawe, "Public policy comes out of the judicial closet," *The Kingston Whig-Standard,* 19 April 1989, 1.

34. "The Judicial Role in a Democratic State," www.ontariocourts.on.ca/coa/en/ps/ speeches/judicialrole.htm (accessed 21 February 2009).

SOURCES AND ACKNOWLEDGMENTS

The main source for this book was the written word. I read a large number of Supreme Court judgments, and many books, articles in law reviews, and magazine and newspaper stories about the court and related subjects. They are referenced in the endnotes.

I formally interviewed a variety of people. I talked informally, over dinner or coffee, or sitting on a park bench in the summer sun, with many more. Given the sensitive nature of the subject, it was clear from the start that most people would not talk to me if they were to be identified in the text, by name or otherwise. I decided early on, despite some misgivings, to conduct interviews on a not-for-attribution basis (with three exceptions—see below).

I spoke to five of the eight living retired Supreme Court judges, and found them remarkably candid and helpful. I interviewed a dozen former law clerks; initially, I had planned to speak to more, but as I've described in Chapter 14, the Supreme Court took steps to discourage former law clerks from speaking to those writing about the court, and many that I asked for an interview turned me down. I talked to a number of senior lawyers who appear frequently before the court, several journalists and writers, and a handful of academics. All of these people gave me valuable background and interesting insights, and I thank them.

In April 2010, I wrote separately and simultaneously to the chief justice and each of the other sitting judges, describing this book and asking for an interview. Jill Copeland, the court's executive legal officer, wrote back, "Due to the heavy demands of the workload at the Court, and the large number of requests for the justices to attend events and do interviews, it is the practice of the Court not to have all nine members of the Court participate in a given interview or event." Chief Justice McLachlin and Justices Louis LeBel and Marshall Rothstein agreed to meet me; I interviewed them, on the record, in May and June 2010. Thank you to them.

My wife, Cynthia Wine, read a draft of the book and made many good suggestions. Her job was to spot legal mumbo-jumbo that would be incomprehensible to a layperson, and to check my tendency to be a smart aleck. I hope that her influence shows, although I doubt she was entirely successful in her efforts. My daughter, Gabrielle Domingues, provided very useful research assistance. Diane Turbide, my publisher, was her usual excellent self, and did her best to turn a sow's ear into a silk purse. Thanks as well to my editor, Lynn Schellenberg, who combined dedication and diplomacy to exactly the right degree. And I am grateful to Beverley Slopen, my agent, who always encourages me to have realistic expectations about book sales and everything else.

The book is dedicated to my late father, Raymond Slayton, and my mother, Valerie Slayton.

December 31, 2010

INDEX